NETANYAHU'S ISRAEL

Netanyahu's Israel

RISE OF THE FAR RIGHT

Jotam Confino

VALLENTINE MITCHELL

LONDON • CHICAGO

First published in 2025 by Vallentine Mitchell

Catalyst House,
720 Centennial Court,
Centennial Park, Elstree WD6 3SY, UK

814 N. Franklin Street,
Chicago, Illinois,
IL 60610 USA

www.vmbooks.com

Copyright © 2025 Jotam Confino

British Library Cataloguing in Publication Data:
An entry can be found on request

ISBN 978 1 80371 073 0 (Paper)
ISBN 978 1 80371 074 7 (Ebook)
ISBN 978 1 80371 075 4 (Kindle)

Library of Congress Cataloging in Publication Data:
An entry can be found on request

To Natalie and my parents

Contents

Acknowledgements

This book was written during perhaps the busiest time of my life, and the most chaotic situation in Israel's history.

I couldn't have written it without the full support from Justin Cohen and Richard Ferrer, my editors at Jewish News. They both gave me moral backing and allowed me to let my work on the book become a part of my daily work for the paper.

I also couldn't have written the book without the support of my partner, Natalie Lisbona, who has been nothing but patient and helpful during the incredibly intense period in which it was written. Lastly, my family's history and connection to Israel gave me all the motivation and inspiration I needed to write it.

Introduction

This book was written during the biggest crisis in Israel's history, with the threat of a civil war continuing to loom over the country. It isn't the first time Israel is experiencing a deep societal rift. From the outset of the birth of the nation in 1948, the left-and right-wing argued viciously, but never about the need for Israel to remain, first and foremost, a democratic country based on liberal values. 75 years later, that is no longer the case. The liberal values, promoted by left-wing, secular Zionists, are slowly but surely eroding. Fascist and religious values are becoming more and more popular, for a variety of reasons that this book seeks to examine.

Warnings about fascism in Israel were aired from the very beginning. On 4 December 1948, a letter was published in the New York Times, protesting an upcoming visit to the United States by Menachem Begin, the leader of the right-wing Herut party in the newly established state of Israel. The letter, signed by Albert Einstein, Hannah Arendt and 25 other prominent Jews, accused Begin's Herut party of being 'closely akin in its organization, methods, political philosophy and social appeal to the Nazi and Fascist parties. It was formed out of the membership and following of the former *Irgun Zvai Leumi*, a terrorist, right-wing, chauvinist organization in Palestine.' Begin, who had gained notoriety for his role in the Jewish underground organization *Irgun* in the years leading up to Israel's establishment, would go on to become Israel's first right-wing prime minister in 1977. He was arguably also the first prominent political leader in Israel to be accused by his critics outside and inside Israel of being a fascist. His fierce rival, David Ben-Gurion, Israel's first prime minister, called Begin a 'Hitlerist type: a racist, willing to destroy all the Arabs for the sake of Greater Israel; he justifies any means for the sacred end – absolute rule.' But despite his militant views on Arabs and Palestinians, Begin became the first prime minister to concede territory to an enemy state when he signed a peace treaty with Egypt in 1979. It earned him a Nobel prize, but it didn't appease his political rivals, who continued to label him a fascist.

The accusations against Begin during the election campaign in 1981 illustrated just how deep the division in Israel had become. Jerusalem

Mayor Teddy Kollek said that Begin's political bloc had 'fostered a hysterical personality cult which arouses fears of the growth of fascism in this country.' Labour party leader Shimon Peres went as far as comparing Begin to the Supreme Leader of Iran, saying: 'We won't permit Israeli democracy to be turned into autocratic rule, with an idolized leader, with Khomeini-like statements. I see the battle today as being over Israel's democratic soul.' The statements made by Peres and Kollek over 40 years ago are almost identical to those made against Prime Minister Benjamin Netanyahu today. But when comparing the two leaders and the government's they've led, Begin comes off as what would be considered almost centrist in today's political landscape in Israel. His strong beliefs in expanding settlements and cracking down harshly on Palestinian terrorism are shared by the majority of parties in Knesset today, including those positioning themselves as centrists.

Begin's Likud party is all but a shadow of its former self, with almost none of its values kept from the time of its formation in 1973. But perhaps the biggest difference between Begin's Likud and Netanyahu's Likud is how far to the right the latter took the party. Begin never hid his loathing for the Palestinians, but he respected Israel's judicial system and rejected the most extreme voices in the country. In fact, he signed an administrative detention order against Meir Kahane, one of the most extreme, Jewish racists in Israel at the time, on suspicion that he and members of his *Kach* party planned on planting bombs on buses in Hebron. Begin signed the order despite being vehemently opposed to administrative detention. Kahane, who would become a member of Knesset in 1984 only to be barred from politics in 1988, was described as 'crazy' and 'dangerous' by Begin. In contrast, Netanyahu normalized the racist ideology of Kahane by forming a coalition with the Jewish Power party, whose ideology descends from Kahane's *Kach* party (which was later outlawed as a terrorist organization). Its leader, Itamar Ben-Gvir, himself a disciple of Kahane, is arguably as extreme as him. But despite being convicted of supporting a terrorist organization (Kach) and inciting to racism, Ben-Gvir wasn't shunned by Likud or barred from Knesset. Instead, he was catapulted into the centre of power when Netanyahu appointed him National Security Minister in 2022.

The far-right in Israel under Begin was still considered fringe and wasn't nearly as organized as today. That is not to say they didn't exist, or that they weren't violent. The 'Jewish Underground' in the early 1980's, which consisted of some of the most radical settlers in the West Bank, planned on bombing the Al-Aqsa Mosque on Temple Mount in order to rebuild the Jewish temple. The numerous violent attacks committed by radical settlers against Palestinians also became more frequent and normal in the 1970's and 1980's.

Begin strongly supported building Jewish settlements on Palestinian land in the West Bank but his predecessors from the Labour party did the same. In fact, it was under their leadership that Israel took control with the West Bank in 1967, implemented military laws in the Occupied Territories and gradually began building Jewish settlements considered illegal under international law. Begin only continued their path. One can argue that the election of Begin as prime minister in 1977 paved the way for the far-right years later. But as this book seeks to argue, it's indisputable that the change in political culture and atmosphere under Netanyahu's reign accelerated the rise of the far-right to the position of power they are in today.

1

From Yitzhak Rabin to Benjamin Netanyahu

Killing peace

The assassination of Israel's Prime Minister Yitzhak Rabin on 4 November 1995 in many ways marked the beginning of the end of Israel's left-wing. The events leading up to the assassination of Rabin have been scrutinized, analyzed, and debated since and continue to divide Israel to this day.

Conspiracy theories blaming Israel's Internal Security Agency, the Shin Bet, for Rabin's assassination were spread on the eve of Rabin's 26th memorial in Israel's parliament, the Knesset, by the leader of the far-right Religious Zionism party, Betzalel Smotrich. His baseless accusations sparked widespread condemnation, ripping up an old wound which the nation hasn't healed from. It serves as a testament to how divided Israel still is almost three decades after the assassination.

The person at the center of the division is astonishingly the same now as it was then: Benjamin Netanyahu, the opposition leader who railed against Rabin for signing the Oslo Accords with the Palestinians. Netanyahu understood then that Israel was undergoing a massive societal change, managing to tap into the anger, frustration and fear that many Israelis felt when Israel agreed to give up territory to the Palestinians.

The incitement against Rabin began after the signing of the Oslo Accords in 1993 when he shook hands with Palestinian leader Yasser Arafat in Washington. As the Oslo accords were slowly but surely implemented, establishing the Palestinian Authority and removing Israeli soldiers from parts of Gaza and the West Bank, Hamas and Palestinian Islamic Jihad launched a series of suicide attacks in Israeli cities. The two suicide attacks at bus stops in the cities of Afula and Hadera in April 1994 killed 13 Israelis. With every attack, the anger at Rabin for signing a peace deal with the Palestinians rose exponentially.

Demonstrations in front of the Prime Minister's Office in Jerusalem and Rabin's private home in Tel Aviv led to clashes between angry protestors and Israeli security forces. Arafat's return to Gaza in July that year, after 27 years in exile, was met with fury among Israeli right-wingers. The suicide bombing in Tel Aviv's Dizengoff street just three months later killed 22 people, marking the deadliest attack in Israel's history. Netanyahu, already a skilled media hawk from his time as Israel's ambassador to the UN, showed up at the scene of the attack, which looked like a warzone, telling international and Israeli media that Rabin 'bears a grave responsibility.'[1] Dan Meridor, who was a senior Likud official at the time, said he told Netanyahu he didn't like that he was going to the scenes of terror attacks for political gain. 'It's the same thing that Itamar Ben-Gvir is doing today,' Meridor said, referring to the far-right extremist who became Israel's National Security Minister in Netanyahu's government three decades later. Demonstrations became more frequent and more hostile, while Netanyhau and the Likud party attacked Rabin for wanting to 'divide Jerusalem,' something he vehemently denied. 'I'll put it simply: It's a political outrage. There is no disagreement regarding the unity of Jerusalem, our sovereignty over it or its continuation as the capital of Israel,' Rabin said in July 1994.[2]

As the demonstrations grew bigger and more aggressive, the idea of justification for killing Rabin began spreading in radical religious groups, circulated by rabbis. They applied the concept of *din rodef*, or the 'law of the pursuer,' a provision in Jewish law permitting extrajudicial killings if someone intends to harm them. The rabbis interpreted Rabin's concession of 'Jewish' land to Palestinians as a direct threat to Jews, hence the need to apply *din rodef*.

The director of Israel's Shin Bet intelligence agency Ya'akov Peri, who would resign in early 1995, nine months before Rabin was assassinated, said some extreme rabbis, mostly from the settlements of Hebron and Kyriat Arba in the West Bank, were 'absolutely' using *din rodef* as a way of justifying an 'elimination' of Rabin. Sensing the seriousness of the atmosphere at the time, Peri said Shin Bet visited some of the rabbis and groups in the West Bank leading the incitement to try and put a stop to it. His successor, Karmi Gillon, also visited the heads of the Yesha settler Council in the West Bank, but they refused to take responsibility for the incitement, saying it didn't come from them. A number of rabbis, however, kept repeating the *din rodef* argument. U.S. Middle East envoy Dennis Ross said he was visiting Rabin one night, where demonstrators were chanting outside his house, asking him if he wasn't worried about the situation. 'He said "no." It wasn't that he was completely dismissive of it, but he kind of took it as a given. He knew in a sense what was coming and simply accepted it,' Ross said.[3]

One incident, that would become almost synonymous with the inciteful atmosphere at the time, and which would be discussed heavily many years later, was a young Itamar Ben-Gvir, then an unknown radical, who was interviewed on Israeli TV holding an emblem he had snatched from Rabin's car, saying 'just like we got to his car, we can get to him'. Ben-Gvir was also demonstrating against the Deputy Minister of Foreign Affairs, Yossi Beilin, due to his involvement in the Oslo Accords. In one incident, he showed up at the Hilton Hotel in Jerusalem where Beilin was scheduled to deliver a speech. 'My bodyguard told me that there was a guy named Itamar Ben-Gvir who said that if Yossi Beilin would come and deliver the speech he would not get out alive,' Beilin said.

In the summer and autumn of 1995, the incitement against Rabin reached new heights. In a demonstration led by Netanyahu in July, a mock funeral was held with Rabin's name on a fake coffin. 'You don't need the head of Shin Bet to explain to the public, and the prime minister in particular, the significance of Rabin's coffin at a mock funeral at the demonstration in Ra'anana,' Gilon said in 2012.[4] Fearing the increasing incitement could lead to an assassination of Rabin, Gillon asked him to wear a bulletproof vest and to drive in an armoured car, which he refused. The incitement culminated with a massive rally in Zion Square in Jerusalem in October 1995, where angry members of the crowd were chanting 'Rabin is a murderer, Rabin is a traitor,' and 'with blood and fire we will expel Rabin.' Some were holding banners depicting Rabin as an SS officer and in a Palestinian *keffiyeh* headscarf. In 2023, Rina Matzliach, one of Israel's most famous journalists, said Ben-Gvir physically gave her a poster of Rabin wearing an SS uniform at the demonstration in Jerusalem that night. Netanyahu, standing on a balcony overlooking the crowd alongside other senior Likud members, held a speech, once again warning that Rabin wanted to 'divide Jerusalem.' But for some Likud members, the demonstration was too much. 'I left the demonstration at Zion Square in Jerusalem, because I didn't agree with what was going on, the violent atmosphere,' Meridor said.

Assassination and blame game

Yossi Beilin, widely considered one of the architects of the Oslo Accords, said he never thought the agreement would receive such backlash on the Israeli side. 'I never imagined to see something like Baruch Goldstein. Such a massacre wasn't on my horizon,' Beilin said, referring to a Jewish far-right extremist who killed 29 Palestinians on 25 February 1995 at the Ibrahimi

Mosque in Hebron. 'Suicide bombings by Hamas were also beyond my horizon. And of course we never imagined an assassination of the prime minister. Rabin imagined the threat would come from the Palestinians, not from Israelis. And that was the big mistake of all of us,' Beilin said.

On 4 November 1995 Rabin held a peace rally at the King of Israel square in central Tel Aviv, where more than 100,000 supporters showed up. The atmosphere was a contrast to the many demonstrations against Rabin around the country, and gave the feeling of a divided nation. 'This rally must send a message to the Israeli people, to the Jewish people around the world, to the many people in the Arab world, and indeed to the entire world, that the Israeli people want peace, support peace. For this, I thank you.'[5] Those were Rabin's last words to the public before he was assassinated shortly after as he was trying to get to his car. Yigal Amir, a Jewish, religious extremist, had managed to sneak up behind Rabin and shoot him with a semi-automatic pistol. Rabin was rushed to the hospital. At 11:15 PM the same night, Rabin's chief of staff Eitan Haber announced 'shock, sorrow and deep grief, the death of Prime Minister and Defense Minister Yitzhak Rabin, who was murdered by an assassin, tonight in Tel Aviv.'[6]

Crowds that had gathered outside the hospital broke down in tears, while some exploded with anger, chanting 'Bibi is a murderer' and holding signs saying 'Bibi, Rabin's blood is on your hands.' A clearly shocked Netanyhau was interviewed on TV, saying his 'heart was crying.' An intense debate over Netanyahu's role in which he denounced the incitement against Rabin erupted immediately. When asked in an interview with CNN to what extent she held Netanyhau and the Likud responsible for the assassination, Rabin's wife Leah said 'I do blame them. The rally in Zion Square in Jerusalem that showed him in the uniform of a Nazi. Mr. Netanyahu can say from now and to eternity that he didn't support it and didn't agree with it, but he was there and he didn't stop it.' Netanyhau himself denied playing any role, referring to incidents wich denounced the incitement, such as telling an angry crowd in 1995 that 'Rabin is a political opponent, but he is not a traitor. He is mistaken. ... We are dealing with political rivals, not enemies. He is not a traitor.' In a TV interview prior to Rabin's assassination, Netanyahu also said that calling Rabin a traitor is 'inappropriate. It is immoral and it is untrue. I urge those people doing this to stop, because we will all denounce you.'[7] Those close to him at the time, such as advisor Eyal Arad, called it a 'cheap political propaganda trick' in order to 'delegitimize' him and the Likud. Meridor, who would soon become Finance Minister in Netanyahu's government, also said he didn't think it was right to say Netanyahu played a role in the assassination of Rabin. Ehud Olmert and

Ehud Barak, who would both later become prime ministers, said many years later that Netayahu did indeed incite. Olmert went as far as saying that 'the truth is that the extreme right was inciting against Rabin and they were responsible for creating the atmosphere which contributed to the assassination. And no one can be relieved of his responsibility for creating this atmosphere, first and foremost Netanyahu.'[8]

For Shin Bet, the assassination marked a catastrophic intelligence and security failure. Amir was not on Shin Bet's watch list of Jewish extremists in what they referred to as the underground, a movement that had risen since the 1970's with the first Jewish settlements in the West Bank. Amir had managed to slip under the radar by avoiding associating too much with the extremists that were being followed and watched by the Shin Bet. Dvir Kariv was among the first Shin Bet officials to speak with Amir after he had assassinated Rabin. Kariv was an intelligence analyst in a division in the Shin Bet which dealt exclusively with non-Palestinian extremists, therefore often referred to as the 'Jewish Division.' Kariv recalled how difficult it was for him to face Amir so soon after he killed Rabin. 'It was very intense. Amir was very happy and smiled because he had succeeded in two things, killing Rabin and escaping from the assassination alive,' Kariv said. Amir felt like he had acted in the interest of Israel and that while he might have killed Rabin it was the Israeli public that had pulled the trigger, metaphorically speaking. In other words, Amir felt like he had the backing of the people.

As the public was trying to heal from the shock, Peres became acting prime minister. Having already served as prime minister once in 1984, Peres was a highly esteemed statesman, who had played an instrumental part in establishing the state of Israel. Peres did, however, not enjoy the same public popularity as Rabin did. But polls showed he would have beaten Netanyhau by a landslide had he called elections immediately after the assassination. A senior Likud official at the time recalls that the day after Rabin was killed Netanyahu said it was a bad thing because he could have beaten him in the election if he was alive. The official said he was taken aback as to why someone would think about their own political chances in a situation like this. Luckily for Netanyahu, Peres decided to delay elections to 29 May the following year. Both Beilin and Meridor later said it was a big mistake on Peres' part. 'If Peres had gone to elections right after Rabin was killed, he could have quite easily have won. But he didn't want to win on Rabin's back,' Beilin said. In the following months, a string of suicide bombings in Jerusalem, Tel Aviv, and Ashkelon killed 59 people.

Netanyhau's election campaign centered around bringing back security to Israel, using the slogan 'Peres will divide Jerusalem' as a way to remind

Israelis of one of the most sensitive issues in the conflict with the Palestinians. Going head to head with Peres in a TV debate three days before elections, Netanyhau's on-camera skills proved extremely useful, coming off as vibrant, hungry and eloquent. Peres, 72 at the time, meanwhile came off as stiff and monotone and assumed he would win the election easily due to his vast political experience in the Labour party, compared to the political novice sitting next to him in the studio. Netanyahu used what proved to be extremely persuasive in rallying support behind him: fear. Referring to the suicide bombings on busses in Jerusalem earlier that year, he said:

> Our children are afraid to get on a bus. Many of you who are watching us now are getting up in the morning and asking themselves whether the next attack will happen today. Mr. Peres, you brought our security situation to a nadir.[9]

Netanyahu, as expected, avoided any mention of Rabin, seeing that the wounds were still fresh. Peres, however, had every intention of reminding the public. 'Rabin was murdered in front of my eyes. Otherwise it would have been him who would be sitting here in my place. The messenger was murdered, but not the message,' he said.

The general elections in 1996 marked the first time that Israelis would have to vote separately for prime minister and for Knesset. Polls leading up to the election had shown Peres leading marginally over Netanyahu. Knowing every vote counted, senior Likud official Ariel Sharon used his connections in the ultra-orthodox communities to secure support for Netanyahu. After meeting rabbis from *Chabad*, an ultra-orthodox Hasidic movement, the community decided to put their weight behind Netanyahu, posting huge banners across Israel with the slogan 'Netanyahu. It's good for the Jews'. Netanyahu's ties with the ultra-orthodox community grew stronger and would eventually become his most loyal allies.

Dr. Gilad Malach, Director of the Ultra-Orthodox in Israel Program at the Israel Democracy Institute, said:

> Netanyahu created a synonym between right-wing and Jewish. And they (ultra-orthodox) supported him. It gave them the feeling that they need to go with the right-wing, because they are traditional and want a Jewish state. It has now become quite clear in the past 20-25 years that the ultra-orthodox are right-wingers. Netanyahu's second success was that he became the most adorable secular politician for the ultra-orthodox. They adore him.

On election night, the race proved much tighter than expected. The first exit polls showed Peres had a slight lead, with some commentators predicting it was game over for Netanyahu. The results, however, started changing overnight. Israelis woke up the next morning to the news about Netanyahu receiving 50.4 percent of the votes, beating Peres by a hair's breadth. The historic win both heralded a comeback for the right-wing in Israel, while exonerating Netanyhau from having played a role in the assassination of Rabin, at least in a slight majority of the public's eyes. The newly elected prime minister, the youngest in Israel's history, was met by an enthusiastic Likud crowd, chanting 'King Bibi', a nickname that would stick with him among his supporters for decades.

Meeting Arafat

Netanyahu's government consisted of the far-right National Religious party, the right-wing parties *Gesher, Tzomet,* the ultra-orthodox parties Shas and United Torah Judaism and the newly established *Ysrael BaAliyah* party. It didn't take long before Netanyahu had to deal with the Israeli-Palestinian conflict himself. Railing against Arafat and the Palestinians was a luxury only opposition lawmakers could afford. In the first couple of months Netanyahu had refused to meet Arafat while approving new homes in Jewish settlements in the West Bank, causing Arafat to accuse the Israeli government of 'declaring war' against the Palestinians. Netanyahu understood that meeting Arafat and implementing the Oslo Accords was inevitable.

On 4 September, Netanyahu met Arafat at the Erez crossing separating Gaza from Israel. The meeting came about after pressure from the U.S., Jordan, and Egypt, and after Israel's President Ezer Weizman said if Netanyahu wouldn't meet Arafat, he would do it himself. Reaching across the table to shake his hand, Arafat caught Netanyahu in a moment that would taint him in the eyes of his voters, as well as other right-wing hawks in his government who criticized him harshly. He had suddenly found himself doing the exact same as what he had so harshly condemned Rabin and Peres for doing: shaking the hand of a leader he had referred to as a terrorist.

This became the start of a four month long intense negotiation over how to proceed with implementing the withdrawal of Israeli troops from Palestinian areas of Hebron, as was stipulated in the Oslo Accords. But on 23 September 1996, Netanyahu's first real security crisis erupted, threatening to disrupt the baby steps he had taken to make progress with the Palestinians. Netanyahu gave the greenlight to allow for Israeli archaeologists, under the protection of Israeli soldiers, to create a new opening of the Western Wall tunnels in the Muslim Quarter of Jerusalem's Old City, which previously could only be entered from the Jewish Quarter. The work began at around midnight, just hours after the end of Yom Kippur, the holiest day of the year for Jews. The following morning, Jerusalem Mayor Ehud Olmert announced the opening of the newly created exit. Shin Bet chief Ami Ayalon said he 'couldn't believe his ears' when he found out that the tunnel had been opened without coordinating with him, or the Palestinians, something he had specifically advised Netanyahu to do before making any unilateral move.[10] Netanyahu, however, said that Ayalon had encouraged him to open the tunnel, not going into further into detail.

For Palestinians, the opening of the tunnel was a highly provocative move, penetrating the holy site of the Temple Mount, or *Haram al-Sharif* as it is known to Muslims, upon which the Al Aqsa Mosque is located. Arafat responded to the opening of the tunnel by calling on Palestinians to respond. Riots quickly broke out in the Old City, with Palestinians throwing stones at Israeli security forces as well as Jews praying at the Western Wall. The riots spread to Gaza and the West Bank, with Palestinian security forces taking part in the clashes against Israeli soldiers.

Netanyahu, meanwhile, was on a diplomatic tour in Europe when the clashes erupted but ended up cutting the trip short and returning to Israel. Netanyahu said he called Arafat when he returned to Israel that day, telling him he had 'thirty minutes to call off' his forces and accept a complete cease-fire. 'If you don't, I will send in our tanks and destroy your regime,' to which Arafat replied: 'I understand.'[11] The riots lasted four days in total, leaving 17 Israelis and over 100 Palestinians killed. The incident caused Ayalon to consider handing in his resignation but said he didn't out of a sense of duty to the country.

On 2 October 1996 President Clinton hosted Netanyahu, Arafat and Jordan's King Hussein at the White House, relaunching the negotiations between Israel and the Palestinians. On 17 January 1997 the Hebron agreement was finally signed, with Israel agreeing to withdraw its troops from 80% of the city. According to Yossi Beilin, Clinton was the deciding force behind the Hebron protocols, not Arafat, despite his pressure on Netanyahu to implement the Oslo Accords. Beilin said:

> The Americans are the only ones Netanyhau cares about, and even with them he is playing games. The fact that he not only shook Arafat's hand but said he had found a new friend, that was the

surprise, not so much that they met. Arafat used to kiss me (on the cheek) everytime we met, which was quite inconvenient.

While Netanyhau was applauded by Clinton and Arafat for signing the Hebron protocols, his right-wing base fumed. 'The agreement that was signed here today is a complete capitulation by Benjamin Netanyahu. I am shocked, amazed and hurt,' spokesman for the Hebron settlers Moshe Ben-Zevra said following the agreement.[12] And among the more extreme right-wingers, a new movement was established in reaction to the Hebron agreement. 'Hilltop Youth' was a gang of young and extreme Jewish settlers in the West Bank who believed that any territorial concession to the Palestinians was a crime against the Jewish people. Their response was to establish new settlement outposts just south of Hebron, illegally built on Palestinian owned land. This phenomenon would later be known as 'price tag' attacks, a tactic meant to extract a price for any territorial concession made by the government or to punish Palestinians who killed Jews in terrorist attacks.

Analysts and experts differ in their views on when the price tag attacks began. While some say it can be traced to the period of Israel's withdrawal from Gaza in 2005, Kariv assessed that the outposts established following the Hebron agreement marked the beginning of the phenomenon. The attacks would later come in many shapes and forms, such as establishing illegal outposts, vandalizing Palestinian property, physically attacking Palestinians, and attacking Israeli military and police when they were ordered to remove settlers on illegally built land. In some cases, the price tag attacks would be extremely violent, killing innocent Palestinian women and children. For Kariv, whose division dealt with Jewish extremists, the Hilltop Youth would become a major headache due to their terrorist activities. His division, which only made up 1% of Shin Bet, used agents to infiltrate the movement, while surveilling its most dangerous members. Kariv said Jewish extremists had kept a low profile for a while following the assassination of Rabin, but that their activities continued, especially after the Hebron agreement was signed. The biggest challenges came from violent extremists from the settlements of Yitzhar and Itamar, both located just south of the Palestinian city of Nablus in the northern part of the West Bank.

While Shin Bet was busy keeping the Hilltop Youth in check, a total of 42 illegal outposts were established during Netanyahu's first term. Meanwhile, the number of settlers in the West Bank had grown from 146,900 to 183,900 in that period, and roughly 10,000 construction starts had been approved (including in Gaza).[13] But despite the government in many cases turning a blind eye to the outposts, Kariv said Netanyahu was still a target among the most extreme Jewish settlers. 'They don't distinguish between left and right-wing prime minister. Whoever poses a threat to Israel (in their eyes) is a target,' Kariv said. Knowing he had to do something to calm his right-wing constituents, Netanyahu approved the building of new Jewish homes in the Har Homa neighborhood of Jerusalem, considered illegal under international law. It infuriated Clinton and Arafat and Netanyahu's relationship with the Clinton administration remained uneasy throughout his term. Clinton thought Netanyahu was deliberately slowing the peace process by expanding Jewish settlements in the West Bank at the same time as he was negotiating with Arafat. Netanyahu on the other hand thought Clinton was unsympathetic to the Israeli cause, while appeasing the Palestinian Authority, an institution Netanyahu still considered a terrorist organization. U.S. Secretary of State Madeleine Albright used the word 'torture' to describe her negotiations with Netanyahu, something he later described as a compliment. Negotiations between Netanyahu and Arafat nevertheless continued, culminating with the signing of the Wye River agreement in Maryland on 23 October 1998.

The agreement was based on the 1995 Interim Agreement, also known as Oslo II, which was built on the land-for-peace concept. Israel agreed to transfer 13% of West Bank land to the PA, which would fight terror, enhance security cooperation with Israel, crack down on incitement and reduce illegal weapons. But the pressure from his right-wing constituents remained intact. The Settlers Council of the West Bank and Gaza had sent a delegation to Wye to remind Netanyahu not to give in to American pressure. Netanyahu argued that the territory transferred to the Palestinians wasn't of any historic or strategic importance to Israel. To his right-wing constituents, Netanyahu had done the exact same he had accused Rabin and Peres of, namely ceding territory to the enemy.

Arafat's nephew and Palestinian Foreign Minister from 2005-06, Nasser Alkidwa, said that Netanyahu in many ways did more for the Palestinians in that period, compared to what Ehud Barak and Ariel Sharon (the two following prime ministers) would. Alkidwa described him as a 'big opportunist' who would respond as a politician to any pressure. 'There is a famous story that says the American national security advisor held Netanyahu by the neck in Maryland, telling him "You are playing with the future of my president, and I will not allow that." Finally, Netanyahu signed the Wye River agreement. So, in a sense Netanyahu was the one making a lot of negative noise, but he was the one who took a few small steps in the right direction,' Alkidwa said. According to him, it wasn't difficult for Arafat to deal with Netanyahu because he 'understood what he was all about, which was right-wing noise, but opportunistic enough to do some business with.'

Clashing with security

While Netanyahu begrudgingly accepted that he had no choice but to continue his predecessor's peace negotiations with the Palestinians, a different conflict slowly but surely unfolded between him and the defense echelon. Clashes between the IDF Chief of Staff Amnon Lipkin-Shahak and Netanyhau were leaked to the Israeli media. According to Aviv Bushinksy, Netanyahu's media advisor from 1998-99, the IDF leaked information about Netanyahu's intentions to conduct certain military operations, in order to stop him from doing it. 'At the beginning he had tremendous respect for the military. His meetings with them were sacred. He didn't like them but he respected them,' Bushinsky said. Netanyahu thought that the defense echelon was in bed with the left-wing, and thought of Shahak as a 'left-winger' according to Bushinsky. The media reported on frequent clashes between Netanyahu and IDF officials, with one headline suggesting Netanyahu had 'silenced' Shahak at a cabinet meeting.[14] While some saw Netanyahu as indecisive, both Peri and Bushinsky saw a leader who 'listened' carefully to the advice given to him. 'He listens, sometimes too much. It doesn't matter if you are his hairdresser, media advisor or his wife. When I was his chief of staff (2003-4) my target was sometimes to lock him in a room and to minimize his friction with other people, fearing he would change his mind,' Bushinsky said.

Danny Yatom, Mossad chief at the time, experienced exactly that in 1997, when Hamas launched suicide bombs in Jerusalem, causing Netanyahu to ask the military and intelligence to present plans to punish Hamas. Yatom said he presented Netanyahu with a plan to eliminate Hamas targets in an undisclosed third country, which he initially approved. But not long after, Yatom received a phone call from Netanyahu's military secretary who informed him that the prime minister had changed his mind after meeting with Defense Minister Yitzhak Mordechai and Shin Bet chief Ami Ayalon. They had persuaded Netanyahu to go after the Hamas leadership in Jordan. 'I was furious,' Yatom recalled, saying he phoned Netanyahu and asked for an explanation. Eventually Yatom accepted the change of plans. The target they chose was Khaled Mashal, Hamas' leader who resided in Jordan's capital Amman. The operation, however, went terribly wrong. Two of the Mossad agents who had managed to spray poison in Mashal's ear as he left his office were caught. The assassination attempt immediately sparked a diplomatic crisis with Jordan's King Hussein, who felt Israel had betrayed him by operating in his country without approval. Yatom's soon to be successor, Efraim Halevy, was hurried back from Europe to Israel by Netanyahu, who asked him to negotiate with King Hussein on behalf of him. Halevy had been instrumental in bringing about peace with Egypt just three years earlier and had a good relationship with King Hussein, based on mutual trust. Backed into a corner, Netanyahu agreed to save Mashal's life by sending an antidote to Jordan, as well as free Hamas' spiritual leader Sheikh Yassin from Israeli jail, in exchange for the release of the Israeli Mossad agents in Jordanian custody.

Netanyahu, who for years had argued that one cannot and should not negotiate with terrorists, found himself once again going against his own doctrine. In the span of a less than a week, Netanyahu went from approving the assassination of a Hamas leader to saving his life and releasing another from jail. Halevy said the decision to release Yassin was 'difficult' for Netanyahu, but it wouldn't be the last time he released Hamas terrorists with Israeli blood on their hands. Following the Mashal affair, Yatom joined the ranks of high-level security officials who fell out with Netanyahu. Their relationship had up until then been 'very good' and 'based on mutual trust,' according to Yatom, who said Netanyahu gave him the 'green light' for almost all the operations he wished to carry out. But when leaks about Netanyahu's intentions to find a new Mossad chief flooded the news, Yatom felt that 'the famous machine of Netanyahu was working behind my back. I immediately understood the sources leaking to the media came from Netanyahu's office. Our relationship became so bad I didn't trust him anymore.' Yatom eventually resigned and Netanyahu named Halevy the new Mossad chief.

In his three year-term, Netanyahu managed to fall out with both the IDF chief of staff, the defense minister and the heads of Shin Bet chief and the Mossad. Defense Minister Yitzhak Mordechai, who was fired by Netanyahu in 1999 over differences on the issue of negotiations with Palestinians, would even break from Likud to establish the new Center Party along with Shahak. Meridor, who had been named finance minister by Netanyahu, also resigned in 1997, joining Mordechai and Shahak. 'Our relationship soured. I could not agree with some of his behavior. Netanyahu did what he wanted to do. Years later he told me out of the blue it was Lieberman who wanted me out. People told me I was seen as a political rival,' Meridor recalled, referring to Avigdor Lieberman, the director general of the prime minister's office. Lieberman also ended up resigning, establishing his own party; *Israel Beitenu*. He would eventually become one of Netanyahu's fiercest rivals and contribute to his short-lived downfall many years later.

The pattern of clashing with colleagues was something that caused instability in Netanyahu's first term as prime minister but would eventually become a natural, almost sacred part of his leadership style. Anyone deemed a threat, whether it be old friends or political talents, would find themselves either crushed by Netanyahu or becoming his bitter rivals. One of the biggest threats was the media, whose relationship with Netanyahu became increasingly toxic after he defeated Peres in the 1996 elections. For Netanyahu, the bad relationship had already started when he returned to Israel to run for Knesset in 1988 after having served as Israel's ambassador to the UN. 'The media monopoly's antipathy would ultimately become my most potent opponent, acting effectively as the main opposition party,' Netanyahu said many years later.[15] The media largely held Netanyahu responsible for creating an atmosphere where incitement against Rabin ran wild. Bushinsky said that he was 'shocked' to find out how much attention Netanyahu gave to how the media portrayed him. 'Netanyahu believes that the media is the most important thing,' he said. At the same time Bushinsky knew that the media was 'very tilted to the left,' supporting the Oslo Accords and blaming Netanyahu for creating obstacles. 'The media chased him vigorously. I did think they were biased against him. I came from the media so I knew my colleagues from the inside. I knew how they worked and their political views. And it penetrated into their coverage,' he said. Little did it help that Netanyahu made efforts to try and change the Israeli media landscape's view of him. Whatever he did was portrayed in a cynical way. Bushinsky said:

> Netanyahu thought once he signed the Wye River agreement he would be treated differently by the media. But he wasn't. And I think this was a turning point with his attitude toward the media. He thought no matter what he did, the media wouldn't like or respect him.

Netanyahu eventually understood he needed to do two things; never betray his electoral base and establish a right-wing media in Israel, something that didn't exist at the time. In the years after he lost the election, Bushinsky said Netanyahu was looking for a media mogul who could buy an outlet that would promote him, ending up finding the American Jewish billionaire

Sheldon Adelson who established the free daily newspaper Israel Hayom in 2007. The war between Netanyahu and the media would only worsen throughout the years, reaching a low point never seen between an Israeli prime minister and the media in the country's history.

Notes

1   Netanyahu TV interview with Associated Press, 19 October 1994: Israel – Tel Aviv Bus Bomb Outrage Reactions.
2   Scott Kraft, 'Rabin Accuses Israeli Rightists of Scare Tactics: Mideast: Protests against Arafat's return continue in Jerusalem. Prime minister calls claims he will turn city over to Palestinians an 'outrage', *Los Angeles Times*, 4 July 1994.
3   Frontline PBS, 'Netanyahu at war', 2016.
4   Sony Picture Classics, 'The Gatekeepers', 2012.
5   International forum for peace, 'The last speech of Prime Minister Yitzhak Rabin', 5 November 2014.
6   Greer Fay Cashman, Eitan Haber, former advisor to Yitzhak Rabin, passes away at age 80', *Jerusalem Post*, 7 October 2020.
7   Staff, 'Netanyahu rejects left's allegations he incited against Rabin', *Israel Hayom*, 13 November 2016
8   Jotam Confino, 'Former prime minister warns Israel could see another political assassination', *Jewish News*, 7 November 2022.
9   Serge Schmemann, 'Peres and his foe do verbal battle in sole TV debate', *The New York Times*, 27 May 1996.
10 Ami Ayalon, *Friendly fire: How Israel became its own worst enemy and its hope for the future*, (Steerforth Press, Lebanon, New Hampshire, 2020), pp. 147-155.
11 Benjamin Netanyahu, '*Bibi: My Story*' (Simon & Schuster, New York, 2022) pp. 288-290
12 Serge Schmemann, 'Netanyahu and Arafat agree on Israeli pullout in Hebron', *The New York Times*, 15 January 1997.
13 Israeli Central Bureau of Statistics (CBS).
14 Y. Peri, The "Democratic Putch" of 1999, in *Generals in the cabinet room: How the military shapes Israeli policy* (United States Institute of Peace Press, Washington, D.C. 2006), pp. 77-90.
15 Benjamin Netanyahu, '*Bibi: My Story*' (Simon & Schuster, New York, 2022) pp. 198.

2

'You'll be back'

Retirement

Netanyahu returned to Israel from Maryland facing immediate political backlash among some of his hawkish Likud colleagues for signing the Wye River agreement. Two months later his government collapsed when he was defeated in a vote of no confidence at the Knesset.

Elections were called for 17 May 1999. Ariel Sharon, who had accompanied Netanyahu to Maryland, was waiting for his inevitable downfall, preparing himself to take control of Likud. In the meantime, Israel's most decorated soldier, Ehud Barak, had been named new Labour party leader, succeeding Peres. Barak, who had served in most senior positions in the IDF, including chief of staff, was fired up and ready to assume control of the highest office in the country.

Netanyahu knew that his attempt to act like a responsible statesman by dealing with Arafat and honouring the Oslo Accords had hurt him badly among right-wing voters. The settlers had turned their backs on him, and so had many of Israel's centrist voters who had opted for Netanyahu instead of Peres in 1996. The final nail in Netanyahu's coffin was planted during a TV debate between Netanyahu and Mordechai, who was now vying for the same votes as Netanyahu in his new Center party. Barak had been advised to sit this one out, fearing he wouldn't gain much from entering a three-way debate. Mordechai famously asked Netanyahu to look him in the eye when he asked him about his alleged intentions to give up the Golan Heights in a peace deal with Syria. Netanyahu was visibly uneasy with the question and didn't manage to convince the viewers with his answer.

On election day, Barak beat Netanyahu by a landslide, winning 57% of the votes against 43% for Netanyahu. The defeat was a hard blow to Netanyahu, who shortly after resigned from the Knesset and announced his political retirement. Netanyahu later recalled that Clinton called him to bid him farewell, telling him 'You'll be back.'[1] In his own mind, however, he thought his political career was over. Sharon, Netanyahu's nemesis, was named Likud's new leader. With his hawkish military background and his deep connections in the ultra-orthodox community, Sharon was preparing for a complete takeover of Israeli politics. Meanwhile Barak created a broad government with many of Netanyahu's previous partners. It consisted of Labour, *Gesher,* the Center Party, the religious Zionist *Meimad* party, the ultra-orthodox parties United Torah Judaism and Shas, the left-wing *Meretz* party, the National Religious party, and *Yisrael BaAliyah.*

Barak, full of confidence, prepared to kickstart negotiations with Arafat. Yossi Beilin, who was now Justice Minister in Barak's new government said both he and Barak thought that it was the right thing to 'accelerate efforts towards a permanent agreement.' Watching from the sideline how his rival was welcomed warmly by Clinton at the White House, about to offer the Palestinians wide-reaching concessions, Netanyahu struggled to accept his new life as a political has-been, touring the U.S. as a speaker to make money. Meanwhile Barak soon got in big trouble at home for his eagerness to strike a peace deal with the Palestinians. Interior Minister Natan Sharansky who headed *Yisrael BaAliyah,* would be the first to resign from the government after he discovered that Barak had been negotiating secretly with the Palestinians without the government's knowledge. Sharansky said:

> One day I got a message from Washington, I still to this day can't say from whom, but it said that Barak was secretly negotiating with the Palestinians in Europe. And in those negotiations, he was including everything, which meant Jerusalem. I asked the other ministers if they knew anything about it and they didn't. So, I challenged Barak on this in one of our government meetings, but he denied it. I checked again with my source who insisted it was happening, and that one of the points was a division of Jerusalem where the Western Wall would become neutral territory. I sent a letter about this to him and all the party leaders, and then almost immediately after he went public and said there were negotiations taking place. The day he flew to Camp David I resigned from the government.

Barak faced widespread backlash from all sides of the political spectrum on the issue of Jerusalem. Netanyahu accused Barak of 'breaking all the red lines held by all Israeli governments,' while Yitzhak Rabin's widow, Leah, said 'Yitzhak is certainly turning in his grave.... Yitzhak would never have agreed to compromise on the Old City and the Temple Mount.'[2] The political crisis in his own government escalated when several parties defected over the summer, among them the large ultra-orthodox Shas party, leaving him in a minority government. Shas had demanded more financial support for the ultra-orthodox, which Barak had refused. 'They are extorting us in the diplomatic, political sphere. Even if he wants to transfer Tel Aviv to the Palestinians, we would have to vote yes,' Shas lawmaker and the Deputy Finance Minister Nissim Dahan said at the time.[3]

The breakdown of the Camp David summit between Clinton, Arafat and Barak, and the ensuing second *Intifada* marked the end of the peace process that had begun seven years earlier with the signing of the Oslo Accords. For the Palestinians, Israel's consistent settlement expansion remained a core issue of the conflict and a crucial obstacle in its goals of establishing a state. The number of settlers living in the West Bank had doubled in those years, from roughly 100,000 to some 200,000 in 2000. For Israel, the continuation of terror attacks in that period proved that it had no peace partner.

The *Intifada*, which was sparked after Opposition Leader Ariel Sharon visited the Temple Mount on 28 September 2000 surrounded by heavy security, would ultimately bring Barak down. Sharon's visit caused anger among Palestinians, and led to violent clashes with Israeli security forces in Jerusalem, Gaza and the West Bank in the following days. Sharon's role in sparking the *Intifada* continues to this day to be a source of deep agreement among Israelis. For Beilin, there was no doubt about Sharon's responsibility. He said:

> This was the excuse and the reason for the second *Intifada*. There is no question about that. To say that the land was already fertile for an *Intifada* might be right, but you always need to ignite it. And Sharon was the pyroman,

To Sharon, the visit was a political move, which both showed his willingness to make sure 'every Jew can visit the sacred' Temple Mount, while at the same time exposing the fragile security situation for Jews if Barak 'divided' Jerusalem.[4] The *Intifada* grew stronger day by day, leaving hundreds of Palestinians and 51 Israelis killed. Barak ultimately announced his decision to resign as prime minister on 9 December 2000. Elections were called for 6 February the following year, and with Netanyahu out of the picture, Barak thought he could beat Sharon and form a different coalition that would stabilize him for years to come. Netanyahu, who had briefly considered returning to Israeli politics to try and beat Barak, decided not to run in the end.

Sharon

Sharon won the elections in February with 62%, causing Barak to retire from the Knesset. The right-wing in Israel had once again won an election against a left-wing government failing to adequately contain Palestinian terror attacks. Despite a resounding defeat, Labour would become part of Sharon's new government under the leadership of Binyamin Ben-Eliezer. His government also included Shas, United Torah Judaism, the Center party, *Yisrael Ba'Aliyah*, the National Religious Party, *Yisrael Beitenu, Gesher*, the newly established New Way party as well as an alliance of right-wing parties called National Union.

The latter was made up of several parties, some of which were secular while others were influenced by the ideology of religious Zionism. National Union, however, represented a significant shift to the right. One of the parties, *Tkuma*, was created by two lawmakers who defected from the National Religious Party in 1999 as a response to Netanyahu's signing of the Wye River agreement. National Union represented hardcore anti-Palestinian and pro-settlement views which would soon become headaches for Sharon. But more importantly, their inclusion in the government was a sign of the beginning of a new political reality in Israel, namely the acceptance and normalization of far-right parties, such as *Tkuma*. Up until the formation of National Union, the National Religious Party had largely represented settlers and religious Zionists. According to Dr. Assaf Shapira, PhD in Political Science from the Hebrew University of Jerusalem, the National Religious Party wasn't the main driving force behind the expansion of settlements. Dr. Assaf said the real political forces pushing the settlements were rather Likud and Labour. The National Religious Party had up until the 1970's been moderate and aligned with the left-wing. Although it had a history of being considered a centrist party from its establishment in 1956 and onward, the party became increasingly right-wing with time and was influenced by *Gush Emunim*, an ultranationalist, Orthodox movement established in the early 1970's.

The movement was founded by followers of ultra-nationalist Orthodox rabbi Zvi Yehuda Kook, a religious fundamentalist who believed in the coming of Messiah, something that could be hastened if Jews settled all over biblical Israel. Rabbi Haim Druckman also helped establish *Gush Emunim* and would become a member of Knesset on the National Religious Party list in 1977. That decision, however, was made because his mentor Rabbi Kook wanted Druckman to serve in the Knesset, to further the cause of religious Zionism. Druckman himself said he didn't want to enter politics.

Despite being seen as a moderate and moral spiritual leader for thousands of religious Zionists, including the Religious Zionism party (an offshoot of National Religious Party) as well as the highly controversial anti-LGBTQ *Noam* party, Druckman eulogized Meir Kahane, an American Israeli extremist who was banned from running for Knesset in the 1988 elections over his racist views. Kahane was assassinated in 1990 in New York by an Egyptian-American extremist. Druckman's praising of Kahane's 'soul' was a sign of the direction in which the religious Zionist movement was headed.

With the inclusion of National Union, and an increasingly right-wing National Religious Party, Sharon had now opened the gates to controversial far-right politicians like Efraim 'Effi' Eitam, a former Israeli brigadier general who was first named minister without portfolio and then minister for national infrastructure. Knesset had already had its fair share of controversial and racist lawmakers in the country's short history, most notably Kahane, whose *Kach* party was later deemed a terrorist organization. Kahane was shunned by both right- and left-wingers at the time, with Prime Minister Yitzhak Shamir famously walking out of the Knesset during one of his speeches. His spirit and ideology were kept alive among the most extreme settlers and would ultimately rise again through his disciples in the Jewish Power party that was established many years later, on the ruins of *Kach*.

Other lawmakers had also drawn negative attention for their ultranationalist views. Prime Minister Menachem Begin was considered an extremist and a fascist by the left-wing in Israel. Israel's founding father and first prime minister David Ben-Gurion called him a 'racist' and a 'Hitlerist type' who was willing to 'destroy all Arabs for the sake of Greater Israel.'[5] Sharon himself was also an arch enemy of the left-wing, who saw him as a violent warmonger and cynical right-wing extremist, who as defense minister under Begin was responsible for the Israeli invasion of Lebanon in 1982. Rehavam Ze'evi, another secular far-right lawmaker, had also been condemned for advocating for the transfer of Palestinians from the West Bank and Gaza to neighboring Arab countries. Ze'evi had been part of Shamir's government in the early 1990's but resigned after the peace conference between Israelis and Palestinians in Madrid in 1991. Coincidentally, Ze'evi's *Moledet* party joined National Union and Ze'evi was named minister of tourism under Sharon. In October 2001, he was assassinated at a hotel in Jerusalem by four Palestinians.

With Ze'evi killed, Eitam, who was part of National Religious party, was now one of the most controversial ministers in Sharon's new government, which arguably contributed to the normalization of racist and violent rhetoric seen among senior Israeli ministers today. Eitam would refer to Israeli Arabs as 'cancer' and call for Arab-Israeli lawmakers to be expelled from Knesset, a view that Israel's national security minister would also express repeatedly 24 years later.[6] It took less than a year before the National Union left Sharon's government over his decision to pull back Israeli troops from Hebron who had been deployed to fight Palestinian attacks against Jews during the *Intifada*.

As Sharon took office, the *Intifada* had escalated quickly, with Hamas and Islamic Jihad having already launched terrorist attacks during the election campaign. Throughout 2001 and 2002, suicide bombings in malls, bus stops, train stations and night clubs left Israel more vulnerable than ever. As Sharon approved several targeted killings of Hamas and Islamic Jihad commanders in retaliation, the crisis only worsened, peaking with a suicide attack at a hotel in Netanya on Passover eve in 2002. 30 Israelis were killed and 140 injured. Deciding to increase the pressure on the Palestinians, Sharon approved a military operation in the West Bank called Operation Defensive Shield. Soldiers and tanks rolled into Jenin, Nablus, Bethlehem and Ramallah, where Arafat was effectively under siege in his headquarters. Nablus and Jenin were particularly hard hit. Images of dead Palestinians on the streets, and the rubbles left by Israeli tanks caused an international uproar. 'Many business owners left Nablus after the invasion because the city was closed off. We couldn't leave by car freely for six years (after Operation Defensive Shield),' Dr. Hijjawi, Mayor of Nablus, said. U.S. President George Bush called on Sharon to immediately halt the operation. In the meantime, Sharon's government approved a plan to build what would be known as the West Bank barrier, a security wall separating the West Bank from Israel to prevent terror attacks. The wall would sometimes cut into West Bank territory, leaving some Palestinian villages surrounded by the wall.

For Sharon, this was a clear sign that he intended to eliminate Palestinian terror, no matter the international outrage over the barrier. For him, dealing with his long-time enemy Arafat was a nightmare, but a top priority. The man he had hunted in Lebanon twenty years earlier was suddenly allowing Palestinian terror attacks to be unleashed at Israel. According to Ben-Eliezer, who had been named defense minister, Sharon would be furious in the aftermath of attacks, screaming 'bomb Arafat' only to take it back after he had calmed down.[7] Nasser Alkidwa described the animosity between Sharon and Arafat as both 'personal and ideological.'

The unraveling security crisis, however, brought Netanyahu back on the political scene. He persuaded Sharon to let him do a PR campaign in the U.S. to defend Israel's actions against the Palestinians. Netanyahu embarked on a media blitz and spoke out against the Bush administration in a meeting with U.S. Senators. Netanyahu found himself doing what he did best, getting his message through via the American media. 'Netanyahu always told me that if you want to convince the Americans, you need to do it through the media,' Netanyahu's former advisor and chief of staff, Aviv Bushinsky, said.

On 6 November 2002, Netanyahu was thrown straight back to Israeli politics, having accepted the offer from Sharon to take over from Peres as foreign minister. The position became open when the Labour party quit the government a week earlier, citing disagreements over funding for settlements in Gaza and the West Bank. Without a majority-led government, Sharon called for new elections on 5 November, with parliament voting to dissolve itself. Despite Sharon's popularity in the public, Netanyahu saw the political chaos as an opportunity, even if it meant working under his old rival. Ehud Olmert, who would soon be named Vice Prime Minister in Sharon's new government, said Sharon told him several times about how he loathed Netanyahu, whom he referred to as 'garbage', and that the only reason he named him foreign minister was to get him out of Israel as much as possible. Nevertheless, Netanyahu was back in business. His return to return to politics, he said, was a combination of wanting to liberalize Israel's economy, which would also affect its military and thus its status in the region and focusing on one issue that nobody else seems to care about, namely stopping Iran from developing nuclear weapons. The latter would become Netanyahu's, and in continuation of that, Israel's almost obsession in the coming decades. Netanyahu said he had pointed out to Sharon that focusing on Iran's nuclear program should be a top priority to him, but to no avail. Halevy would, however, many years later point out that he dedicated about 50% of his time for Iran during his years as Mossad director, a period that spanned from 1998-2002.

Gaza disengagement

Much like Sharon's decision to disengage militarily from Gaza and remove some 8,500 Jewish settlers, the second *Intifada* became catalysts for Israel's increasing shift toward the right. And for Netanyahu, both issues would become both a curse and an opportunity politically. But first, he had to fall in line under Sharon's leadership after the ageing Likud leader won yet another election on 28 January 2003. Sharon's Likud party became the biggest party in Knesset with 38 seats, beating Labour which received just

19 seats. His new government excluded the ultra-orthodox party Shas, but included the liberal secular *Shinui* party, which became the third biggest in Knesset, as well as National Union and National Religious party. *Yisrael Ba'Aliyah* meanwhile merged with Likud. The ultra-orthodox *Agudat Israel* party, which normally ran with *Degel Hatorah* as part of United Torah Judaism, joined in 2005 along with Labour and *Meimad*. Sharon appointed Netanyahu the next finance minister, a decision he referred to as a shocker. Israel's economy was in a bad shape, with sky-high interest rates and negative growth two years in a row. The appointment was a way for Sharon to keep his rival in check. The ungrateful task of having to recover Israel's economy would put Netanyahu in a difficult situation where he had to make unpopular moves while getting little or no credit if he succeeded. It would however become one of the periods in his life that both rivals and allies would look back at as one of Netanyahu's most successful.

Cutting the welfare sector, which had become a financial liability for the economy, hit the ultra-orthodox hard since they relied more than anyone on handouts from the state due to a high unemployment rate. Ultra-orthodox men mainly studied the Torah for a living, while the women stayed at home taking care of their large families. Dan Meridor applauded Netanyahu for showing leadership when he did what was 'good for the economy but wasn't popular.' The economic reforms carried out during Netanyahu's term as finance minister proved fruitful, gradually turning Israel into a capitalist free-market nation.

But it was his clash with Sharon over the disengagement from Gaza that would stand out politically in that period. While Sharon was seen as the settlers' patron, someone who actively promoted the expansion of settlements in the West Bank going back to the 1970's, Netanyahu's deals with Arafat to implement the Oslo Accords were still remembered among the hard-core right-wingers. A lesson he would never forget, and which caused him to harden his support for the settlers. Sharon would soon turn from hero to traitor in the eyes of the settlers, causing much greater outrage than Netanyahu's deal with Arafat.

On 18 December 2003, Sharon shocked the nation when he announced his intention to withdraw from Gaza unilaterally, a small strip of land Israel occupied after the 1967 war. Four other settlements in the northern West Bank would also be evacuated. Moshe Ya'alon, who was IDF chief of staff at the time, said many years later that the decision, which shook him, was made without proper consultation with Israel's security establishment and that the Americans had been informed long before the relevant and responsible parties in Israel. For the residents in Gush Katif, the Jewish settlement bloc established in Gaza in 1977, the feeling of betrayal was absolute. Anita Tucker, whose family helped establish Gus Katif with the help of the Israeli government, said that Sharon had visited their town a few months before his announcement, telling them they needed to build faster. 'He wanted more communities and was very warm and friendly to everyone,' Tucker said, recalling how devastating Sharon's decision was to the residents of Gush Katif. Tucker said:

> I remember thinking how unethical and immoral it was. It's not only a threat to me but to everyone living in the Gaza Strip, including our Arab friends that we knew for generations. Everyone knows that if you want peace with someone you need to live next door to them. If there is a wall between you there can never be peace, because you have no connection. So, we coordinated with the Yesha Council (West Bank) on how to demonstrate.

Public Security Minister Tzachi Hanegbi, a close confidant of Sharon, said he didn't think anyone knew the reason for his sudden turnaround vis-a-vis Gaza. Hanegbi, among the Likud hawks who intended to vote against the disengagement plan, said Sharon asked him for a 'for a very intimate meeting and asked me to abstain (the vote). He made me feel that it was a personal request. It wasn't about the settlers anymore, or about policy or Israel. It was a personal issue, that he stands between defeat and success. And I told him, "Arik there are things I cannot abstain. I cannot make a decision not to make a decision."'[8] One person who wasn't shocked about Sharon's Gaza plans was his number two, Vice Prime Minister Olmert, who said he initiated it. About a month before Sharon's big announcement, Olmert had himself advocated publicly for a withdrawal from Gaza as well as large parts of the West Bank. He did so at a memorial for David Ben-Gurion, standing in for Sharon who was sick.

> I said things that devastated everyone. I also gave an interview to *Yediot Ahronot* (Israeli newspaper) shortly after where I said that Israel should pull out of most of the territories, including Jerusalem. This quickly became the talk of the country, and large parts of the world. I didn't say anything to Sharon about this, so I was curious to hear what he thought. When he called me, he asked if I was in Jerusalem, because he wanted to meet. I said yes, I was at home. He asked me if it was the part of Jerusalem I had given to the Palestinians or the one that we would keep to ourselves. We were

laughing, and he said he was very impressed with my speech and that he had his own thoughts about pulling out of Gaza. So, we started planning it.

Several Likud officials thought it was a big mistake to withdraw from Gaza, including Hanegbi and Netanyahu. They feared it would make Israel look like it was surrendering while paving the way for Hamas. Tucker said the Palestinians in Gaza told them that their culture was different than the Jewish: 'If you are strong, we will respect you. If you show any weakness, we will step all over you.' The tensions between Sharon and the residents of Gush Katif residents, as well as the West Bank settlers, caused Minister of Housing and Construction, Tzipi Livni, to arrange a meeting between him and the settler leaders. The meeting, she said was 'tough' and very moving. 'For many years Sharon saw Gaza as part of Israel's security. The need to be there and control the sea but during that time he understood there was no use for it,' Livni said.[9]

In the 18 months following his explosive announcement in Gaza, Sharon would repeatedly clash with Netanyahu, as well as other right-wingers in his government. Netanyahu, seeking to delay what he saw as his inevitable resignation from the government, tried to persuade Sharon to change the conditions of the Gaza disengagement plan. Despite a referendum among Likud members showing that 60% were against the disengagement, Sharon proceeded with the plan, having a majority backing in Knesset, including from the ultra-orthodox *Agudat Israel* party, whom the Gush Katif residents tried to convince to support them. Tucker said they met with party member Moshe Gafni, 'who really wasn't nice. He said "go to someone who will pray for you because Sharon is going to do it anyway. Too bad for our money that we need for the yeshivas, that's why we are voting for it."'

Netanyahu meanwhile felt a pressure to resign given his vocal criticism of Sharon. After he voted for an interim bill on compensating the settlers slated for eviction, Netanyahu was ridiculed in the media, calling his threats to resign a bluff. It only made matters worse after he threatened to resign if Sharon didn't allow for a national referendum on the plan, only to walk back that threat. But in Netanyahu's eyes, he was doing the only responsible thing, hanging on to his position as finance minister to see that his reforms as well as the state budget would be approved in March 2005. The National Union as well as the far-right National Religious Party did however back their threats with actions, with both parties resigning from Sharon's government in 2004. Sharansky, who described his relationship with Sharon as 'excellent' would also resign from his role as minister of Jerusalem affairs in response to the Gaza disengagement. Sharansky said:

> I couldn't believe it. The disengagement plan was so strange. It came out of nowhere. (President) Bush also didn't expect it, so Sharon didn't do it because of American pressure. Sharon said that by leaving Gaza we would get 10 years where we could do what we want. One shot from Gaza and we would go in. I told him I didn't think we would even get 10 days (of peace).

Netanyahu also ended up resigning from his position as finance minister on 8 August. Eight days later, the military implemented the plan, moving into the Gaza settlements with bulldozers to evacuate the settlers and tear down their houses. Tucker was among the last of the residents to leave her home, recalling how the Palestinians who worked with them were crying as well.

While Sharon's decision was applauded in the international community as 'courageous,' hundreds of thousands of right-wing Israelis took to the streets to demonstrate against Sharon across the country. Several influential rabbis also raged against Sharon. According to Olmert, many of those were 'dumb, 'narrowminded, and useless. Because they had adopted extreme positions, they immediately gained a certain prestige that made them very influential. People were anxious to be inspired by some great ideas, and the center and left-wing couldn't provide them any inspiration. But the right-wing and the rabbis managed to enthuse people, by the idea of a "return to greater Israel". While most of the demonstrations were peaceful, a handful of settler extremists engaged in price tag attacks to punish Sharon for evacuating Jews in what they saw as their homeland. Among them was Betzalel Smotrich, a future Israeli minister, leader of the religious Zionist movement and crucial Netanyahu ally. Smotrich was arrested in 2005 by Dvir Kariv and other members of the Shin Bet's 'Jewish Division' on suspicion of planning an attack. The biggest newspaper in Israel, *Yediot Ahronot*, reported that Smotrich and four others had been arrested with 700 liters of gasoline, allegedly planning to block and damage a major highway in Israel in protest of the disengagement.[10] Smotrich spent three weeks in Shin Bet custody but was never charged. To this day he denies the report that he intended to carry out any attack. 'He is trying to tell a different story than what really happened,' Kariv said. Other price tag attacks were much more violent.

On August 17, Jewish extremist Asher Weisgan from the settlement Shvut Rachel killed four Palestinians near another West Bank settlement,

Shiloh. Weisgan committed the attack in response to Sharon's disengagement plan. Others settled for harsh verbal condemnation of Sharon. Shas' spiritual leader, Rabbi Ovadia Yosef, spoke out against his old ally, saying 'How cruel is this evil one who does such things? The Holy One wants us all to return to the Torah, and then he will strike him with one blow and he will die. He will sleep and never wake up.'[11] Far-right Knesset member Orit Strock's harsh verdict on Sharon when he died in 2014 was another clear example of exactly how dangerous it would be for any right-wing leader to ever make deep concessions to Palestinians, something Netanyahu had already gotten a taste of in his first term as prime minister. Strock said:

> The truth must be said: Sharon was one of the great builders of the land of Israel, and its greatest destroyer. Someone who knew to defeat terror, and someone who caused all the south of the country to be hit by terror. His great firmness and ability to decide and act enabled him to reach impressive achievements, as well as disastrous processes. Alongside our thanks and honor of the great contributions of Sharon to the state of Israel, it is impossible not to also thank G-d, that Sharon was taken from our public lives before he managed to carry out on the residents of Judea, Samaria and the "Judea Samaria belt" the disaster he conducted on residents of Gush Katif and the Gaza Strip.[12]

Tucker said that the residents of Gush Katif never forgave Sharon for kicking them out of their homes in Gaza. 'The feeling of disgust and disappointment is bigger than ever and the longing for home grows stronger with time,' Tucker said. Uzi Benziman, the author of 'Sharon: An Israeli Caesar,' said Sharon didn't have any problem with dismantling settlements, which he had done once before in 1982 with Yamit, a Jewish settlement of some 2,500 residents on the on the Gaza-Egypt border. Sharon, then defense minister, ordered the evacuation of the settlement himself as part of the Egyptian-Israeli peace treaty in 1979. Benziman described Sharon as a 'pragmatist' and an 'opportunist' lacking any ideology.[13] This, he said, made it easier for him to carry out controversial actions, such as disengaging from Gaza.

Yair Golan, who was then the IDF commander of the Judea and Samaria Division, said the disengagement was a 'shock' to the settlement movement because it went against their 'divine plan.' They came out of the disengagement 'terribly beaten.' Therefore, they decided on a new strategy to rise again. Simply speaking, Golan said, the movement tried to install their people in 'the most influential positions that could affect the prosperity of settlements. But not just politically, but also in the military, police, Shin Bet, and the interior ministry. Everywhere, really. It wasn't like there was a committee that sat down and decided this. It was more a public understanding. And what we have seen since then is that more and more extreme people holding high positions.'

End of an era

Rabbi Ovadia Yosef's curse proved almost prophetic when Sharon suffered a brain hemorrhage and fell into a coma in January 2006. Just two months before in November 2005, Sharon had announced his decision to leave Likud, establishing his own party named *Kadima*, and dissolving Knesset at the same time. 'The Likud in its present form cannot lead the country to its national goals,' Sharon said when he announced his new party, a clear signal and blow to Netanyahu and those who remained loyal to him.[14]

It became a groundbreaking moment for Likud, splitting the party in two; those who supported Sharon and those who feared the Gaza disengagement was just the beginning of territorial concession. Netanyahu belonged to the latter and would be elected Likud leader once again in December that year. Several senior Likud ministers followed Sharon to his new centrist party, including Tzipi Livni, Ehud Olmert, and Tzachi Hanegbi. Shimon Peres, the Labour icon, also decided to join *Kadima*. Olmert said that parts of the Likud party had already started becoming 'extreme' and too right-wing. When Sharon was declared incapacitated by doctors after he fell into a coma, Olmert who was Vice Prime Minister became Israel's acting Prime Minister overnight. A position Netanyahu said he had asked Sharon to receive, but that was given to Olmert as compensation for not being named finance minister. Netanyahu found himself back in a position of power, but in a party that had been significantly weakened by Sharon's departure. He now had to rebuild the party from almost scratch, while appealing to voters further on the right.

The following elections in 2006 dealt a harsh blow to Likud, which ended up with just 12 seats, causing Netanyahu to consider retiring once and for all. Sharon's *Kadima* party, now led by Olmert, received 29 seats. Olmert could continue as prime minister, establishing a government with Shas, Labour, *Yisrael Beitenu* and the centrist *Gil* party. Netanyahu, being a rival of Olmert, was left out of the coalition, instead becoming opposition leader. Olmert meanwhile had a lot of imminent security issues to deal with, internally as well as externally. One of the first incidents he had to deal with came soon after he assumed the role of acting prime minister, when Israel's Supreme Court finally ruled that the settlement of Amona, established in 1995 in the West Bank, was indeed illegal according to Israeli law, built on private owned Palestinian land, and therefore had to be evacuated. Olmert, who was in the middle of an election campaign, said he was advised by legal and military officials around him to postpone the evacuation, because it could hurt him in the election. Olmert said:

> 'Amona was a very important test-case. It was the first evacuation of a settlement after the Gaza disengagement. There was a feeling in Israel that we shouldn't do that because it could end violently. I had a discussion with all the top military and legal advisors to the government, including the IDF chief of staff and the Attorney General, and they told me: "Prime Minister, you don't have to do this before election, which may cost you a lot of votes. If we ask the Supreme Court for an extension, they will give it to us." The Attorney General told me to postpone it. And I said "you guys don't understand me. I don't want to postpone it. I want to pass a message. I want everyone in Israel to know what I am after, so that nobody will tell me after the elections they didn't know what I was going to do, like they did with Sharon." They told me it would be violent, and I replied that if someone chooses to be violent, we will handle him in a firm manner. (The evacuation) created a lot of bitterness among the settlers, and these guys were looking for action. And that helped, already then, the strengthening of the far-right parties.

Defense Minister Shaul Mofaz eventually ordered the military to evacuate the settlement on 1 February. Thousands of soldiers, policemen and security personnel carried out the order, but met fierce resistance by over 300 settlers. One of them was the extremist lawmaker and former Sharon ally, 'Effi' Eitam, who was still a member of Knesset. Olmert felt the rage of the settler movement for the first time, something all his predecessors had experienced at one point in their career, some more than others. Eitam spoke directly to Olmert from the hospital in Jerusalem where he had been sent after suffering a head injury in scuffles with Israeli security forces. Eitam said:

> You are far from being the successor of (Prime Minister Ariel) Sharon. You have proven today that you are frightened, confused and

manipulative. You have acted with stupidity and narrow-mindedness. This is not the way to build premiership. We would have known how to control this incident like in Gush Katif, but the police officers were ordered to act with violence against the children and public leaders. This is a pogrom against young people. [15]

The unprecedented attack on Olmert was backed up by his former colleague in Likud, Uzi Landau who said 'Ehud Olmert wants confrontation at all costs. His refusal to compromise with the settlers proves we face a struggle not over the rule of law, but a political manoeuvre aimed at distracting the public from his role in Hamas' victory. He cannot fight terror, so he turns the settlers into the enemy.'[16] The disdain among the most right-wing lawmakers for the Supreme Court and their loyalty to the settlement movement was a sign of what was to come in Israeli politics. It would take another 11 years before the evacuation was complete, with the military barring civilians from returning to the illegal outpost. According to Yair Golan, who was then the IDF commander of the Judea and Samara division, overseeing the evacuation, Amona was a watershed moment for the settlement movement. Golan said:

> Amona was kind of a rehabilitation process for the extreme right. Tactically, the government, the IDF and police were terrific. We did exactly what we wanted to do. By the end of the day, all eight buildings were flattened. But at the time, we couldn't understand that strategically, for the settlers it was kind of a victory, because it enabled them to reconsolidate their power. They were in a void after the Gaza disengagement. Amona was another shock but a positive one. Now they understood they needed to be more sophisticated, devoted, aggressive and organized and that they shouldn't hesitate when it comes to "price tag" attacks. They were going to fix the destiny of Israel, whether the citizens wanted it or not.

While the Amona evacuation illustrated that the Supreme Court and military were keeping a sense of law and order in the territories, the increasing power of the settlers had become evident. Nadav Weiman, who at the time served as a sniper in the Israeli elite unit known as Sayeret Nahal, explained how he slowly realized what the IDF's purpose was in the West Bank; serving the interests of the settlers and disrupting the lives of the Palestinians at the same time. In terms of protecting the settlers no matter what, Weiman recalled an incident where his unit was asked to keep an eye on a group of settlers who had decided to visit *Homesh*, an illegal outpost that had been evacuated under the 2005 Gaza Disengagement Plan. Weiman said:

> It was (Israel's) Independence Day, and we were supposed to go back to our homes and celebrate but they (IDF) stopped us at the last minute, telling us we needed to give covering fire to settlers who were going to (visit) Homesh. And we told them "Listen, they are not supposed to visit that place, it's illegal. It's all over the media. We need to stop them." Our commander told us we were right, but it wasn't our job to stop them. It doesn't matter if they (settlers) are doing something illegal. We had to cancel our vacation and spend 24 hours in a camouflage tent and protect them. That was the minute I understood who controls everything. The settlers do. We were one of the most experienced units which is why we had the courage to question the decision. But we didn't want to disobey a direct order because we could end up in military jail. And our commander was a settler from Hebron, so he supported (the decision). His father was one of the key figures in the settlement movement and a member of the Jewish Underground in the 1980's. We felt like we were soldiers to the Palestinians and to the settlers we were their private security company.

As for disrupting the daily lives of the Palestinians, Weiman recalled numerous incidents where his unit was taking part in erecting what is known as 'flying' checkpoints, which is a temporary and unannounced checkpoint set up by the army for security reasons. Weiman, however, said that while they were told to erect that type of checkpoints to catch Palestinians on the way to commit terror attacks, reality was different. The checkpoints created huge traffic jams, and the soldiers didn't check every Palestinian car. 'You suddenly understand that you are there so that they (Palestinians) can see who controls them. But you start justifying why you are doing it. You must,' he said. Weiman had been a big supporter of the settlers in the West Bank before his time in the army. He even looked forward to serving and combatting terror. But his experiences changed his view on both the IDF and the settlers, causing him to join 'Breaking The Silence' in 2011, an Israeli NGO which collects testimonies of soldiers who expose the daily life in the occupied territories. The testimonies range from abusing Palestinians to night raids, arrests, killings and of course settler violence.

Hamas rises

In Gaza, Palestinians were jubilating over Sharon's disengagement, which also saw an end of the second intifada, leaving over 1,000 Israelis and over 3,000 Palestinians killed. 'In retrospect, I think there was some kind of deal between Hamas and Sharon. Suddenly Hamas seized its suicide bombings without the usual review of the religious authorities. Not even to avenge the (Israeli) assassination of Hamas spiritual leader Sheikh Yassin (in Gaza in 2004),' Nasser Alkidwa said. The days of suicide bombings were over, but soon Israel would have to deal with a new terror challenge, such as indiscriminate firing of rockets from Gaza.

The Israeli withdrawal from Gaza left a power vacuum that Hamas would soon capitalize on. Alkidwa said Hamas was able to portray it as a 'win for the resistance,' and that 'Israelis were running away' from Gaza. Tzachi Hanegbi, Netanyahu and many other right-wingers saw it the same way. After Arafat died in 2004, Mahmoud Abbas took over as Palestinian President, but soon found that the void he had left in the Palestinian movement would be an opportunity for Hamas to take power. Palestinian elections were called in 2006, which ended up with Hamas being the big winner. After a bloody conflict with Abbas' Fatah party, Hamas seized power in Gaza in 2007. The fact that Hamas managed to take over Gaza with Israeli soldiers standing a few hundred meters away, Alkidwa said, is proof that there was a deal in place: 'One must be dumb to think all this happened by chance. There was, and still is, an Israeli interest in splitting Gaza from the West Bank.'

Not long after Olmert had established his new government, he was confronted with two imminent security threats simultaneously. On 27 June, Hamas kidnapped Israeli soldier Gilad Shalit on the border with Israel, bringing him into Gaza. And just three weeks later, a cross-border attack by Hezbollah on the Israeli Lebanese border left three Israeli soldiers killed, while two Israeli soldiers were kidnapped by Hezbollah. With two disastrous situations unfolding, Olmert refused to negotiate release terms with Hamas for Shalit and decided to embark on two military operations at the same time. With the capture of Shalit and repeated rocket attacks by Hamas from Gaza since the disengagement a year before, Olmert launched a ground invasion. It would take four months before Hamas and Israel reached a ceasefire.

The ground invasion failed to bring back Shalit and only marked the beginning of many wars to come between Hamas and Israel. Both the issue of Shalit and Hamas would seriously challenge Netanyahu in the years to come and serve as never ending sources of criticism among his rivals. At the same time as the Israeli military was pounding Gaza, Olmert ordered a military operation against Hezbollah in Lebanon to bring back the kidnapped soldiers, which ended in a full-fledged war that lasted five weeks. Nearly 1,200 Lebanese and 170 Israelis were killed in the war. The IDF left Lebanon seriously damaged, and Hezbollah fired some 4,000 rockets at civilians in Israel. Not long after the two simultaneous military confrontations, peace talks with the Palestinians were launched once again, with U.S. President Bush hosting Olmert and Palestinian President Abbas in Annapolis in 2007. Olmert, who believed peace was within reach, was ready to offer concessions similar those made by Barak seven years earlier at Camp David. Sharing Jerusalem with the Palestinians, as well as mutually agreed land swaps were on the table.

As usual, the backlash from hardcore right-wingers was strong. On the day of Rabin's memorial, incitement was again running wild, with football fans at Jerusalem's soccer stadium booing during a minute of silence for the late prime minister, as well as posters hanging in Jerusalem, depicting now Shimon Peres, now the Israeli President, in a Palestinian headdress. Hundreds took to the streets, carrying torches through Jerusalem to demonstrate against Olmert's offer to share Jerusalem with the Palestinians.

Two of Israel's biggest newspapers, *Yediot Ahronot* and *Ma'ariv* warned that about the implications of the incitement. 'A new era is beginning, a stormier, dramatic and — as we saw yesterday — also an ugly one. And ugly is an understatement,' wrote *Yediot Ahronot,* while *Ma'ariv* ran a headline saying 'Incitement is back.'[17]

While negotiations continued until 2008, Abbas eventually rejected Olmert's offer. In the meantime, a report on the Lebanon war two years earlier was released, damaging Olmert significantly. The Winograd Commission concluded that while Olmert had based his decision to launch the military operation on 'honest assessments' the war was full of 'serious failures', ending in no clear military victory, which both the military and political leadership bore a responsibility for.[18]

Netanyahu, smelling blood from the damning report, called on Olmert and the 'amateurish' government to resign.[19] The Likud leader would get what he wanted later that year, but for different reasons. After it became evident that he was facing an indictment for corruption, Olmert announced his resignation as prime minister with elections to be held on 10 February 2009.

Notes

1   Benjamin Netanyahu, *Bibi: My Story* (Simon & Schuster, New York, 2022) pp. 309.

2   Ehud Barak, *My Country, My Life, Fighting for Israel, Searching for Peace,* (Martin's Press, New York, 2018), pp. 384.

3   Deborah Sontag, 'Shas party resigns Israeli coalition, but leaves Barak time to negotiate a reversal', *The New York Times,* 21 June 2000.

4   CNN, 'Ariel Sharon visits Temple Mount', 29 September 2000.

5   Tom Segev, 'Why did Ben Gurion call Begin a "Hitlerist Type"', *Ha'aretz,* 2 July 2009.

6   Judy Maltz, 'Plan to name former right-wing politician to head Yad Vashem enrages holocaust survivors', *Ha'aretz,* 26 October 2020.

7   Ari Shavit, 'Dear God, this is Effi', *Ha'aretz,* 20 March 2020.

8   David Landau, *Arik: The life of Ariel Sharon,* (Vintage Books, a division of Random House, New York, 2014), pp.

9   I24NEWS, 'Israel marks 15 years since Gaza disengagement', 16 August 2020.

10 I24NEWS, 'Israel marks 15 years since Gaza disengagement', 16 August 2020.

11 Moran Azoulay, 'Arrested by Shin Bet before disengagement: 9th on Bennet's list', *Yediot Ahronot,* 11 January 2015.

12 Amiram Barkat, 'Ovadia Yosef off the hook – no criminal investigation for Sharon taunt', *Ha'aretz,* 10 March 2005.

13 David Lev, 'Dayan: They don't like Struck because they fear her', *Arutz Sheva,* 16 January 2014.

14 BBC documentary, 'Sharon: Israel's Iron Man,' 13 January 2013.

15 David Landau, *Arik: The life of Ariel Sharon,* (Vintage Books, a division of Random House, New York, 2014), pp.

16 Efrat Weiss, 'MK Eitam: Amona was a pogrom', *Yediot Ahronot,* 2 February 2006.

17 Efrat Weiss, 'MK Eitam: Amona was a pogrom', *Yediot Ahronot,* 2 February 2006.

18 Joseph Nasr, 'PM slams Israeli rightists' provocations over peace', *Reuters,* 5 November 2007.

19 Tobias Buck, 'Olmert bruised by Lebanon war report', *Financial Times,* 31 January 2008.

20 Gil Hoffmann, 'Bibi: "Amateurish PM must resign', *Jerusalem Post,* 31 January 2008.

3

Bibi is back

Two states?

In the middle of the election campaign, the outgoing government had launched a cross-border operation in Gaza to destroy Hamas tunnels which Israel said was built to kidnap Israeli soldiers. The operation ended with Israeli soldiers killing six Hamas members, causing Hamas to retaliate by resuming rocket firing at Israel. Not long after, the Israeli military launched a ground invasion dubbed Operation Cast Lead, which lasted three weeks and ended up killing some 1,400 Palestinians, including 600-700 Hamas members. Ten Israeli soldiers and three civilians were killed during the three-week conflict.

Netanyahu, eyeing a political comeback, promised to topple Hamas and bring an end to rockets being fired at Israel. The videoclip would be played repeatedly in the media in the years to come every time Israel faced Hamas in yet another military stand-off. But both Yair Lapid and Naftali Bennett, two future prime ministers, would make the same promise years later, only to learn that toppling Hamas wasn't as easy as it seemed.

In this election, Netanyahu had finally managed to break the centrist-left media landscape that was inherently hostile to him and had never forgiven him for his role in the demonstrations against Rabin. Las Vegas casino mogul and multi-billionaire, Sheldon Adelson, had been persuaded by Netanyahu to launch a right-wing and free newspaper in Israel that would change the Israeli media landscape forever. *Israel Hayom* had been launched in 2007, with a clear goal; to offer Israelis a different view on politics, in particular Netanyahu. The paper, which would later be referred to as '*Bibiton*' (a wordplay on Netanyahu's nickname 'Bibi' and the Hebrew word for newspaper '*iton*') became the most read newspaper just four years later. For Netanyahu, this was a game changer. The newspaper was circulated for free across Israel and could be found on stands at train stations. Adelson denied that the newspaper was intended to help Netanyahu get re-elected, but the significant positive coverage he received made it clear to other journalists as well as Netanyahu's rivals that it was nothing short of propaganda. For Prof. Motti Neiger, who served as the

President of the Israel Communication Association between 2006-09, Israel Hayom changed the media landscape 'dramatically', and the criticism against the new paper by other journalists and lawmakers was completely justified. Associate Professor at the School of Communication at Bar-Ilan University, said:

> Israel HaYom was a platform constructed to work for Netanyahu. Just a small example; it was published that from 2012 to 2015, Benjamin Netanyahu made 230 calls to the chief editor of Israel HaYom at that time, Amos Regev, and an additional 120 calls to Sheldon Edelson. Netanyahu conducted 15 such calls in the 19 days before the 2013 elections. We can see a direct line between the political agenda of Netanyahu and the front pages' headlines. I can't imagine any other news outlet allowing such an intervention. The paper supported all of Netanyahu's interests and was very critical of his opponent, both from the left and the right. In the 2006 elections, Netanyahu and the Likud party gained only 9% of the votes leading them to the opposition. In the 2009 elections, they gained more than 21% of the votes that crowned Netanyahu as PM and maintained this position for 12 consecutive years. Israel HaYom is not the only factor for that, but it certainly had a meaningful contribution.

For Netanyahu, this was just an attempt by a Jewish American billionaire to invest in a media industry controlled by the left-wing elite. Going into the elections on 10 February 2009, Netanyahu was hungry and ready to prove that he was the only one who could bring back stability for Israelis. Tzipi Livni's *Kadima* party ended up becoming the biggest party in Knesset with 28 seats, but Netanyahu, whose Likud party received 27 seats, had more lawmakers backing him as prime minister. What had seemed unimaginable ten years earlier was now a reality. Netanyahu had made a historic comeback, becoming Israel's next prime minister.

His new government consisted of Labour, *Yisrael Beitenu*, Shas, United Torah Judaism, and the newly established Jewish Home party, another right-wing spin off made up by members from the National Religious party. Meanwhile, National Union again transformed, including the newly established far-right *Eretz Israel Shelanu* party which had merged with another far-right party, Jewish National Front. The latter was founded by Baruch Marzel, a Hebron based activist and close follower of Meir Kahane's racist ideology. After Kahane was assassinated, Marzel became the leader of the outlawed *Kach* party, continuing to promote his idol's racist views.

Israel's Supreme Court barred Marzel from running for Knesset in 2019 on the grounds of incitement to racism. Marzel, who had been arrested numerous times since the age of 14, had called Baruch Goldstein (who killed 29 Palestinians in 1994) one of the 'purest' people on earth, and believed Jews were in a religious war with Arabs.[1] The National Union deemed Marzel too extreme, opting instead for Michal Ben-Ari, another member of Jewish National Front. Ben-Ari, who was also a follower of Kahane and a member of his *Kach* party, was elected member of Knesset on the National Union party's list. Ben-Ari would, much like Eitam, become notorious for his racist remarks, such as calling on deporting Arabs from Israel, as well as complaining that the IDF didn't kill enough Palestinians in Gaza in the 2012 war.[2]

From the outset, Netanyahu had his work cut out for him with newly elected American president, Barack Obama, who had his eyes on trying to solve the Israeli-Palestinian conflict. Obama also sent strong signals to the Muslim world that he wanted to amend ties with the U.S. in the aftermath of 9/11 and made a symbolic yet strong gesture to the Palestinians by making President Abbas his first phone call after taking office. Netanyahu knew he was facing his exact opposite in Obama, but he had to keep his constituents and right-wing coalition partners happy by expanding settlements and keeping a hardline vis-a-vis Palestinians, and at the same time please the American superpower. Obama was by any standard a pro-Israel president, ending up signing the biggest ever American aid package to Israel. He was even portrayed wearing a kippah on the cover of New York Magazine with the title 'The First Jewish President' due to his strong backing in the American Jewish community. But his sharp views on Israeli settlements in the West Bank, as well as his diplomatic approach to the issue of Iran's nuclear program almost immediately brought Netanyahu and Obama on collision course.

Netanyahu's solution to Obama's pressure to kickstart peace negotiations was to pay lip service to him while stalling for time and proving that the Palestinians weren't interested in peace. The first big clash happened on the first meeting at the White House between the two newly elected leaders. Obama told Netanyahu in private and later in their press conference that he demanded Israel freeze all settlement construction immediately. Netanyahu was shocked and outraged and would later describe something Obama told him as 'shocking' and 'offensive'.[3] Two weeks after the traumatic meeting, Netanyahu got another slap in the face when Obama held a speech in Cairo in June 2009 on his first trip abroad as president. The speech sent a strong signal to the Palestinians that the U.S.

was backing their right to a State and to end the 'intolerable' situation they were living in.[4] Michael Oren, Israel's ambassador to the U.S. at the time, said the Israelis were completely caught off guard by Obama's speech, which contained fundamental changes to U.S. policy in the Middle East. Oren said:

> There is a long-standing practice in U.S.-Israel relations about no surprises. It means that when you are going to make major policy announcements, you give the Israelis a heads up. We had no warning of it whatsoever. Nor did we ever have any warning about any presidential speech (during the Obama administration).

To make matters worse, Obama also visited Saudi Arabia and Turkey but didn't stop in Israel, which was interpreted as a clear message in Israel. Netanyahu, clearly feeling the pressure from the new administration to fall in line and restart peace negotiations, held a speech at Bar Ilan University just 10 days after Obama's speech in Cairo. Knowing full well which trap he had found himself in with Clinton and Arafat 12 years earlier, Netanyahu tried his best to stress Israel's right to defend itself against Palestinian terrorism, and its right to live in the biblical land of Israel. But one thing stood out and would come back to haunt him again.

After he had called on Palestinians to restart peace negotiations 'immediately without prior conditions', Netanyahu said Israel was willing to accept a 'demilitarized Palestinian state.'[5] The speech was welcomed by his coalition partners in the Labour party, but strongly rejected by the more hawkish members of Likud and *Yisrael Beitenu*. Knowing full well that departing from his old promise never to allow a Palestinian state to be established would upset the right-wing, Netanyahu warned his Likud party ahead of the speech. His argument was that Israel had to pursue a dual track with the new administration in Washington by negotiating with the Palestinians while pushing the U.S. on a tougher Iran policy.

In November 2009, under heavy pressure from the Obama administration, Netanyahu agreed to a 10-month freeze of settlement construction in the West Bank. The freeze, however, would not be imposed in East Jerusalem, whose status remained a highly disputed issue between Israelis and Palestinians. The freeze would also not include synagogues, schools, kindergartens and public buildings. A few months before, Ehud Barak who was now an ally of Netanyahu and served as defense minister in his government, had approved 455 new housing units in the West Bank. The move was seen as a deliberate attempt to ease the settlers before the announcement of a 10-month freeze. It did little to please the Yesha Settler Council, with its chairman, Dani Dayan calling it an 'awkward compromise'.[6] After Netanyahu's announcement of the freeze, settlers began demonstrating in the West Bank. Some reacted violently by attacking Israeli officers to prevent them from enforcing the building ban, and others torched cars and tractors belonging to Palestinians near Nablus. Ben-Ari was among the far-right lawmakers who demonstrated against Netanyahu's settlement freeze, declaring that the periods in which the 'settlers were suckers' was over. 'What are we, schnitzel that Netanyahu cooked in his kitchen? We have an opportunity to teach Netanyahu, Obama and Sarkozy (French President) and the world that Jewish building cannot be frozen,' he said.[7]

The Obama administration was pleased with the settlement freeze but would soon be humiliated when Vice President Joe Biden visited Israel. An announcement of 1,600 new apartments in Jerusalem's Ramat Shlomo neighborhood was made the same day Netanyahu welcomed Biden. Netanyahu claimed he was unaware of the decision and that it was a deliberate attempt by a left-wing member of Jerusalem's municipal council to embarrass him and cause bad blood with Netanyahu. 'Biden was embarrassed. If it was up to Netanyahu, it wouldn't have happened. He would have waited. He (Biden) came for three days. Couldn't it have waited?' then director general of the Prime Minister's Office, Ran Ichay, said.

The announcement did indeed infuriate Washington. Secretary of State Hillary Clinton called Netanyahu the next day and said the announcement was a personal insult to Obama. Meanwhile Netanyahu was trying to expose the lack of willingness on the Palestinian part to engage in peace negotiations. President Abbas thought the settlement freeze was insufficient since it didn't include East Jerusalem and allowed for already planned construction in the West Bank to continue. Netanyahu was risking his reputation among his right-wing constituents but got nothing in return. Obama kept pushing Netanyahu to solve the dispute over construction in Jerusalem to make the Palestinians come to the table but knowing that such a move had the potential to cause a deep rift with the right-wing, Netanyahu pushed back. The issue was still contentious, but Abbas eventually agreed to finally meet Netanyahu in the autumn 2010. The informal meetings in Sharm El-Sheikh in Egypt and later in Jerusalem, however, amounted to little.

Soon after, the Arab Spring would break out, toppling Egypt's President Hosni Mubarak, whom Obama had called on to resign after mass protests erupted in Cairo. Netanyahu, fearing an Islamic takeover of Egypt, thought Obama and other Western leaders who cheered on the demonstrators were naïve. The Muslim Brotherhood, whose ideology Hamas was founded on, won the election after Mubarak had resigned, proving to Netanyahu that he had been right in worrying. When Abbas's Fatah party reconciled with Hamas in 2011 after four years of internal fighting, the fragile situation between Israel and the Palestinians deteriorated. Netanyahu had refused to extend the 10-month settlement construction freeze after it ended in September 2010, arguing that the Palestinians had shown no willingness to start negotiating.

In May 2011 the relationship between Netanyahu and Obama reached a new low following the breakdown of negotiations between Israel and the Palestinians, and Obama's continued pressure on Israel. The day before Netanyahu was scheduled to meet Obama in the White House, the president reiterated in a speech that the border between Israel and the Palestinians should be based on the 1967 lines with mutually agreed swaps. Although this view had been consistent throughout previous U.S. administrations, Netanyahu was furious. He felt that Obama didn't give Israel a break, and that he was the only one being asked to make any concessions. The following day, Netanyahu would push back at Obama at a press conference in the White House in what would later become known as an unprecedented history lecture given by an Israeli Prime Minister to an American President. 'I have never seen a foreign leader speak to the president like that, and certainly not in public and certainly not in the Oval Office,' Obama's advisor Ben Rhodes would later say.[8] Ambassador Oren, however, said that the lecture could have been a lot worse, had it not been for the Israeli staff trying to calm Netanyahu down. Oren said:

> While Bibi was in the air, flying to Washington, Obama gave his speech. At least half of it was about Israel-Palestine and it changed American policy. When Bibi landed there was smoke coming out of his ears. That led to the famous lecture in the White House. There was no rational reason for doing this. We had to sit on him (Netanyahu), he was so angry. The lecture he was going to give was much worse. Oh boy. This was the most difficult period in U.S.-Israel relations. There is nothing that really came close to it.

According to Yoaz Hendel, then Director of Communications and Public Diplomacy for Netanyahu, the international community was 'far away from reality' when it came to the Israeli-Palestinian conflict. The urge to push for a two-state solution was proof of that. Hendel, who himself was part of the Israeli negotiating team during the attempts to renew the peace process with the Palestinians, said it was difficult to know whether Netanyahu, whom he described as a 'Machiavellian' leader, was ready to make any concessions to the Palestinians because his personal needs always come first. Netanyahu 'knew how to manipulate and maneuver the international community in order to keep Israel safe,' Hendel said, adding that the American attempt to bring the parties together was a 'waste of time.'

The situation between the Palestinians and Israel had also reached a new low with the phenomenon of 'price tag' attacks running wild. In 2011, settler attacks against Palestinians rose 57% according to UN's Office for the Coordination of Humanitarian Affairs.[9] The attacks ranged from damaging property to stoning Palestinian cars and throwing a Molotov cocktail into a Palestinian home. Some were seen as a response to a brutal Palestinian terrorist attack committed against a Jewish family in the settlement of Itamar in March 2011. The family of five were killed in their beds, including three children, one of whom was an infant who was decapitated. Netanyahu 'unequivocally' rejected the concept of 'private militias' and that 'those who break the law will be dealt with accordingly.'[10] But the widespread anger among settlers after the family had been killed caused him to approve hundreds of new housing units in the major West Bank settlement blocs of Gush Etzion, Maale Adumim, Ariel and Modiin Ilit.

For the Palestinians, the Israeli government and the military weren't doing enough to prosecute Jewish extremists committing 'price tag' attacks. The settler attacks were however not limited to Palestinians. The IDF had become a more frequent target for extremists in the West Bank who saw the military as an obstacle to the settlement enterprise. The head of IDF Central Command, Avi Mizrahi, said in 2012 that the hatred the military saw from Jews was something he hadn't seen in his 30 years of service. While peace talks between Israel and the Palestinians were going nowhere in 2011, a different set of negotiations had opened with an unlikely partner: Hamas.

The kidnapping of Israeli soldier Gilad Shalit in 2006 on the Gaza border had been haunting Netanyahu since he took office. Bringing back soldiers from enemy territory had always been a top priority for Israel. Knowing Shalit was alive and kept by Hamas in Gaza was an unbearable situation for his parents and for the many other Israelis who watched the years of captivity go unresolved. After months of shuttle diplomacy between Israel and Hamas, brokered by Germany and Egyptian mediators, an agreement was finally reached in October 2011. Netanyahu believed that he could link the prisoner swap with the public support he needed for a strike on Iran. Hamas agreed to release Shalit on the Israeli-Gaza border where Netanyahu would be welcoming him. But the price was steep. More than 1,000 Palestinian prisoners were released, many of whom were convicted terrorists who had killed civilian Israelis. Netanyahu was once again going against his own beliefs by cutting a deal with terrorists. Among the prisoners was Yahya Sinwar, a Hamas official who had been sentenced to life in prison in 1989 for orchestrating the abduction and murder of two Israelis. Sinwar was welcomed as a hero in Gaza and would end up becoming the leader of Hamas in 2017.

Iran

As Netanyahu was trying to appease the Obama administration on Israel's conflict with the Palestinians, he instructed the IDF and Mossad to prepare for a possible military attack on Iran's nuclear program. Israeli intelligence had discovered that the Obama administration had been negotiating secretly with Iran in Oman, leading Netanyahu to once again feel hoodwinked by the U.S. Dan Meridor, who was deputy prime minister and minister of intelligence at the time, recalled how a secret group of ministers would discuss the plan to attack Iran. Meridor said:

> We had serious differences of opinions on Iran. I thought that the proposed military action (attacking Iran without American consent) would not achieve the target. Netanyahu established a group of six ministers, which eventually became eight, to discuss sensitive defense issues, mainly Iran. It was an open forum, where everyone could say what they wanted, but it was closed in the sense that nothing leaked. This group made the security cabinet irrelevant because we did all the serious defense discussions. If we had gotten American approval for a strike against Iran, it would have been a different story. But we didn't. It was clear to me that if we did, the goal would not be reached, Iran wouldnt have been stopped and could have even enhanced its nuclear program.

While Netanyahu and Barak were in favour of an attack against Iran, even without U.S. approval, the heads of Mossad, IDF and Shin Bet were against. Netanyahu tried to convince Obama that sanctions and military threats were the only way to handle Tehran but would soon find that his arguments fell on deaf ears. The top military and intelligence brass were united in the assessment that a military strike would at best delay the program a few years but would simultaneously risk an all-out war with Iran. Hezbollah, Iran's proxy in Lebanon, would likely be activated by Tehran, sending thousands of rockets at Israel, in addition to what Iran might send Israel's way.

Barak and Netanyahu, on the other hand, believed that it was Israel's last chance to stop Iran from going nuclear once and for all. This debate would continue for many years to come. Despite the continued opposition in the security echelon to launch a military strike against Iran without U.S. approval, Netanyahu kept reminding Obama that he didn't need his green light. 'Many times, I was asked by President (Barack) Obama... "no surprises. Please tell us before you do anything." And I said, "No, sometimes I will. Sometimes I won't",' Netanyahu said many years later when asked about his frictions with Obama over Iran.[11] But despite the implications and possibly even in reaction to Netanyahu's hints that Israel was preparing to attack Iran, the Obama administration kept negotiation with Tehran. Israel's campaign to get tougher on Iran and back harsh sanctions with credible military threats were replaced with direct negotiations over its nuclear program. When it became clear that the U.S. and world powers would sign a nuclear agreement with Iran in 2015, Netanyahu once again infuriated the Obama administration. In what he would later describe as one of the proudest moments in his career, Netanyahu attacked the pending nuclear deal in a speech in the U.S. Congress, calling it a 'very bad deal.' A senior U.S. official slammed Netanyahu's speech which he said contained 'literally not one new idea; not one single concrete alternative; all rhetoric, no action.'[12] The speech marked the lowest point in the relationship between Netanyahu and Obama, with the president feeling humiliated by an ally in his own house.

Notes

1   Noam Osband, 'The Radical Jew', 2016.
2   Asher Shechter, 'Michael Ben Ari, bugbear of the left', *Ha'aretz*, 11 January 2013.
3   Benjamin Netanyahu, *'Bibi: My Story'* (Simon & Schuster, New York, 2022) pp. 422-23.
4   The White House, 'Remarks by the President at Cairo University', 4 June 2009.
5   Staff, 'Full text of Binyamin Netanyahu's Bar Ilan speech', *Jerusalem Post*, 14 June 2009.

6   Isabel Kershner, 'Israel tries to placate settlers by allowing some construction before freeze', *The New York Times*, 7 September 2009.

7   Tohav Lazaroff, 'Michael Ben-Ari: Jewish settlements cannot be frozen like schnitzel', *Jerusalem Post*, 9 December 2009.

8   Frontline PBS, 'Netanyahu at war', 2016.

9   Tom Perry, 'In West Bank, settler violence seen on the rise', Reuters, 14 July 2011.

10 Herb Keinon, 'Netanyahu condemns settlers' 'price tag' violence, *Jerusalem Post*, 9 March 2011.

11 Jotam Confino, '"More of a wild-card": What a Netanyahu comeback could mean for US-Israel relations', *USA TODAY*, 26 October 2022.

12 Stephen Collinson, 'Netanyahu warns Congress: Deal will lead to Iranian nuclear bomb', *CNN*, 3 March 2015.

4

New government

Seeking a new mandate from the public to deal with what he saw as Israel's biggest challenge (Iran's nuclear program), Netanyahu urged fresh elections in May 2012. But it would take another five months before Knesset finally voted to dissolve itself, with elections set for January 2013. As Israel was gearing for another round of elections, a familiar conflict erupted in Gaza.

A week after Knesset had voted to dissolve itself Netanyahu ordered Israeli airstrikes at a shipment of weapons in the Sudanese capital of Khartoum. 40 containers of missiles from Iran en route to Hamas in Gaza were destroyed in the attack. Netanyahu also sent a message to Sudan's dictator Omar Al-Bashir that if he didn't seize the smuggling of weapons to Hamas through Sudan he would be assassinated. On 14 November, Israel assassinated Hamas military leader Ahmed Jabari in Gaza in an airstrike. Jabari had been behind the abduction of Shalit in 2006, which had cost Israel and Netanyahu dearly, releasing over 1,000 Palestinian prisoners in exchange.

Israel's military operation in Gaza dubbed 'Operation Pillar of Defense' was aimed at weakening Hamas and Islamic Jihad and stopping rockets from being fired at Israel. The operation would last eight days and ended up killing 177 Palestinians and six Israelis. Israel's newly developed Iron Dome missile defense system had proved useful, shooting down 400 of the 1,500 rockets and missiles fired at Israel, some of which failed to cross the border. But the 2012 Gaza conflict marked the first time Hamas successfully launched Iranian made missiles at Tel Aviv and Jerusalem. The conflict ended with another Egyptian-brokered ceasefire that would last less than two years until a widescale war erupted in the summer of 2014.

Netanyahu's election campaign centered around the security threats Israel faced, mainly from Iran but also from Palestinian groups in Gaza. Winning 31 seats Likud remained the largest party in Knesset, but the big surprise of the election was the newly established *Yesh Atid* party, led by former journalist Yair Lapid. A centrist, secular party focused on socio-economic issues, *Yesh Atid* won 19 seats, making it the second biggest party in Knesset. Netanyahu no longer had the option of forming a pure right-wing government with his old ultra-orthodox partners, opting instead for a government with *Yesh Atid*, the Jewish Home party, which was now led by Netanyahu's old chief of staff Naftali Bennett, and the newly established centrist party, *Hatnua*, led by Tzipi Livni.

With a stable 68 seat majority, Netanyahu's new government was an ideal formation of mutual interests. At least on paper. The two ambitious and younger party leaders, Bennett and Lapid, weren't Netanyahu's cup of tea, and would eventually replace him as prime minister years later. Bennett was an ultranationalist and religious politician, whose policies were largely aligned with Netanyahu's Likud party. Having made a fortune in high-tech, and with a history as the Yesha settler Council leader, Bennett was ideologically driven. He transformed the Jewish Home party after taking over as its chairman, winning 12 seats in the 2013 election. Together with Ayelet Shaked, another young ideologue, the two would transform Israeli politics in the years to come. Shaked was a firebrand politician, right-wing to the bone. But unlike the Jewish Home party she was secular and had grown up in Tel Aviv. Both Shaked and Bennett were considered far-right in their political views, supporting annexation of Jewish settlements in the West Bank while staunchly opposing a Palestinian state. The party also brought other ultranationalist and extreme politicians to Knesset, such as Orit Strock, who would be condemned for her remarks on Sharon a year later when he died.

Strock, an ultra-orthodox settler leader from Hebron was among the most extreme lawmakers in the party and worked to expand settlements in the West Bank as well as legalizing outposts that were deemed illegal according to Israeli law through the Land of Israel lobby in Knesset. Another lawmaker from Jewish home who would draw headlines for his racist remarks were Eli Ben-Dahan, who said Palestinians 'are like animals, they aren't human,' and that 'a Jew always has a much higher soul than a gentile, even if he is a homosexual.'[1] Jewish Home, which in many ways was built on the ruins of the National Religious party, attracted the hard-core right-wing settlers, offering them the ideology of religious Zionism combined with ultranationalism. Their hardline views, especially on the Palestinians, were a sign of the changing times in Israel and what would be permissible for senior ministers to say publicly. Likud itself had also started changing its DNA, with new politicians replacing the old 'princes' such as Dan Meridor. 'In 2013 I understood that there was a change of policy in Likud. Instead of trying to get votes from the centre, they flamed up the base,' Meridor said. The once rising star of Likud had failed to enter Knesset after receiving a low spot on the list. Instead, new politicians had entered

Likud, such as Moshe Feiglin and Miri Regev. They both illustrated new direction Likud was headed in, with room for provocative and controversial statements.

Feiglin was in many ways a far-right and religious lawmaker who believed Israel should encourage its Arab citizens to emigrate, while questioning why non-Jews should have a say in a Jewish state.[2] Regev, on her part, would become highly influential in Likud, known for her aggressive rhetoric in Knesset debates. Moshe Ya'alon was among the Likud members who detected the change in the party after 2013. 'Likud became a party to which even (Ze'ev) Jabotinsky (Likud's ideological father) and Menachem Begin would not have been elected. Where people such as Benny Begin, Ruvi Rivlin and Moshe Arens are perceived as leftists,' Ya'alon said in his memoirs.[3] Ya'alon, who was named defense minister in Netanyahu' new government, said he quickly discovered the extent of the hilltop youth phenomenon and how Jewish terror had intensified. The price tag attacks were mainly committed in the settlements of Yitzhar, Tapuach and Southern Har Hebron.

Some of the extremists were followers of the notorious Rabbi Yitzhak Ginsburgh, the president of a yeshiva in Yitzhar. According to Ya'alon, Ginsburgh's worldview could be compared to that of Hitler's *Mein Kampf*, stating that the Jewish race is superior while Arabs are inferior.[4] Ya'alon could see why the hilltop youth flocked around him, offering them a fascist and racist worldview with charm. Ginsburgh was a classic example of an influential and dangerous rabbi in the West Bank who influenced young settlers, like those who advocated for the religious concept of *din rodef* to be applied to Prime Minister Rabin in the 1990's. Ginsburgh had previously praised Baruch Goldstein and had made several inflammatory and racist remarks throughout the years, referring to Arabs as cancer. His teachings, however dangerous, continued to attract hilltop youth extremists who believed that every inch of biblical Israel should be settled by Jews, whatever the costs. The education ministry decided to close the yeshiva in 2011 after some of its students were arrested on being involved in 'price tag' attacks. In 2014, Ya'alon went a step further by letting the IDF turn the yeshiva into a military base in reaction to settler attacks against soldiers. Itamar Ben-Gvir, a future key minister in Netanyahu's government who in the 1990's was heavily engaged in demonstrations against Rabin, had now become a lawyer, representing Jewish extremists, among them members of Yitzhar. Ben-Gvir reacted strongly to Ya'alon's decision to take over the yeshiva, warning it would only lead to more 'price tag' attacks.

The rising tensions between Israel and Palestinians only made Obama, who had also been re-elected, keener on trying to solve the mother of all conflicts. John Kerry had replaced Hillary Clinton as secretary of state and would lead the new negotiation team. On the Israeli side, Livni, who had been appointed justice minister, would conduct negotiations, while Kerry appointed Martin Indyk as Middle East envoy. Indyk had previously served as U.S. ambassador to Israel during Netanyahu's first term as prime minister. The two weren't fond of each other, to put it mildly. The Palestinian negotiator would be Saeb Erekat, a diplomatic veteran who also didn't care for Netanyahu or the Israeli right-wing in general. Between Kerry, Indyk, Erekat and Livni, whom Netanyahu accused of wanting to concede too much to the Palestinians, a nightmare had been born for the Likud leader.

Meanwhile the vastly different attitudes toward the negotiations inside the new government made it difficult to present a unified position. Likud and Jewish Home were skeptical of the American efforts to broker a peace deal with the Palestinians, while the two other factions in Netanyahu's government, represented by Livni and Lapid, were more open to negotiations. With annexation remarks from Bennett one day and Livni endorsing Kerry's initiatives aimed at reaching a two-state solution the next, Netanyahu's partners sent different signals, causing great confusion about the Israeli position. As the teams were negotiating terms for relaunching proper peace negotiations, the Israeli government, military and intelligence agencies faced another kidnapping crisis. On 12 June, three Israeli teenagers, Gilad Sha'ar, Naftali Frankel and Eyal Yifrach had disappeared in the West Bank, leading Israeli authorities to believe they had been kidnapped. As Israeli security forces arrested hundreds of Palestinians in the West Bank, including senior Hamas members, Hamas had responded by firing rockets at Israel. As the days passed without any news of the missing teens, frustration and anger exploded among government officials as well as civilians. A Facebook page with 10,000 likes called on Netanyahu to execute a Palestinian terrorist every hour until the teenagers had been found. The anger also spilled over to Jewish-Arab relations. Left-wing extremist lawmaker Haneen Zoabi called IDF's search for the perpetrators in the West Bank 'terror', causing widespread condemnation among Jewish lawmakers. Foreign Affairs Minister Avigdor Lieberman called Zoabi a terrorist, saying that the 'sentence of the kidnappers and that of Zoabi, who is inciting and encouraging abductions, must be the same,' while Likud lawmaker Miri Regev said Zoabi should be 'expelled to Gaza.'[5]

After an 18-day manhunt, the three bodies were found hidden in a Palestinian village. It turned out they had been killed on the spot by their

Palestinian abductors. Hamas later took responsibility for the attack. The killings were condemned internationally, with Obama calling it a 'senseless act of terror against innocent youth' and UN Secretary-General Ban Ki-moon calling it 'heinous act by enemies of peace.'[6] As the nation mourned the killing of the three teenagers, the frustration and anger reached a boiling point among the most hard-core right-wing extremists. A Facebook page named 'The People of Israel Demand Revenge' got 35,000 likes in the two days it existed. The day after the funeral, on 2 July, three Jewish extremists seeking revenge, decided to commit a gruesome 'price tag' attack. They kidnapped a 16-year-old Palestinian boy, Mohammed Abu Khdeir, from the Shuafat refugee camp in East Jerusalem and burned him alive in the Jerusalem Forest. The terror attack was condemned internationally. With both Jewish and Palestinian anger spreading to the streets, Netanyahu convened his cabinet to decide how to respond to Hamas.

According to both Ya'alon and Netanyahu, Bennett had leaked information from the cabinet meeting about his proposal to destroy Hamas' vast tunnel system which had been discovered by Israel, trying to take credit for the plan. Ya'alon, who had attended cabinet meetings since 1995, both in capacity of his military and political positions, said he found a shallow cabinet when he was appointed defense minister in 2013. Members of the cabinet didn't bother to read up on the issues at hand and many tried to destroy Netanyahu, while leaking information from the meetings for political use.

On 7 July, Israeli airstrikes hit one of Hamas' tunnels, killing several Hamas members. As expected, Hamas retaliated by firing rockets. On 8 July, the cabinet approved the mobilization of 40,000 reservists, preparing for a widescale ground invasion of Gaza. 'Operation Protective Edge' would become Netanyahu's first real war. In the initial stage, Israel mainly used aircrafts to target Hamas rocket launchers and infrastructure and only nine days later would the ground invasion be launched, with tanks and soldiers on foot. As the casualties on both sides rose, and the images of a bombarded Gaza filled the news coverage, international pressure on Israel mounted.

Netanyahu preferred using Egypt's new military dictator Al-Sissi as mediator, instead of Turkey and Qatar, which had close ties with Hamas. The military operation received widespread support in the Israeli public. Israelis living in the south near the Gaza border were fed up with years of endless rocket attacks, which caused post-trauma among Israeli children. In Gaza, the situation was much more severe. Humanitarian crises from several military confrontations with Israel, poverty, lack of freedom of movement, and of course living under Hamas' rule had brought Gazans to their knees. After 50 days of fighting, Israel and Hamas finally agreed on a ceasefire. Over 2,000 Palestinians were killed. Israel claimed two thirds belonged to Hamas, Islamic Jihad or other Palestinian terror groups. That number, as in previous conflicts in Gaza, was disputed by UN, which said some 1,462 were civilians, of whom 551 were children. Hamas executed 21 Palestinians it said had collaborated with Israel.

On the Israeli side, 67 Israeli soldiers and five civilians were killed, while over 4,500 rockets were fired from Gaza. The Iron Dome had improved significantly since the last Gaza conflict two years earlier, shooting down 86% of the rockets. Two Israeli soldiers, Oron Shaul and Hadar Goldin, were killed in Gaza and their bodies captured by Hamas. As of 2023, their bodies were still held captive, despite efforts by the families to have them released in a prisoner exchange. The leaks by cabinet ministers as well as political profiteering during the war had caused internal fights in Netanyahu's government. Ya'alon on his part was furious with Bennett for going in the field to visit soldiers without coordinating with him, as was required. Ya'alon also accused Lieberman of leaking information and proposing that Israel destroy Hamas in one of the meetings, only to leave before it was discussed. The differences over West Bank settlements also drove a wedge between the parties. Bennett had continued to push for annexation of settlements, causing both Lapid and Livni to threaten with quitting the government. Lapid said in June 2014:

> If even one settlement is unilaterally annexed, Yesh Atid won't just quit the government, it will topple it. There is no reason to continue to build settlements in areas that will not remain part of Israel in any future agreement or to invest billions in infrastructure that at the end of the day will be given as a present to the Palestinians. [7]

John Kerry's efforts to bring Israel and the Palestinians to the table had failed after broken promises on both sides, as well as Palestinian requests to become members of 15 UN organizations. The daylight between the most right-wing and centrist members of Netanyahu's government was becoming clearer in the aftermath of the Gaza war.

Netanyahu believed that both Livni and Lapid were plotting to oust him and that Livni met in secret with Palestinian President Abbas in May that year, going against a cabinet decision. In early December, Netanyahu decided to fire Lapid, who had served as finance minister, after he rejected Netanyahu's demand to support a bill that would declare Israel the nation state of the Jewish people. He also fired Livni, accusing her and Lapid of plotting a *putsch* by negotiation with the ultra-orthodox parties to form a new government without Netanyahu. Lapid fired back at Netanyahu, saying he was the one who had negotiated with the ultra-orthodox to speed up elections. Livni criticized Netanyahu's decision harshly, calling his firing of her an attempt to remove the 'gatekeeper of Israeli democracy.'[8] The short-lived government collapsed, and Netanyahu called fresh elections scheduled to be held in March 2015.

Notes

1   Tamar Pileggi, 'New deputy defense minister called Palestinian animals', *Times of Israel,* 11 May 2015.

2   Jeffrey Goldberg, 'Among the settlers: Will they destroy Israel?', The New Yorker, 24 May 2004.

3   Moshe Ya'alon, *'The longer, shorter path',* (Geffen Publishing House, Jerusalem, 2020), pp. 296-297.

4   Moshe Ya'alon, *'The longer, shorter path',* (Geffen Publishing House, Jerusalem, 2020), pp. 307-309.

5   TOI Staff, 'Hanin Zoabi: IDF operation in West Bank is terrorism', *Times of Israel,* 21 June 2014.

6   JPost staff, 'LIVE BLOG: Search for Israeli teen ends in tragedy', *Jerusalem Post,* 1 July 2014.

7   Tohav Lazaroff, 'Lapid: If even one settlement is annexed, we'll topple the government', *Jerusalem Post,* 9 June 2014.

8   Jonathan Lis, 'Netanyahu calls for new elections, accuses Livni and Lapid of plotting 'putsch'', *Ha'aretz,* 2 December 2014.

5

Jewish Nation-State

'Arabs are voting in droves'

As Netanyahu returned from having delivered an unprecedented speech in the U.S. Congress against a sitting president, election campaigns in Israel were heating up. Netanyahu was slammed in the Israeli media for attacking Obama's nuclear deal with Iran, with commentators warning that he was jeopardizing the relationship with Israel's most important ally. Netanyahu stood his ground, arguing that he had done exactly what he was elected to do; looking out for Israel's interests. Most of his election campaign centered around what he called an existential threat posed by a nuclear armed Iran. With Obama soon to be out of office, and after years of failed peace negotiations with the Palestinians, Netanyahu said his speech from 2009, in which he voiced support for a demilitarized Palestinian state, was no longer relevant. Israel had no partner for peace, he said. Two of Netanyahu's rivals in the centre-left of the political map, Labour and Livni's *Hatnuah* party, decided to run on a new joint list: Zionist Union.

The union, which ran on relaunching peace negotiations with the Palestinians among other topics, was headed by Isaac Herzog, an experienced politician who had served as minister under Sharon, Olmert and Netanyahu. Another party, *Kulanu*, also emerged on the list, established by former Likud lawmaker Moshe Kahlon. *Kulanu* was considered a centrist party, whose aim was to tackle the rising cost of living in Israel. As election day neared it became clear that the race would be close, with some polls indicating that Zionist Union would be bigger than Likud. Both Herzog and Netanyahu refused the possibility of a unity government where they would each serve as prime minister in a rotation agreement. Netanyahu warned there was a 'real danger' that he would be ousted as prime minister, while his Likud party slammed President Peres for endorsing Herzog ahead of elections, saying 'it's obvious that Peres, an avowed leftist, supports (Herzog) and Tzipi. He is the architect of the Oslo Accords, an enthusiastic supporter of the disengagement, and a proponent of withdrawal from the West Bank.'[1]

Netanyahu also departed from his near boycott of the Israeli media, deciding to give interviews to get his message out. The *Gevald* (Yiddish word for sounding alarm) campaign was in full force, alarming Likud voters that if they didn't vote, the right-wing would fall. This campaign had been used by other politicians before and would be used many times later, by Netanyahu as well. With the polls favouring Zionist Union, Netanyahu made a highly controversial statement in a video meant to get Likud supporters out and vote. 'The rule of the right is in danger. Arab voters are moving in droves to the polling stations. Left-wing organizations are busing them in,' Netanyahu said. His rivals were quick to condemn him, accusing him of making derogatory remarks against Israel's Arab minority. Whether his video message worked or not, scaring right-wing voters about Arab Israeli voter turnout, remains unclear. His Likud party did, however, win 30 seats, becoming the largest faction in Knesset, against all odds and polls. Zionist Union received 24 seats and became the second biggest party. Netanyahu was forced to apologize for his for his comment about Arab voters after being scolded by President Reuven Rivlin, Herzog and Arab Israeli lawmakers. Herzog said that Netanyahu 'humiliated 20 percent of Israeli citizens for the sake of his election campaign (with those remarks). His first action must be to repair his ways – and not in empty words – and the severe fissure he has caused in doing so. He has to do everything to turn them into citizens with equal rights,' and that his comments were 'the most fraudulent and racist utterances that exist.'[2] Netanyahu eventually apologized, admitting that that it had 'hurt some Israeli citizens' and that he saw himself as the prime minister of all Israelis 'without differentiating between religions, races and sex.'[3] But his apology did little to calm the Arab Israeli lawmakers. The leader of the Joint Arab List, Ayman Odeh, said Netanyahu 'will keep pushing the racist legislation and will sit with Bennett to legislate the Jewish nation-state law. That isn't a true apology.'[4] Odeh referred to a law in the making that would define Israel as the nation state of the Jewish people.

'Extortion'

With Netanyahu's surprising election result, he found himself in a position once again with a majority of lawmakers backing him for prime minister. But Foreign Minister and *Yisrael Beitenu* party leader Avigdor Lieberman dropped a bombshell when he announced that his party wouldn't join Netanyahu just two days before the coalition deadline. Lieberman argued that the coalition was 'purely opportunistic' and wasn't nationalistic enough, while he accused Netanyahu of caving into ultra-orthodox demands to change laws on Jewish conversion and for not toppling Hamas in the 2014 Gaza war.[5]

Lieberman's surprise decision put Netanyahu in an extremely uncomfortable situation, with just 61 seats, the bare minimum needed for a majority government. This meant that he was susceptible to political pressure from the coalition parties, which included Shas, United Torah Judaism *Kulanu* and Jewish Home. The latter, led by Bennett, demanded that his party colleague Ayelet Shaked be named justice minister and that the party would receive another senior portfolio. Bennett and Shaked had their eyes on the justice ministry as part of their plan to carry out a judicial revolution that would curb the Supreme Court and appoint right-wing justices across the judicial system. Netanyahu was reluctant to hand Jewish Home the justice ministry, fearing it would lead to a full-on confrontation with the Supreme Court. Ironically, Likud would make a U-turn on this topic just five years later, launching a campaign to significantly weaken the Supreme Court. With Jewish Home being the only party Netanyahu hadn't signed a coalition deal, just hours before deadline he finally caved and gave Shaked the keys to the justice ministry. The ultimatum, which Netanyahu saw as extortion, marked the beginning of the bad blood between him and the ambitious and shrewd far-right duo, Shaked and Bennett. Bennett was named education minister and his party got the chairmanship of the Knesset Law and Constitution committee. Shaked chaired the powerful Ministerial Committee for Legislation and the Judicial Appointments Committee. The party had immense power over the judicial system, with Shaked at the top. With just eight seats Jewish Home had managed to get crucial influence in Netanyahu's new government. Uri Ariel, a far-right lawmaker from Jewish Home, was named agriculture minister and both Bennett and Shaked had gotten a seat at the security cabinet. As with every new Knesset, a few new lawmakers had been elected while some had either retired or didn't make it. One of them was Betzalel Smotrich, the religious right-wing extremist who had been arrested by Shin bet 10 years earlier, reportedly with 700 liters of gasoline on his way to launch an attack on one of Israel's highways. Smotrich, whose far-right *Tkuma* party had run on a joint platform with Jewish Home, would become one of the most extreme lawmakers in Israel's history and would quickly challenge Bennett and Shaked in far-right views.

Knife intifada

The wounds from the 2014 Gaza war were still fresh as tensions brewed between Israel and the Palestinians in the summer of 2015. On July 31,

21-year-old Jewish extremist Amiram Ben-Uliel firebombed the home of the Palestinian Dawabsheh family in the village of Duma in the West Bank, killing an 18-month-old baby and its two parents. 'Revenge' and 'Long Live King Messiah' had been spraypainted on the wall by Ben-Uliel and another extremist. The terrorist attack sparked immediate outrage among Palestinians and in the international community. Netanyahu phoned Palestinian President Abbas to condemn the attack and called it a 'reprehensible and horrific act of terrorism in every respect' while Israel's President Rivlin said that to 'to my great sorrow, until now it seems that we have been lax in our treatment of the phenomena of Jewish terrorism. Perhaps we did not internalize that we are faced with a determined and dangerous ideological group which aims to destroy the fragile bridges which we work so tirelessly to build.'[6] Lawmakers from across the political spectrum in Israel, as well as the Yesha settler Council united in condemning the terror attack. Lapid, now in the opposition, issued a particularly harsh condemnation, politically loaded and with a clear message to other 'enemies' of Israel. Lapid said:

> We're at war. He who burns a Palestinian baby declares war on the State of Israel. He who stabs young people on a Pride March declares war on the State of Israel. He who burns down a church declares war on the State of Israel. He who threatens to attack the Supreme Court with a D9 bulldozer declares war on the State of Israel. He who throws rocks at the security services declares war on the State of Israel. The members of "Lehava" (far-right group) are traitors who assist the enemy at a time of war. The young people who attacked Arabs in Jerusalem, traitors. Anyone who chants "Death to the Arabs" at a Beitar Jerusalem match, a traitor to our homeland.[7]

But as lawmakers were seemingly united in their condemnation, Defense Minister Ya'alon recalled a reluctance among certain security cabinet members to accept that it was an act of Jewish terror. Ya'alon also said he was 'disgusted' to learn that some politicians had visited the home of Ben-Uriel, and that he saw a clear connection between a 'forgiving' attitude toward 'price tag' attacks by the hilltop youth and the escalation of Jewish terror.[8] Conspiracy theories had begun spreading about the Shin Bet torturing settlers who had been arrested following the attack, after the security cabinet had approved the use of administrative detention for Jewish terror suspects, a method normally used for Palestinian suspects. A few months later, a video of young extremists Jews at a wedding started circulating, showing them celebrating the murder of the Dawabsheh family and stabbing a picture of the toddler. Once again Netanyahu was forced to issue a condemnation.

While it took months for Israeli intelligence and security apparatus to get a breakthrough with the suspects who had been arrested, Hamas instantly called for a 'Day of Rage' and for Palestinians to carry out 'Lone Wolf' terror attacks against Israeli soldiers and civilians. As the Jewish high holiday of new year was nearing, Israel prepared for an escalation with Palestinians on the Temple Mount, the holiest site in Judaism and home of the Al-Aqsa Mosque, the third holiest for all Muslims. Almost every year, the Temple Mount became a flashpoint in the Israeli-Palestinian conflict. Sharon's visit in 2000, which sparked the second *Intifada*, was the best example of that. When Israel conquered East Jerusalem in 1967, an agreement was made with Jordan about the Temple Mount. Jordan, which remained the custodian of the site, allowed Jews to visit but not to pray. The status-quo agreement had been sacred ever since and seen as a cornerstone of the relationship between Jordan and Israel. Over many years, Jews visiting the Temple Mount would be limited to a few hundred annually. But with the rise of the religious Zionism movement, the idea of visiting the holy site and of changing the status-quo agreement so that Jews were allowed to also pray became popular. The number of Jews visiting the Temple Mount had risen to some 10,000 a year, and some Jews had been caught praying in secret at the site in violation of the status-quo agreement. The religious Zionists who believed in restoring the Jewish Temple ignored a decree by the Chief Rabbi of Israel who said it was forbidden for Jews to visit the holiest site in Judaism.

One of the biggest advocates of allowing Jews to pray was far-right activist and rabbi, Yehuda Glick, who survived an assassination attempt in 2014 by a member of Islamic Jihad, who according to Glick wanted to kill him for visiting Al-Aqsa. But Jewish Home lawmaker Uri Ariel and Likud lawmaker Miri Regev were also vocal in their support for allowing Jews to pray at the site. Netanyahu, however, would repeatedly reject the calls to change the status quo. On the eve of the Jewish New year some 300 Jews visited the Temple Mount, including Ariel who was seen praying at the site. Their visit sparked rumours among Palestinians that Israel was trying to change the status-quo, igniting a wave of violence that spiraled quickly. Palestinian car-ramming, stabbings and shooting attacks became an almost daily occurrence for Israel. The 'Knife *Intifada*' was born. To quell the high tensions at Temple Mount, Netanyahu banned both Jewish and Arab lawmakers from visiting the site in October. The move was criticized by

Ariel who called it unreasonable, as well as by Arab lawmakers who said they would ignore the ban. Ahmad Tibi, the leader of the Ta'al party, defied Netanyahu's ban. 'I went there. I said I wasn't going to the Temple Mount but to the Al-Aqsa Mosque. And a Muslim shouldn't ask for permission to go there,' Tibi said. As violence escalated, both Bennett and Netanyahu accused President Abbas of incitement, an allegation Abbas denied. In the Knesset, Arab and Jewish lawmakers would also accuse each other of fanning the flames. In February 2016, three Arab lawmakers from the far-left *Balad* party were suspended by the Knesset's Ethics Committee and barred from attending the Knesset plenum after visiting the families of Palestinian terrorists. Lawmakers Haneen Zoabi and Basel Ghattas were suspended for four months while Jamal Zahalka got two months suspension. Their visit, in which they had reportedly held a minute silence for a Palestinian terrorist who had been killed by Israeli security forces after attacking Jews, was widely condemned by Jewish lawmakers from across the political spectrum. Netanyahu slammed their behavior, saying there is such a thing as 'national pride', while Zoabi criticized Knesset, telling Army Radio: 'There is a racist atmosphere; there is even a fascist atmosphere that empties democracy of its content. Already, I have to ask right-wing Knesset members if they will let me deal with things that are in public interest and now, I have to ask them if I can deal with humanitarian issues?'[9]

The rift between Arab and Jewish lawmakers would only worsen in the years to come, especially between the *Balad* party and the Joint Arab List. As the daily terror attacks continued to kill civilians and Israeli soldiers, the army and the Shin Bet stepped up its efforts to put an end to it. The 'Knife *Intifada*' would last until around May 2016, killing 38 Israelis and over 200 Palestinians. Most of the Palestinian attacks were carried out in the West Bank and East Jerusalem.

Elor Azaria

As the 'Knife *Intifada*' was still raging, the debate about how to deal with terrorism reached its peak when an Israeli soldier executed a Palestinian terrorist in the West Bank. Two Palestinian men, Abdel Fattah al-Sharif and Ramzi al-Qasrawi, were both shot after stabbing an Israeli soldier in Hebron. Al-Qasrawi was killed on the spot while al-Sharif was left wounded, lying on the ground. A few minutes later, Elor Azaria, a medic from the battalion stationed in Hebron, arrived. When he saw al-Sharif was still alive he pulled his M-16 and shot him in the head. A video of the killing quickly circulated and reached Israeli and Palestinian media. As expected, the killing was condemned by the Palestinian Authority, but in Israel, the issue became the centre of a political campaign, showing the deep divide between right and left-wingers. Netanyahu, along with Defense Minister Moshe Ya'alon and IDF Chief of Staff Gadi Eisenkot quickly issued a statement condemning Azaria, who had been arrested after the incident. But other lawmakers in Israel were quick to defend Azaria, including Education Minister Bennett, Likud lawmaker David Bitan and *Yisrael Beitenu* party leader Avigdor Lieberman. Bennett called Azaria's parents to show support while a member of Lieberman's party even visited the family.

Shortly after, a political campaign to free Azaria of any charges was launched. In a court hearing to extend Azaria's custody, several lawmakers showed up to support him, including Lieberman, newly elected Likud lawmaker Oren Chazan, former far-right lawmaker Moshe Feiglin, as well as Jewish extremist Baruch Marzel and another Meier Kahane supporter Ben-Zion 'Bentzi' Gopstein. A demonstration at Tel Aviv's Rabin Square drew thousands who called for Azaria's release. Posters with signs reading 'Kahane Lives', a reference to the racist Jewish extremist Meir Kahane, was seen at the demonstration, a highly controversial sight at an event in Tel Aviv. Likud lawmaker Oren Chazan encouraged Israelis to join the demonstration, saying 'Love of the Land of Israel and supporting the IDF is not a matter of politics but of free love. The story of Elor is the best story of all of us. This is the time to demonstrate unity and show support for the men.'[10] Ya'alon, who fully supported the IDF in its investigation, quickly became a scapegoat and the focus of criticism from far-right lawmakers who supported Azaria.

Netanyahu had initially stood on Ya'alon and the IDF's side, unequivocal in his condemnation of the incident, but his rhetoric changed as the political storm raged. Netanyahu called Azaria's father, Charlie, telling him he felt his pain and promised that his son would get a chance to defend himself. When asked about the phone call months later, Netanyahu compared it to calling parents of fallen soldiers, which immediately sparked a backlash, forcing him to apologize for the comparison shortly after. 'I apologize if my remarks were misunderstood. I did not intend in any way to compare the suffering of bereaved families, a suffering I am very familiar with, to the situation of other parents in distress. There is no comparison and can be no comparison,' Netanyahu said.[11] As the public debate over Azaria intensified, Ya'alon announced his resignation as defense minister. Ya'alon had clashed repeatedly with Netanyahu over security related affairs, but the Azaria affair was the last straw. He would later say that the Likud he joined in 2009 was no longer the same party, which had undergone a 'radicalization' with new lawmakers who led a rhetoric that was 'brash and disrespectful.'[12]

Just five days later, Netanyahu appointed Lieberman as defense minister, expanding his shaky coalition with five more seats. Lieberman, who had refused to join Netanyahu's government a year earlier, was now the second most powerful man in the country. While he had almost two decades of influence as a politician, he had very little experience in security affairs, unlike his predecessor. Former Defense Minister Moshe Arens, a Likud icon, called Netanyahu's decision a 'mistake', arguing that the importance of the IDF in Israel required the 'best possible person in that position.'[13] Lieberman, an ultranationalist and a defense hawk who lived in the Nokdim settlement in the West Bank, had been highly critical of the 2014 war in Gaza. About a month before his appointment, Lieberman had promised that if he became defense minister, he would order the killing of Hamas leader Ishmael Haniyeh in Gaza within 48 hours if he failed to return the bodies of Israeli soldiers. And with his support of Azaria, the defense minister was suddenly at odds with the army, which was investigating and supporting the trial. However, when a military court convicted Azaria of manslaughter and sentenced him to 18 months in a military prison in February 2017, Lieberman changed his tune, saying the verdict should be respected. Other senior minister and lawmakers called immediately for pardoning Azaria, including Bennett, Transportation Minister Yisrael Katz, Housing and Construction Minister Yoav Gallant, and Likud lawmaker Miri Regev.

The Palestinian authority called the trial a 'farce', slamming the lenient sentence. The same did Arab lawmakers and civil rights activists. Lawmaker Youssef Jabareen from the Arab Joint list said the sentence did not reflect the 'severity of the act and it sends the harsh message that Palestinian blood is worthless. The case of Azaria is not an isolated incident but part of a widespread manifestation of the army, supported by the politicians, and nourished by not prosecuting soldiers,' while former chief of the Peace Now organization called the sentence 'embarrassing in its leniency.'[14] The most significant reaction came from Netanyahu, who had joined the chorus calling on a pardon for Azaria. The impact on having the prime minister, as well as senior ministers, going against the army and the court showed a tremendous division in Israel. The decades old accusations by the right-wing that the IDF and the judicial system were infected by the 'left-wing' only strengthened after the Azaria affair.

Judicial revolution part 1

The inevitable clash between the newly appointed Justice Minister Ayelet Shaked and the Supreme Court was evident in her first speech as minister. Addressing the Israel Bar Association, Shaked explained her philosophy on the judicial system. Shaked said:

> In recent years it seems a large part of the public has been under the impression that this outlook (of judicial restraint) has diminished. It seems decision making – governance – is no longer under the control of the people – their elected officials in the Knesset – but is held by the judiciary. The issue is the heart of a contentious public debate. Those objecting to this process of the erosion of powers, myself included, are labeled as "sons of darkness", while those who support disenfranchising the public from their right to deice through their elected officials are labeled as "sons of light". I reject this division and reject those characterizations.[15]

Her speech was a clear warning sign of the direction Israel was headed in. Not long after, Shaked elaborated on her philosophy on Israel's judicial system in a manifesto published in the *HaShiloach* periodical. Shaked wrote:

> Precisely as we want Israel to undergo processes of advanced democratization, it is our obligation to deepen its Jewish identity in turn. These identities certainly do not conflict. On the contrary: I believe they strengthen one another. I believe we will be a more democratic state the more we are a Jewish state, and we will be a more Jewish state the more democratic we become. [16]

Her arguments were completely in line with the Jewish Nation-State Law which would be passed 2018. Shaked had effectively set the wheels in motion for a radical change of Israel's judicial system, laying the groundwork for the complete overhaul that would be pushed just eight years later. Her legal philosophy and harsh criticism of the Supreme Court's power was shared by several Likud lawmakers, including Transportation Minister Yariv Levin, and Absorption Minister and Jerusalem Affairs Minister Ze'ev Elkin.

Levin had long railed against the Supreme Court, believing it to be infected by left-wing activists who prevented Knesset from enacting certain laws. Elkin and Levin had even submitted a bill in 2011 seeking to require public hearings for Supreme Court nominees, allowing the Knesset Constitution, Law and Justice Committee the right to veto an appointment. Netanyahu, however, a believer in the separation of powers and a self-declared supporter of the liberal icons such as Jock Locke and Montesquieu, had long defended the Supreme Court and its importance, and therefore dismissed the proposal. In 2012, Netanyahu said he had prevented radical proposals to curb the Supreme Court's power, which he referred to as pillars of democracy. But for Shaked, as well as a growing number of right-wing lawmakers, Knesset should be allowed to pass whichever law it wanted without the Supreme Court being able to strike it down. The Supreme Court's oversight of Knesset legislation was meant as way to keep the politicians in check by defending civil rights, preventing Israel's Basic Laws from being violated. Another clear target for Shaked was the appointment of Supreme Court judges, which was made by a committee consisting of Supreme Court judges, two government ministers, one coalition lawmaker and one opposition lawmaker, and lastly two representatives of Israel's Bar Association. Shaked wanted to dissolve the committee, adopting the American model which allows for politicians to appoint Supreme Court judges, whose elections would be subject public hearings in Knesset. In other words, politicize the appointment of judges.

The difference between the U.S. and Israel was that the US an actual constitution, guaranteeing civil rights. Israel, on the other hand, has quasi-constitutional 'Basic Laws' which aren't protecting rights in the same way. One of Shaked's first big clashes with the Supreme Court erupted after the court overturned a gas deal between the government and companies operating Israel's offshore gas fields. The court had found that one of the clauses in the agreement was unconstitutional. It stated that the government promised that Knesset wouldn't make any regulatory changes that could affect the companies in the following ten years. Shaked called the ruling a phenomenon of 'irresponsibly wielding authority' and that the Supreme Court had once again 'turned itself into a venue for arbitrating on purely political and macroeconomic questions.'[17] Her attack on the Supreme Court was backed by Netanyahu who accused its ruling of 'seriously threatening development of Israel's gas reserves. Israel is seen as a country with excessive judicial intervention that's hard to do business in.' Supreme Court President Miriam Naor responded by slamming the 'harsh, vitriolic' statements against the Supreme Court and its justices made in recent days.[18]

The ruling was seen as a perfect example of the Supreme Court's judicial activism which had been promoted during the tenure of its former president, Aharon Barak, in the 1990's. Barak wanted the Supreme Court to take a clearer stand on protecting minorities and interpreting laws more freely. This had been noted by scholars across the world who would consider it one of the most activist judiciaries in the world, while some considered the Supreme Court to be among the best in the world. The Supreme Court would, however, often rule in favour in cases seen as highly favourable to the far-right, such as greenlighting new settlements in the West Bank as well as allowing demolitions of homes belonging to families of Palestinian terrorists and Palestinian homes considered to be built illegally. Shaked had the exact opposite view on the judicial system than Barak, vowing to reverse some of the marks he made. Shaked's toxic relationship with the Supreme Court would only worsen throughout her tenure, often embarking on attacks in speeches held at the Bar Association. One such speech took aim at the Supreme Court for failing to consider Zionism in comparison to that of individual and human rights. Her comment came after the Supreme Court ruled that the unlimited detention of African asylum was prohibited and that they couldn't be deported against their will. One of Shaked's biggest victories in her path to revolutionize the judicial system came in early 2017 when the Judicial Appointments Committee elected four new Supreme Court judges, three of whom were conservatives backed by Shaked, who praised the decision as historic. Despite President Naor and Shaked ending up agreeing on the final nominees, a huge public fight had erupted between the two in the months preceding. In an unusually harsh-worded letter, Naor accused Shaked of 'putting a gun on the table' after she had promoted new legislation that would remove justice's veto power on new Supreme Court judges. Naor's public letter to Shaked read:

> I am compelled to notify you that along with Deputy Supreme Court President Rubinstein and Justice Joubran, that we have no intention of continuing to pre-discuss and consult with you at this time with regard to formulating a list of candidates and with regard to possible compromises.[19]

Shaked's public arguments with the Supreme Court would occasionally be defended by Netanyahu. But her far-reaching judicial reforms to curb the Supreme Court's power was still a radical proposal in Netanyahu's eyes. When Shaked was justice minister, at least for part of her term, Netanyahu still held that belief, making it impossible for her to implement all the changes she had intended.

The biggest marks Shaked would leave on the judicial system would be the appointment of conservative judges throughout the country, an estimated 300 according to her, as well as presiding over the appointment of six new Supreme Court judges. Shaked also took credit for co-sponsoring the highly divisive Jewish Nation-State Law. But her other far-reaching reforms, such as curbing the Supreme Court's power and making sure the government could appoint Supreme Court judges, failed. She did, however, kickstart a revolution to change Israel's judicial system, which would eventually become the biggest societal issue in Israel's history.

Notes

1 TOI staff, 'Final polls show Likud trailing behind Zionist Union', *Times of Israel*, 13 March 2015.

2 Jonathan Lis, 'Herzog; Netanyahu humiliated Israeli Arabs to garner votes', *Ha'aretz*, 21 March 2015.

3 Jonathan Lis, 'Netanyahu "sorry" his comments offended Israeli Arabs', *Ha'aretz*, 23 March 2015.

4 Ha'aretz, 'Joint List leader: A real apology from Netanyahu would be true equality for Arabs', *Ha'aretz*, 23 March 2015.

5 Amir Tibon, 'Avigdor Lieberman's failed plan to topple Netanyahu', *Tablet Magazine*, 11 May 2015.

6 Jonathan Beck, 'After Palestinian baby killed in firebombing, Abbas condemns settler groups as terrorists', *Times of Israel*, 31 July 2015.

7 Marissa Newman, 'PM condemns "horrific, heinous terror attack on Palestinians"', *Time of Israel*, 31 July 2015.

8 Moshe Ya'alon, '*The longer, shorter path*', (Geffen Publishing House, Jerusalem, 2020), pp. 310-311.

9 Isabel Kershner, 'Reprimands for 3 lawmakers rekindle debate about Israel's minority', *New York Times*, 9 February 2016.

10 Ben Hartman, 'Thousands at Tel Aviv rally call for release of IDF soldier charged in Hebron shooting', *Jerusalem Post*, 19 April 2016.

11 JTA, 'Netanyahu apologizes for comparing Hebron shooter's parents to fallen soldiers', *The Jewish Telegraphic Agency*, 25 September 2016.

12 Moshe Ya'alon, '*The longer, shorter path*', (Geffen Publishing House, Jerusalem, 2020), pp. 424-425.

13 Isabel Kershner, 'Netanyahu names Avigdor Lieberman Israeli Defense Minister as party joins coalition', *New York Times*, 25 May 2016.

14 TOI STAFF, 'Right-wing politicians call for Hebron shooter Azaria to be pardoned', *The Times of Israel*, 21 February 2016.

15 Revital Hovel, 'Justice Minister Shaked: Governance must return to the people's control', *Ha'aretz*, 18 May 2015.

16 Marissa Newman, 'In manifesto, minister says a more Jewish Israel will be more democratic', *Times of Israel*, 6 October 2016.

17 Sharon Pulwer, 'Justice Minister Shaked attacks High Court over gas ruling', *Ha'aretz*, 4 April 2016.

18 Sharon Pulwer, 'Israel's Supreme Court President slams government for 'vitriol' over gas deal ruling', *Ha'aretz*, 29 March 2016.

19 Yonah Jeremiah Bob, 'Supreme Court severs ties with Ayelet Shaked over gun to the head threats', *Jerusalem Post*, 3 November 2015.

6

State of Israel vs Netanyahu

Cigars and champagne

In 2016, Israel Police began investigating allegations against Netanyahu, suggesting he had received alcohol and cigars worth hundreds of thousands of shekels from Arnon Milchan, a well known Israeli businessman and movie producer in Hollywood. The investigation was revealed in Israeli media in early 2017. The media quickly began digging into Netanyahu's personal affairs, whose name had once again been associated with corruption.

The first corruption allegations against Netanyahu surfaced during his first term as prime minister in 1997. After a three-month long investigation Police recommended Netanyahu be indicted, suggesting he had appointed a new attorney general, Roni Bar-On, as part of a deal with Shas party leader Arieh Dery. Police believed Dery, who was on trial for corruption, had asked Netanyahu to appoint an attorney general who could get him a good plea. In return, Deri promised that Shas would back Netanyahu's Hebron agreement with the Palestinians. In the end, prosecutors decided not to indict Netanyahu, who had dismissed the affair as mere politics. Bar-On resigned less than two days after being appointed attorney general following heavy criticism over his lack of legal experience for such a top job. In the meantime, Eliakim Rubinstein had been appointed attorney general. Despite the lack of evidence to indict Netanyahu, Rubinstein said it was a 'very difficult decision for us to reach, in fact one of the most difficult we have ever had to reach.'[1] Despite admitting to having made mistakes, the 'Bar-On affair' proved to Netanyahu that the judicial system was out to get him too. His frustration and anger with the police as well as branches of Israel's justice ministry exploded with the fresh corruption allegations in 2016.

Not long after the Police investigations into gifts Netanyahu had received from Milchan were leaked to the media, new corruption allegations were revealed in Israeli media. Police were investigating accusations that Noni Mozes, the owner of *Yediot Ahronot,* had been negotiating a deal with Netanyahu that would give him favourable coverage in the newspaper in return for legislation that would limit the circulation of its competitor, *Israel Hayom*. The bombshell reports about illicit gifts and corrupt deals with one of the biggest newspapers in Israel hit Israel like an earthquake. Prime time TV, newspapers and radio all covered the corruption allegations extensively. Netanyahu, however, dismissed the allegations as a 'witch hunt', and a media orchestrated a coup attempt against him. 'In the past few days the media has orchestrated a campaign of unprecedented scope to bring down my Likud government. This campaign is intended to put pressure on the attorney general and others in the prosecution so that they will indict me,' Netanyahu claimed.[2]

Lastly, the most severe corruption investigations were revealed, involving serious allegations about an alleged deal between Netanyahu and the owner of another Israeli news site, *Walla!*. Police suspected that the owner, Shaul Elovitch, had made a deal with Netanyahu, giving him favourable coverage. In return, Netanyahu would secure regulation that benefitted the telecom giant, Bezeq, where Elovitch was the controlling shareholder. The almost daily, juicy leaks about the investigations sparked anger among centrist and left-wing voters who believed Netanyahu should resign as prime minister the same way Ehud Olmert did in 2008 when he was investigated. But while protestors began demonstrating every week, Netanyahu's most loyal voter base, as well as most of his colleagues in the Likud party, defended him vigorously. They believed that Netanyahu was the victim of a conspiracy, orchestrated by the left-wing deep state.

The atmosphere only grew more tense when police announced it would recommend that Netanyahu be indicted for bribery, fraud and breach of trust. Police Commissioner Roni Alsheikh, whom Netanyahu had appointed, had come under intense pressure from Netanyahu's loyalists, urging him to scrap the investigations. When the news broke that Alsheikh recommended Netanyahu be indicted the attacks on him intensified. Likud coalition whip and one of Netanyahu's closes allies, David Amsalem, said 'I have not seen so much evil, cruelty and ingratitude packed into one person as (in the case of) Alsheich. This is persecution by the Israel Police; this is a real coup. Not everyone you appoint turns out to be a decent and honest man and that's what happened to us with Alsheich.'[3] Netanyahu railed against the police chief as well, repeating his accusations that he was the victim of a coup. The attacks only intensified when Attorney General Avichai Mandelblit, whom Netanyahu had also appointed, announced that he agreed with the Police recommendations, and that he would charge Netanyahu with bribery, breach of trust and fraud.

Several Likud ministers and lawmakers defended Netanyahu publicly, backing his claim that the investigations were flawed. Tourism Minister Yariv Levin said:

> These cases should not have been opened. The entire process is invalidated, tainted to the core and prejudiced at all stages by enforcement that was selective and discriminatory in the extreme. We will keep our ranks united and continue as one to fight for our principles and our truth, and we will win.

Both Mozes and Elovitch would turn state witnesses, as would former Netanyahu aides Nir Hefetz and Ari Harow. All four would be key witnesses, offering their full cooperation and providing crucial information in the trial. The unprecedented personal attacks by Netanyahu loyalists against the attorney general, the state prosecutor, the police, and the witnesses intensified with time, and showed how deeply he divided Israel. It also revealed how far-right tendencies had entered the Likud party.

The old conspiracy theory about the left-wing elite controlling everything from the army to the justice system and the media contributed to the deepening division and the growing mistrust in the state institutions among Netanyahu supporters. You were either with Netanyahu or against him. Anyone who didn't support him was branded a 'left-winger' which in their eyes was the same as a traitor. The term 'left-wing' would gradually lose its meaning altogether in the coming year. Anyone could be labeled a left-winger, including IDF chiefs, Supreme Court judges and of course politicians who saw Netanyahu's corruption cases as damaging to the country. It didn't matter if a party or a lawmaker who criticized Netanyahu was inherently right-wing in their policies, supporting settlements and advocated for a hardline against the Palestinians. Most of the Likud party would stay loyal to him from the beginning to the end, cheering him on as 'King Bibi' in one of the faction meetings in Knesset after the corruption allegations had been leaked to the media. The words 'witch hunt' and 'coup' attempt would be repeated over and over by Netanyahu and his allies at Likud rallies and in TV interviews. Opposition lawmakers called, in vain, on his resignation, while the weekly protests against Netanyahu intensified, often met by angry Likud counter-protestors. Netanyahu's refusal to respect the indictment would only harden with time and change his views on the nature of democracy. 'In a democracy, an elected government is replaced at the polls, and not through a calibrated pressure campaign on law enforcement agencies and the attorney general. We can be proud of the fact that the Likud movement has over the years backed its leaders and stood behind them, as opposed to what happens in other parties,' he said in 2017 when the investigations were unfolding rapidly.[4]

Jewish Nation-State Law

As the headlines in all of Israel's media focused on Netanyahu's corruption cases, a different battle took place between the Jewish and democratic character of Israel. Shaked, as well as Lieberman, Bennett, and a range of other right-wing and religious lawmakers had long argued that it was time to once and for all enshrine the Jewish character of Israel into law. The idea had already been floated years earlier by Avi Dichter, lawmaker from the *Kadima* party as well as a former Shin Bet chief. The debate about the wording of the law continued with several proposals that didn't pass in the Knesset. On 19 July 2018, the Jewish Nation-State law passed in the Knesset, with 62 lawmakers voting in favour, 55 against and two abstaining. The new Baisc Law, which has a quasi-constitutional character, stipulated that Israel is the 'national home of the Jewish people.' Right-wing lawmakers hailed it as a long-overdue bill that once and for all declared Israel exactly what it was: the nation-state of the Jewish people. Netanyahu called it a 'defining moment in the annals of Zionism and the annals of the state of Israel.'[5] While some of the principles were less controversial, such as declaring *Hatikva* the national anthem, specifying the colour of the flag and declaring Israel's Independence Day as a national holiday, other clauses drew harsh criticism from Arab and Jewish citizens and lawmakers alike.

The most contentious points in the law included making Hebrew the official language of the state while relegating Arabic from official to 'special,' declaring the right to exercise national self-determination in the State of Israel as unique to the Jewish people as well as stipulating that the state state views the development of Jewish settlement as a national value, promising to act to encourage and promote its establishment and consolidation. The word 'equality' was also missing from the law, which would be one of the main criticisms.

A heated debate erupted in Knesset after the passing of the law, with Joint Arab List leader Ayman Odeh yelling 'apartheid' in the plenum. 'It's an apartheid law. Not all citizens are equal according to this law,' Ahmad Tibi, whose *Ta'al* party was now a part of the Arab Joint List, said. Tibi also argued that the 'fascist' atmosphere seen in Israel today is a direct result of the Nation-State law. Lawmaker Benny Begin, who was one of the last remnants of the old Likud guard, was alone in his criticism of the law, which he warned could spark social tensions and increase extreme nationalism. Leader of the left-wing *Meretz* party, Tamar Zandberg, called it a 'debased and tainted law' passed on a 'shameful night.'[6] Justice Minister Shaked, who had long supported enshrining the Jewish character of the state into law, said that 'there are places where the character of the State of Israel as a Jewish state must be maintained, and this sometimes comes at the expense of equality.'[7]

Shaked also warned the Supreme Court not to strike down the law, after petitions were filed against it. Civil rights organizations and former Supreme Court judges joined the centre and left-wing parties in their opposition to the law, accusing it of discriminating against Israel's non-Jewish citizens. Others, such as former Supreme Court President Aharon Barak, the liberal icon who was a villain in the eyes of the right-wing, said he had 'no inherent objection to the law itself, but the way it was drafted and passed was very wrong. I find the first article in the law (that Israel is the national home of the Jewish people) perfectly acceptable, but there are other aspects of equality that the law does not address properly. Human dignity, for example, is compromised by it.'[8] The country was once again divided over fundamental values defining the country. For Likud and other right-wing parties like *Ysrael Beitenu*, this was a victory and a necessary symbolic law that would remove any doubt about who the country belonged to. But for the far-right parties, this was just another step in a bigger plan. Lawmakers like Smotrich wanted to make Israel more Jewish in all aspects, by increasing religious studies in schools, and ultimately create a state whose judicial system was based on *Halakha* (Jewish laws). They saw the Nation-State law as important, but only stated the obvious and wouldn't have practical impact on the country.

Trump

As Netanyahu was battling the media and the judicial system at home, a gift landed in his lap on 8 November 2016 when Donald Trump was elected president of the United States. With Trump in the White House, Netanyahu seized an opportunity to undo years of friction with the U.S. under Obama. Trump knew very little about the Israeli-Palestinian conflict compared to Obama and wouldn't issue any of the demands his predecessor did. On the contrary, Trump would reverse longstanding U.S. policies on settlements in the West Bank, offering unequivocal support for Israel. For Netanyahu, this was a much-needed break that could divert attention from the media's constant coverage of his corruption charges.

At the same time, Netanyahu had managed to widen the already existing secret diplomatic channels with Arab Gulf states, something previous Israeli governments had done as well, often with the help of Mossad. But in 2016, intense dialogue began between the Israeli government and UAE and Bahrain in particular. Knowing that Trump was looking to strike the 'Deal of the Century', solving the Middle East conflict, Netanyahu knew that if he played him right, the many years of secret talks with Gulf states could become public with Washington's support. But first he made sure to convince Trump of two things; the need to leave the Iran deal and to move the U.S. embassy to Jerusalem. Trump had already promised he would the embassy during the election campaign, and his lack of support for the Iran deal was already known.

It would take less than a year before Trump announced his decision to move the embassy and at the same time recognize Jerusalem as Israel's capital. Trump was praised in Israel, in particular among right-wingers. As expected, the announcement was met with immediate condemnation by the Palestinians, who ended up cutting all ties with the Trump administration. In return, Trump cut all U.S. aid to the Palestinians in 2018, arguing that the U.S. got nothing in return from the Palestinians. $200 million in aid to the Palestinian Authority, earmarked for Gaza and the West Bank were cut, while $300 million to the United Nations Reliefs and Works Agency for Palestinian refugees UNRWA were withheld. The latter had for years been described as a corrupt entity by Israeli right-wingers, including Netanyahu, who praised Trump's decision to cut U.S. funding the 'refugee perpetuation agency', as he referred to it, calling on a complete abolition of UNRWA.[9] Trump's decision caused a huge financial crisis in the agency, which provided crucial humanitarian aid to Palestinians in the West Bank and Gaza. The EU, as well as other donor states would eventually increase their aid to UNRWA to make up for the U.S. loss.

For Netanyahu, things couldn't have gone better on the international scene. His meetings with Trump in the White House, as well as his welcoming of Trump in Israel on his first trip abroad as U.S. President, were warm and friendly. Trump listened to Netanyahu's advice, particularly on Iran. On 30 April 2018 Netanyahu held a press conference, revealing how Mossad had managed to steal over 100,000 secret documents from Iran on its nuclear program. Netanyahu said that the documents proved Iran had lied about its nuclear program, calling on world powers to leave the nuclear deal. On 8 May, a little over a week after Netanyahu's press conference, Trump announced that the U.S. would withdraw from the nuclear deal and that new sanctions would be imposed on Tehran as part of his 'maximum pressure' strategy. Netanyahu and Trump believed that sanctioning Iran to its knees would convince it to either give up its nuclear program or strike a new and more comprehensive deal. For Israel, Iran's financial and military support for groups like Hezbollah, Hamas and Islamic Jihad posed a direct security threat. Any new deal had to include curbing Iran's support for them. In the meantime, Trump's son-in-law Jared Kushner was traveling back and forth between the U.S. and the Middle East to help bridge the last gaps between Israel and the UAE and Bahrain. The 'Deal of the Century', which was supposed to solve the Israeli-Palestinian conflict, was also underway, despite the Palestinians boycotting the Trump administration. In 2019, Trump gave Netanyahu and Israel two more gifts, both of which broke with previous U.S. policies. The U.S., Trump said, would recognize Israeli sovereignty over the Golan Heights, which Israel had conquered from Syria in the 1967 war and annexed in 1981. The area was considered illegally occupied under international law.

The other U-turn, possibly even more significant, was the U.S. change of policy regarding Jewish settlements in the West Bank, no longer considering them in violation of international law. U.S. President Ronald Reagan had also dropped the word 'illegal' to describe the settlements, but his administration still considered them an obstacle to peace. Mike Pompeo, arguably the most pro-Israel secretary of state in U.S. history, reversed what he called a 'bad' longstanding American policy on the settlements, so that they would no longer be considered illegal under international law.[10] The Trump administration also changed an American trade rule so that products imported from West Bank settlements would be branded 'made in Israel.' Both were hugely symbolic as well as practical victories for the right-wing camp in Israel. The importance of the change in U.S. policy on one of the most contentious issues in the Israeli-Palestinian conflict could not be understated.

The settlements, which weren't recognized as legal by any country in the world, all of a sudden got a rubber stamp from the most powerful country in the world. They had created massive obstacles in the peace process and damaged Israel's reputation in the world for decades. For the right-wing nationalists in Israel it was a crucial step in the direction of annexing the West Bank. The list of pro-Israel policies enacted under Trump was unparalleled, rubbing off on Netanyahu as well. But as expected, the far-right wasn't as easily pleased. Being at the mercy of a superpower and having to ask for permission to fulfil a divine plan for Greater Israel was humiliating.

'Peace plan'

On 28 January 2020 Trump finally unveiled his peace plan at the White House, standing next to Netanyahu. The plan consisted of a political and an economic framework that were meant to solve the conflict. While the political plan envisioned a Palestinian state, no Israelis would be uprooted from their homes in the West Bank. With settlements and outposts spread across the West Bank, a Palestinian state would therefore lack territorial contingency. Only parts of East Jerusalem (one of the most contentious issues in the Israeli-Palestinian conflict) would be allocated for the Palestinians. Israel would also maintain security control over the Jordan Valley.

The economic framework saw an opening of the West Bank and Gaza to global markets, as well as investments in infrastructure, electricity and businesses worth billions of dollars. To sum up: the Palestinians would be left with a state that looked like Swiss cheese, surrounded by Jewish settlers, while giving up on its core demands, such as a right of return for Palestinian refugees and having East Jerusalem as its capital. The plan was quickly declared dead on arrival in the international media. Palestinian President Abbas mocked the plan, referring to it as the 'slap of the century.' 'I say to Trump and (Israeli Prime Minister Benjamin) Netanyahu: Jerusalem is not for sale; all our rights are not for sale and are not for bargain. And your deal, the conspiracy, will not pass,' Abbas said after the plan had been unveiled in the White House.[11] Netanyahu, who had previously promised that he would annex Jewish settlements in the West Bank, seized the moment to make it official during his speech at the White House.

Speaking after Trump, Netanyahu said Israel would move immediately to apply sovereignty to all the Jewish settlements, catching Trump off guard. A massive misunderstanding between the Trump administration and Netanyahu had led him to believe that there was a greenlight for annexation. Netanyahu was under the clear impression that he could go ahead and announce it. 'There was a reversal. It wasn't because we had surprised him in any way. In fact, I think it surprised me,' Netanyahu later said.[12] Bur for Kushner, who was the architect of the peace plan, Netanyahu's declaration had not been properly discussed. Kushner later wrote in his memoirs:

> This was not what we had negotiated. Under our plan, we would eventually recognize Israel's sovereignty over agreed-upon areas if Israel took steps to advance Palestinian statehood within the territory we outlined. The two hinged on each other, and it would take time

to flesh out the details…While Bibi had to navigate a difficult political environment at home, this was a step too far. I grabbed my chair so intensely that my knuckles turned white, as if my grip could make Bibi stop. I had explicitly asked Israeli ambassador Ron Dermer to make sure Bibi kept his remarks brief and above the politics of the day. In both tone and substance, the speech was way off the mark. It contained nothing magnanimous or conciliatory toward the Palestinians. It was essentially a campaign speech for his domestic political audience, and it misrepresented our plan. As the prime minister approached the twenty-minute mark, I could tell that Trump was becoming uncomfortable. He was pursing his lips, swaying side to side, and periodically glancing down at Bibi's prepared speech to see how many pages were left. [13]

Netanyahu had overstepped his boundaries with Trump who was furious with him. At the same time, Netanyahu came under fire from the far-right and the settlement movement back at home for agreeing in principle to a Palestinian state. Despite the plan never standing a real chance of being implemented, conceding any territory to the Palestinians was a clear red line for them. A large demonstration against the Trump peace plan was held in front of the prime minister's residence on Balfour Street in Jerusalem in February 2020, organized by the Yesha settler Council. The council's leaders were calling on Netanyahu to dismiss the plan, saying it wasn't up to Kushner or Trump to give away sacred land belonging to Jews. 'We elected you (Netanyahu), not Trump or Kushner,' they raged from the stage. Hundreds of young settlers showed up, dancing and chanting on the street. The energy and increasing political support behind the settlement movement had strengthened significantly since the last serious peace negotiations had been held. They saw no reason to give up a millimeter of sacred Jewish land, having proven that years of stalemate in the peace negotiations only helped their cause. More and more settlements and outposts were built, making any mutual land swap practically impossible. Time was on their side. Bennett showed the first signs of a gradual withdrawal from the hard-core settlement movement which he once led as chair of the Yesha settler Council. Unlike Smotrich, who was representing the most far-right positions, Bennett was willing to accept the Trump peace plan on one condition. Bennett said:

> They've asked us in recent days what Yamina's position would be about the "deal of the century." Our answer is simple. Annex, we'll

support. Don't annex — we'll oppose. If this whole event ends without applying [Israeli] sovereignty now, before the elections, with the American tailwind, then this won't be the deal of the century, but the missed opportunity of the century. [14]

Smotrich, however, had vowed that one of his main goals in public life was to prevent an 'Arab terror state' in the heart of Israel.[15] There was therefore no reason for the settlement movement to compromise whatsoever, despite the peace plan being the most pro-Israel in the country's history. The combination of severe political instability in Israel and the outright Palestinian rejection of the peace plan anyway meant that it never stood a chance. But the vocal protests among the settlers against a once in a lifetime generous peace proposal by the U.S. was a clear sign that they knew there would be no reason to ever compromise again.

Political chaos

Less than two years after Avigdor Lieberman had decided to join the government and become defense minister, he pulled the rug under Netanyahu's feet once again. Lieberman had realized that his policies and ambitions as defense minister were quickly squashed once he sat in the chair.

Prime ministers and defense ministers, the two most powerful people in Israel, would often find themselves rather restrained once they took office. It was a well-known fact those who found themselves in those positions would realize that there was a limit to what they could do. Lieberman was one of those who preferred resigning over compromising. His hardline views on Hamas hadn't changed since the 2014 war where he advocated for a harsher crackdown in Gaza. In early 2018 Palestinians in Gaza began demonstrating along the border fence against the blockade imposed by Israel, which had a tremendous effect on the enclave, both financially and psychologically.

The protests, which were initially arranged by civilians, were quickly endorsed by Hamas and Islamic Jihad and became known as the 'Great March of Return.' Tens of thousands protested every week, with some throwing Molotov cocktails at Israeli soldiers near the border fence. The Israeli army responded by shooting and often killing those who rioted. As the numbers of Palestinians killed during protests rose, tensions between Israel and Hamas and Islamic Jihad boiled over. Lieberman accused Hamas members of constituting the vast majority of the demonstrators, refusing to give in to what he dubbed the 'March of terror.' In November 2018 an undercover Israeli operation in Gaza was exposed. One Israeli special force and seven Palestinians were killed. Hamas responded by firing rockets at Israel, who retaliated by hitting Hamas with airstrikes. After 48-hours, Israel and Hamas agreed on a ceasefire.

Lieberman shocked the nation once again when he announced his resignation shortly after, citing a 'surrender' to terror. 'What we are doing now as a state is buying short-term quiet at the price of serious damage to national long-term security,' Lieberman said.[16] Having previously criticized Netanyahu for allowing fuel and millions of dollars in cash from Qatar to enter Gaza, allowing a cease-fire was the last straw for him. Lieberman also announced that his *Yisrael Beitenu* party would leave the government, leaving Netanyahu with a shaky 61 seat majority once again. IDF's military intelligence chief Tamir Hayman explained how Lieberman differed from the other defense minister's he had worked with, and why he saw no other option than to resign. Hayman said:

> In Gaza, you can't find a good answer to an operation ensuring that it won't end in a total failure eventually. Lieberman was different, because in the initial parts of his term he wanted to create turmoil, trouble or chaos, and he thought that eventually, after a grand scale violence he could redesign the system favourable to him. Time after time he was frustrated that we convinced him what he proposed wasn't rational and that we opposed it in the cabinet and in front of the prime minister.

Lieberman also urged new elections, which weren't due for another year. Eventually, it would be a decades old contentious issue that brought down the government. Since the establishment of the state, ultra-orthodox Jews had been exempted from serving in the army. The first prime minister and the founding father David Ben-Gurion allowed some 400 ultra-orthodox to study the Torah instead, as some sort of a compromise. This deal was initially not a problem, since the numbers of ultra-orthodox in Israel was a tiny minority. Arab-Israelis had also been exempted, for reasons obvious, but every other citizen in the state were drafted. Men served three years and women two years.

Over the years, however, the ultra-orthodox community grew significantly, and by 2019 they would make up roughly 10% of the country. Hundreds of thousands of young men were therefore not drafted but were allowed to spend their time in a yeshiva instead of being sent to the battlefield to protect the country. The special treatment had begun causing a lot of anger among secular Israelis. But for politicians from both the left and right-wing, the ultra-orthodox parties had often been kingmakers in elections. Governments would therefore continue to allow this exemption to continue. But the Supreme Court of Justice would soon get involved in the issue due to community's rising number. In 1998 the Supreme Court ruled that the defense minister wasn't allowed to grant the ultra-orthodox youth exemption from the army. In 2002, Knesset passed new legislation, protecting them from serving in the army but placing strict demands on their studying. Despite noting that this would compromise the principle of equality, the Supreme Court allowed it to be in place until it expired in 2012. New petitions were filed to the Supreme Court, demanding the ultra-orthodox be drafted. But the legal bickering and attempts by the secular *Yesh Atid* party to change the exemption got stuck in the election cycles.

In 2015, United Torah Judaism and Shas conditioned their joining the government on passing a new law that would once and for all seal the exemption. Netanyahu acceded to the demand, and a new amendment to the Equal Service Law was passed, postponing the issue of drafting ultra-orthodox youth. But in 2017, the Supreme Court struck this amendment down, arguing that it was unconstitutional. As expected, the ultra-orthodox parties were furious with the Supreme Court. Much like Shaked, Bennett, Levin, Elkin and other lawmakers who saw the Supreme Court as a power hungry and undemocratic entity, the ultra-orthodox parties echoed their attacks. United Torah Judaism lawmaker Yisrael Eichler said the judges 'proved today that the sole motivation behind its decisions is a dictatorial hunger for power, to oppose the laws of the elected Knesset. The Supreme Court judges will bear personal responsibility for the all-out war on Judaism.'[17] The Supreme Court would continue to grant the government extensions to come up with a new draft law that wouldn't run counter to the principle of equality, but lawmakers failed time and time again to reach a compromise. On 26 December, Knesset dissolved itself, setting elections for March 2019. This once again meant that the issue of the draft law would have to be put on hold. And with increasing pressure over his trial on corruption as well as growing demonstrations against him, Netanyahu entered elections as one of the most divisive figures in Israel's history. Old allies like Lieberman, Elkin, Sa'ar, Bennett and Shaked would soon become his fiercest rivals, creating huge obstacles for his hold on power.

Notes

1   Staff, ''No indictment for Netanyahu', *CNN*, 20 April 1997.

2   TOI Staff, 'Netanyahu accuses media of "unprecedented" attempt to oust him', *Times of Israel*, 16 January 2017.

3   TOI Staff, 'Coalition whip: "Evil" police chief tried to engineer "coup" via Bezeq case', *Times of Israel*, 3 December 2018.

4   TOI Staff, 'PM praised Likud support amid graft probes, vows to stay in office', Times of Israel, 27 January 2017.

5   David M. Halbfinger & Isabel Kershner, 'Israeli law declares the country the "Nation-State of the Jewish people', *New York Times*, 19 July 2018.

6   TOI Staff, 'Netanyahu cheers Jewish state law as a 'pivotal moment' in Zionist history', Times of Israel, 19 July 2019.

7   Revital Hovel, 'Justice Minister: Israel must keep Jewish majority even at the expense of human rights', *Ha'aretz*, 13 February 2018.

8   Yair Altman, 'Former chief justice: Nation-state law important but lacking', *Israel Hayom*, 18 December 2018.

9   Noa Landau, 'Netanyahu: U.S. decision to cut UNRWA funds 'a blessed and important change', *Ha'aretz*, 2 September 2018.

10 Mike Pompeo, 'Never Give an Inch: Fighting for the America I Love', (Broadside Books 2023, New York. NY.), pp. 321.

11 Ali Sawafta & Nidal al-Mughrabi, 'Slap of the century: Palestinians reject Trump Mideast plan', *Reuters*, 28 January 2020.

12 Jotam Confino, 'More of a wild-card': What a Netanyahu comeback could mean for U.S.-Israel relations', *USA TODAY*, 26 October 2022.

13 Jared Kushner, '*Breaking History: A White House memoir*', (Harper Collins 2022), pp. 317-319

14 Jacob Magid, 'Bennett conditions support for Trump peace plan on immediate annexation', Times of Israel, 26 January 2020.

15 Betzalel Smotrich, Facebook post, 30 July 2019.

16 Isabel Kershner, 'Israel's hawkish defense minister resigns and calls for early elections', *New York Times*, 14 November 2018.

17 TOI Staff, 'High Court strikes down law that postponed ultra-orthodox draft', *Times of Israel*, 12 September 2017.

1: Prime Minister Yitzhak Rabin shaking hands with PLO chairman Yasser Arafat (r) on White House lawn as U.S. President Bill Clinton looks on. 1993. Credit: Avi Ohayon, Israeli Government Press Office, hereafter GPO.

2: Burial society members gather body parts from victims of the Hamas terrorist attack on the number 26 bus as it traveled through Ramat Eshkol in Jerusalem. 1995. Credit: Avi Ohayon (GPO)

3: Rescue teams surround the shell of the number 26 bus blown up in Jerusalem by a Hamas terrorist attacker. 1995. Credit: Moshe Milner (GPO).

4: (L-R) MKS Benjamin Netanyahu, Rechavam Zeevi, Moshe Katsav and Shlomo Hillel beside the coffin of slain Prime Minister Yitzhak Rabin lying in state in the knesset plaza. 1995. Credit: Zvika Israeli (GPO)

4: Prime Minister Benjamin Netanyahu (L) shaking hands with Palestinian Authority chairman Yasser Arafat prior to their meeting at an IDF facility at the Erez checkpoint in Gaza. 1996. Credit: Moshe Milner (GPO)

5: US President Bill Clinton announcing at the White House the opening of the "Wye Plantation" summit. On the left, Prime Minister Netanyahu & Yasser Arafat on the right. 1998. Credit: Ya'acov Sa'ar (GPO)

7: Prime Minister Benjamin Netanyahu (right) meeting Prime Minister-elect Ehud Barak, at Jerusalem's "King David" Hotel. 1999. Credit: Avi Ohayon (GPO)

8: Right wing demonstration and memorial service, at Jerusalem's Zion Square, for tourism minister Rechavam Zeevy, who was murdered by a palestinian terrorist. 2001. Credit: Avi Ohayon (GPO)

9: Demonstration against Prime Minister Ariel Sharon's Gaza Disengagement Plan, in front of the Knesset in Jerusalem. In photo, Rabbi Mordechai Eliyahu (right) speaking. 2004. Credit: Amos Ben Gershom (GPO)

10: Anti-disengagement protester carrying a poster with the picture of Prime Minister Ariel Sharon, written in Hebrew "the dictator" at the demonstration near the Knesset, Jerusalem. 2005. Credit: Avii Ohayon (GPO)

11: Prime Minister Ariel Sharon (right) and Foreign Minister Benjamin Netanyahu at the weekly government meeting, Jerusalem. 2002. Credit: Avi Ohayon (GPO)

12: Prime Minister Ariel Sharon visiting IDF forces fighting in Jenin, during operation "Defensive Shield", for elimination of palestinian terror. 2002. Credit: Moshe Milner (GPO)

13: Prime Minister Ariel Sharon's Gaza Disengagement Plan. In the photo: IDF armoured vehicles leave Gush Katif through the Kissufim crossing. 2005. Credit: Moshe Milner (GPO).

14: The evacuation of unauthorized West Bank outpost of Amona. In the photo: baton- wielding policemen clash with protesters during the evacuation. 2006. Credit: Avi Ohayon (GPO)

15: Prime Minister Benjamin Netanyahu visits New York. In the photo: Meeting between Prime Minister Benjamin Netanyahu, U.S President Barack Obama and President of the Palestinian National Authority Mahmoud Abbas (Abu Mazen). 2009. Credit: Avi Ohayon (GPO)

16: Captured IDF soldier Gilad Shalit (second from right) walks with (left to right) Defense Minister Ehud Barak, Prime Minister Benjamin Netanyahu and Chief of Staff Benny Gantz at Tel Nof Air Force Base shortly after Shalit's release. 2011. Credit: Moshe Milner (GPO).

17: A memorial service on the 18th anniversary of the assassination of Prime Minister Yitzhak Rabin, taking place at the Knesset in Jerusalem. Photo, from right to left: Minister of Economy Naftali Bennett, Interior Minister Gideon Sa'ar, Defense Minister Moshe Ya'alon and Prime Minister Benjamin Netanyahu. 2013. Credit: GPO

18: President of the US Donald Trump and Prime Minister Benjamin Netanyahu at the prime minister's visit to the US, White House, Washington D.C. 2017. Credit: Avi Ohayon (GPO)

19: Prime Minister Naftali Bennett lays tefillin at the Blair House in Washington. 2021. Credit: Avi Ohayon (GPO)

20: President of the United States Joe Biden visits Israel. In the photo: (right) Prime Minister Yair Lapid, US President Joe Biden and Minister of Defense Benny Gantz at the welcoming ceremony, Ben Gurion Airport. 2022. Credit: Kobi Gideon (GPO).

21: The swearing in of the 37th government under the authority of Prime Minister Benjamin Netanyahu. In the photo: Amir Ohana, Speaker of the Knesset, and to his left is Itamar Ben-Gvir, Minister of National Security and head of the Otzma Yehudit party. 2022. Credit: GPO.

22: Minister of Defense Yoav Gallant conducting a situation assessment together with IDF Chief-of-Staff, Herzl Halevi, Mossad Director David Barnea and Shin Bet Chief Ronen Bar. 2023 Credits: Ariel Hermoni (IMoD)

23: Mass demonstration in Tel Aviv. 2023. Credit: Jotam Confino

24: Women dressed as "Handmaid's Tale", protesting in Tel Aviv. 2023. Credit: Jotam Confino

25: Israeli police officers on horses, blocking demonstrators from entering Ayalon Highway. 2023. Credit: Jotam Confino.

26: Jewish settlers at the entrance to Palestinian city of Huwara, West Bank. 2023. Credit: Jotam Confino.

27: Israeli military blocking Israeli activists from entering Palestinian city of Huwara, West Bank. 2023. Credit: Jotam Confino.

28: Israeli activist arguing with a young settler outside the Palestinian city of Huwara, West Bank. Sign says: "(standing) with Huwara". 2023. Credit: Jotam Confino.

7

Election marathon

Round one

The elections on 9 April 2019 marked the first time in Israel's history that a prime minister running for re-election was in the middle of a corruption investigation. The demonstrations against Netanyahu and the criticism of him brought the country to a boiling point.

The 'just not Bibi' slogan became a driving force among opposition parties who were willing to form all kinds of coalitions, with the only demand being that it wouldn't include Netanyahu. This led to the establishment of the Blue and White party in February 2019, a joint list consisting of Lapid's *Yesh Atid* party, and two new right-wing parties, *Telem* and Israel Resilience Party. *Telem* was established by former Defense Minister Moshe Ya'alon, who had resigned from his position in Netanyahu's government in 2016. Ya'alon had an old score to settle with Netanyahu, and so did Lapid, who had fallen out with his old boss years ago.

The new and more important player on the scene was Benny Gantz, a former IDF chief of staff under Netanyahu, who had established the Israel Resilience Party in December 2018 when elections were looming. Gantz's claim to fame, like many before him, was his role as IDF chief, something that in Israel had a hero status. The Blue and White party would later include another former IDF chief of staff, Gabi Ashkenazi, who was placed fourth on the list. Lapid and Gantz agreed to co-chair the party, joining forces to bring down Netanyahu once and for all. With three former IDF chiefs in the top four of the party (Ya'alon had also served as IDF chief before entering politics), Blue and White was immediately seen as the biggest threat to Netanyahu, with polls predicting the party would receive 36 seats and Likud 30. The party's manifesto was in many ways similar to other secular right-wing parties like Likud, promising that Jerusalem would remain the undivided capital of Israel, keeping the Jordan Valley under Israel's control, and dismissing a Palestinian right of return. But other campaign promises were directly aimed at Netanyahu, such as limiting the terms for prime minister to eight years or three terms, as well as banning indicted or convicted politicians from running for office.

Sensing the immediate danger that Blue and White posed to Netanyahu, an aggressive campaign was launched to undermine every aspect of the party, ranging from personal attacks against Lapid and Gantz, to warning that it was seeking an alliance with Arab-Israeli parties. Netanyahu accused Gantz, Ya'alon and Ashkenazi of being 'left-wing generals who pretend to be right wing,' and that Gantz and Lapid were 'relying on Arab parties who not only don't recognize the State of Israel' but want to destroy it. But today Benny Gantz is ready to give the premiership to Yair Lapid, whose military experience is a reporter for *"Mahane"*, Netanyahu said, referring to the IDF's newspaper.[1] Having burned most bridges and facing a new party with significant support behind it, Netanyahu and Likud had to make sure every single potential vote went to their bloc.

Bennett, who for years had been seen as the political representative of the religious Zionist movement, left the Jewish Home party to establish a new party together with his long-time companion Shaked. Bennett and Shaked were trying to position themselves as the only alternative for right-wing voters who wanted a partnership between secular and religious people. Their New Right party therefore immediately became threats to both Likud, *Yisrael Beitenu* and the remains of Jewish Home and other far-right parties. Rafi Peretz, who had taken over the leadership of Jewish Home after Bennett, lashed out at him, saying he 'planned to destroy our home. What you (Bennett) did is difficult for me to even call a Jewish deed. This is not how a son of the religious Zionist movement acts… A vote for Naftali is a vote against religious Zionism,' Peretz said.[2] Netanyahu also had good reason to be worried. The first signs of Bennett and Shaked's attempt to break with years of Netanyahu's dominance in Israeli politics emerged on the evening of their announcement of the New Right party. 'We greatly appreciate Netanyahu and his contributions over the years to Israel but the real right, the whole nationalist camp, cannot be captives of one person,' Bennett said.[3]

Bennett's ambitions had already been clear to Netanyahu years earlier when he took advantage of Netanyahu's fragile majority after the 2015 elections to get the justice and education ministry for him and Shaked. After Lieberman had resigned as defense minister in 2018, Bennett had demanded that Netanyahu give him the portfolio. Netanyahu refused to cave, and Bennett eventually backed down from his demand.

The New Right party was quickly slammed by Likud's Miri Regev who called Bennett a left-winger. The familiar accusation was a continuation of Likud's strategy to label anyone a threat to Netanyahu part of the left-wing establishment. Lieberman, who would also compete with Bennett and Shaked for the same votes, said their party was nothing but hot air. When asked whether he would support a law that would prevent a prime minister from being indicted, a specific reference to legislation considered by Likud to save Netanyahu from his corruption allegations, Bennett said he wouldn't. Despite him and Shaked committing to supporting Netanyahu in the election and promising to sit with him, their refusal to help him get rid of his trial was a clear sign that they were no longer to be trusted.

The issue of unconditional support for Netanyahu and adopting his claim that the corruption allegations against him was a left-wing conspiracy, was slowly dividing the entire political map. Bennett and Shaked, as well as *Yisrael Beitenu,* were still wavering, showing early signs of being willing to leave the Netanyahu camp. Predicting a scenario where New Right could end up failing to get enough votes to enter Knesset and thereby waste votes, Netanyahu helped broker a new alliance between small far-right factions. Jewish Home had negotiated with *Tkuma,* now led by Smotrich, as well as the extremist Jewish Power party, the ideological descendant of Meir Kahane. Rafi Peretz, the new leader of Jewish Home, had refused to merge with Jewish Power but accepted it in the end after Netanyahu promised the party two ministerial posts in his new government.

In February, the Union of Right-Wing Parties (URWP) was established, marking one of the most extreme factions in Israel's history. The new far-right alliance sparked immediate backlash over the inclusion of Jewish Power, whose members included extremists like Michael Ben-Ari, Baruch Marzel and Itamar Ben-Gvir. Jewish Power had previously made unsuccessful attempts at running for Knesset, receiving far less votes than required to cross the electoral threshold. It was in many ways still an extremist and fringe party but after merging with UNRW it had a fair shot for the first time since its establishment in 2012. Jewish Power party leader Ben-Ari would take the fifth spot on the list and Ben-Gvir would get the eighth. The party advocated for the deportation of Israel's enemies, annexing the West Bank but without giving Palestinian equal rights, and applying Israeli sovereignty over the Temple Mount. Benny Gantz lashed out at Netanyahu for brokering a deal with people who brought 'Kahanism' back into Knesset (a term used to describe Meir Kahane's ideology). Gantz said:

> (Former Prime Minister Menachem) Begin would be ashamed of Netanyahu. (Netanyahu's inspiration Ze'ev) Jabotinsky would be ashamed of Netanyahu. (Former Prime Minister Yitzhak) Shamir would be ashamed of Netanyahu. But (Meir) Kahane would be proud

of Netanyahu. With Begin in power, Netanyahu would have long been thrown out of Likud. We have to be honest, Begin would not have been welcomed to Netanyahu's Likud. He would have been called an enemy of the state.[4]

The prospect of having the most extreme political party in Knesset since Meir Kahane was met with fierce criticism by other lawmakers. Meretz party leader Tamar Zandberg called it 'appalling that the prime minister is the best man in this... wedding between a Jewish terror group and the Knesset,' while Labour party leader Shelly Yachimovich said Netanyahu had 'crossed a line' by certifying the 'Kahanist fringe.'[5] The news about Jewish Power party's merger with Jewish Home was also criticized in the Diaspora. AIPAC, the powerful Jewish lobby in the U.S., issued a statement saying it had a 'longstanding policy not to meet with members of this racist and reprehensible party', while the American Jewish Committee said it 'felt compelled' to speak out against Jewish Power and its members who don't reflect the core values that are the very foundation of the State of Israel.'[6]

Not long after the announcement of Jewish Power's merger with URWP, the Supreme Court banned Jewish Power party leader Ben-Ari from running in the upcoming elections, citing his history of inciting to racism as the cause. The decision was made by an eight to one majority among the Supreme Court justices, including the newly appointed conservative judges that Justice Minister Shaked had overseen. As expected, Jewish Power reacted fiercely to the decision. Ben-Ari said, 'there is a legal junta that seeks to take over our lives,' but the decision was also criticized by Shaked who issued an unusually harsh statement against the Supreme Court. Shaked said:

> The judges of the Supreme Court have turned themselves into a political factor. Their decision to disqualify Ben Ari and authorize parties that support terror is a blatant and erroneous intervention in Israeli democracy. Tomorrow I will publish my plan for the completion of a judicial revolution in my next term. [7]

Their fury stemmed from the Supreme Court's simultaneous ruling to reverse a decision made by the Central Election Committee earlier that month, that banned the Arab-Israeli joint slate made up of *Balad* and United Arab List, as well as Jewish far-left lawmaker Ofer Cassif. Ben-Ari and his Jewish Power party colleague Ben-Gvir had petitioned against both lists, seeing Arab-Israeli lawmakers as terror supporters due to their sympathy for the Palestinians, including those who were killed in counter-

terrorist actions by the Israeli army. The Supreme Court, despite its support
for establishing Jewish settlements in the West Bank, was considered a de-
facto enemy by the far-right. Banning Ben-Ari was just another example of
the Supreme Court being a direct obstacle to their goals.

As election day drew closer, the verbal attacks between Likud and Blue
and White became more frequent and more personal. Likud launched a
campaign to try and portray Gantz as mentally unstable, sharing a video of
him making weird facial expressions, with horror movie music in the
background, accompanied with the text 'completely stable.' Another Likud
statement lambasted Gantz as 'paranoid, scared and weak.' The attack came
after a voice recording was aired on Israel's Channel 13, in which Gantz was
heard saying:

> If (Netanyahu) had a way that I would be harmed, that they would
> kill me, he would do it. Would regular Benjamin Netanyahu, who I
> know, want me harmed? The answer is no. Would Benjamin
> Netanyahu on the eve of elections want me harmed? Unfortunately
> I would have to say so.[8]

Part of Likud's campaign also focused on the media, attacking and singling
out prominent Israeli journalists who had been particularly critical of
Netanyahu, or had played a role in exposing the corruption investigations
against him. Most of Israel's established media had ramped up their
criticism of Netanyahu since the investigations were revealed two years
earlier. The endless leaks from the investigations made the corruption
allegations the hottest and most widely discussed topic. For Netanyahu, the
established media had for years been one of his worst enemies, going back
to the coverage of his rallies against Rabin. The daily, unabashed criticism
against him and commentators calling on the attorney general to indict him
only reinforced his deep belief that the media had overstepped its
boundaries. They were an integral part of the left-wing conspiracy to topple
him and were therefore a legitimate target.

In the early days of the election campaign, an unprecedented billboard
appeared on one the highways outside Tel Aviv, depicting four of the most
famous journalists in Israel. Pictures of Guy Peleg and Amnon Abramovich
from Channel 12, Ben Caspit from *Maariv* Daily, and Raviv Drucker from
Channel 13 appeared on the Likud billboard with the text 'They will not
decide, you will decide.' Ousting specific journalists, who all covered and
commented on the ongoing investigations, was part of a broader campaign
to delegitimize the established media. Voters were spoon-fed and walked

through every detail of the corruption allegations in the media every day, posing a major threat to Netanyahu's chances of re-election. On 23 January 2019, just three days after Likud had admitted it was behind the billboard, Netanyahu issued a video on his Twitter account, accusing the two biggest TV channels of 'brainwashing' the public. Netanyahu said:

> Propaganda Channels 12 and 13 will try to brainwash you every night with unending false and distorted leaks. Leaks from investigations are a criminal offense with a maximum three-year sentence. For the media, all means are justified to force (the installing of) a left-wing regime against the will of the public. It won't work if you don't let them. [9]

Opposition lawmakers like Yair Lapid and Shelly Yachimovich condemned the attacks on the four journalists, calling it an incitement campaign led by Netanyahu. Referring to the media as propaganda would, however, become an increasingly used accusation by the Netanyahu, as well his son Yair. The debate about whether the mainstream Israeli media was in fact a left-wing bastion, controlled by the elite, had been raging between the political camps for years. And while there were certainly some media that openly declared itself left-wing, like *Ha'aretz* Daily, the TV channels Netanyahu referred to as propaganda were often criticized by left-wing journalists for serving Netanyahu's interests. Professor Neiger said:

> This is a long conversation about whether the Israeli media is truly left-wing (or how much the media promotes peace or resisting occupation). The fact that many Israeli journalists consider themselves center-left doesn't mean that the coverage is leftist. For example, the most influential political commentator in the most popular TV outlet, Channel 12, is Amit Segal, a right-wing journalist born and raised in Ofra, the Israeli settlement in the northern West Bank. As for Israel HaYom, the paper gained power in a new era, the digital age, where journalists' personal views became part of newsmaking. So you can say that, in a sense, the paper contributed to the fact that we hear more views than "news" and that a clear political agenda from both sides is in the front as a legitimate journalistic outcome. But it also contributed to political polarization.

Netanyahu's lawyers also weighed in on the constant leaks in the media, saying they had 'lost all restraint in recent days, and every night we are

astounded to see newscasts open with "new and sensational revelations'"
and that the 'biased' reports were a 'clear attempt to create negative public
opinion of the prime minister ahead of the elections...and to create
improper pressure on the attorney general.'[10] Attacks were also launched at
State Prosecutor Shai Nitzan, whom Netanyahu's associates, according to a
report in Channel 13, claimed was aiming to be remembered as the man
who toppled the prime minister.

In the meantime, Netanyahu perfected social media, using both Twitter,
Facebook and Instagram as his preferred platforms to send out election
campaign messages. Instead of being interviewed by his enemies on the TV
channels or the big newspapers, he could send out unfiltered messages to
his voters on social media. On election day, consensus in both Israeli and
foreign media was that this was a referendum on Netanyahu. Would the
public support him despite his corruption allegations or would they punish
him? The first exit polls revealed an incredibly tight race. As expected, both
Likud and Blue and White emerged as the two biggest parties. Neither,
however, had a clear path to victory, but both parties decided to declare
themselves the winner of the elections that same evening. The big surprise
of the election was the New Right party, headed by Bennett, failing to cross
the electoral threshold. The new political project by the once rising stars in
Israeli politics had failed, with other right-wing parties stealing their votes.

For Netanyahu, this was a blessing in disguise. At least so he thought.
The final results gave Blue and White and Likud 35 seats each, with *Yisrael
Beitenu* becoming the kingmaker with five seats. Netanyahu needed
Lieberman's five seats to get a majority and counted on him to do the right
thing and leave petty differences aside over the draft law. But Lieberman
insisted that he wouldn't back down from his demand to draft ultra-
orthodox men to the army. *Yisrael Beitenu's* campaign had been extremely
critical of the growing influence of the ultra-orthodox in Israel.
Lieberman's party appealed to immigrants from the former Soviet Union
who were mostly secular and were unhappy with Israel becoming
increasingly religious. President Rivlin decided that Netanyahu had the
most realistic chance of forming a government, giving him the first crack
at it. But after weeks of negotiations, it became clear that Lieberman wasn't
bluffing. A day before his deadline expired, Netanyahu realized that he
was essentially held hostage, with nowhere to go. The ultra-orthodox and
Lieberman refused to compromise, seeing each other as mortal enemies.
The shock announcement by Netanyahu on May 30 that he had failed to
form a government was followed by parliament voting to dissolve itself,
sending Israel to unprecedented new elections. Likud raged against

Lieberman, accusing him of secretly trying to topple Netanyahu in a lust for power.

Round 2

As Israel prepared for yet another election, the demonstrations against Netanyahu continued, with protestors accusing him of corruption and for being responsible for a new round of elections. Thousands had gathered in Tel Aviv a few days before his deadline to form a government to protest attempts by the Likud party to pass a law that would make it impossible for the Supreme Court to strike down legislation it deemed unconstitutional. In essence, the same old 'override clause' as Shaked, Levin and a few other right wing and far-right lawmakers had advocated for years. The anti-Netanyahu camp feared that it was the first step in his plan to later pass a law that would make the sitting prime minister immune to indictments.

The issue of the Supreme Court's power and role in Israel would gradually become a central focus point in the public debate as Netanyahu's corruption cases advanced. In the three- and half-month-long election campaign that stretched over the summer it became clear that Lieberman was moving further away from the Netanyahu bloc. *Yisrael Beitenu* signed a surplus agreement with Blue and White that would prevent any votes from being wasted. It also became clear that Gantz, whose entire political platform centered around toppling Netanyahu, was considering joining him if he were to be offered to be prime minister first in a rotation deal. Gantz later walked back his statement, saying Blue and White would replace Netanyahu in the upcoming elections.

In the meantime, Netanyahu made two appointments in his caretaker government that would raise eyebrows in the 'anyone but Bibi' camp. Rafi Peretz, Jewish Home party leader as well as number one on the URWP list, was named interim education minister on 18 June 2019. Less than a month into his new role, Peretz drew headlines across the world after advocating for the controversial 'conversion therapy' for gays. Netanyahu quickly rebuked Peretz, calling his comments unacceptable. The second controversial ministerial appoint was Smotrich, one of the most radical and extreme lawmakers in the Knesset's history, and number two on the URWP list. Netanyahu named him interim minister of transport and gave him a seat at the powerful security cabinet as well. Initially, Smotrich had his eyes on the justice ministry, hoping to base Israel's judicial system on the Torah laws. But Netanyahu instead opted for Amir Ohana from his Likud party. Ohana would become the first openly gay minister in Israel's history, and a stark contrast to Smotrich, who would arguably become the most homophobic minister in the country's history. Opposing gay marriage, boasting of being a 'proud homophobe' and calling gays 'abnormal' were just a few examples of the controversies surrounding Smotrich.

The battle over who represented the real values of the far-right religious Zionist movement eventually came to a halt in the summer months leading up to the September elections. Bennett and Shaked had suffered an embarrassing defeat in the previous elections, while Smotrich and Peretz had replaced them. But neither Bennnett nor Shaked were done fighting. After realizing that they were all competing for the same votes and that they were all jeopardizing their chances passing the electoral threshold if they kept fighting, UNRWP and New Right joined forces under a new name: *Yamina*. Peretz, the leader of URWP, had been fighting with Shaked over who should lead the list. Eventually they agreed that Shaked would be *Yamina*'s leader, Peretz was placed as number two, Smotrich third and Bennett number four. The list was described as a technical bloc, that would split after elections. Bennett described himself as more moderate than both Peretz and Smotrich on issues like religion and state.

One big threat to the new joint list was an old brief ally, the Jewish Power party, which had fallen out with URWP and now ran alone. Polls showed that the extremist fringe party wouldn't cross the electoral threshold, which meant it would waste thousands of crucial votes that would likely go to *Yamina*, Likud or the ultra-orthodox parties. Netanyahu had, according to reports in the Israeli media, again tried to convince Jewish Power to join *Yamina*, but without success. When it became clear that the party would run alone, both Bennett, Shaked and Likud warned right-wingers not to waste their votes on the party. After helping broker a deal between Jewish Power and URWP, Netanyahu was now actively working against the party. After its leader Ben-Ari had been disqualified from running for Knesset by the Supreme Court, Itamar Ben-Gvir took over the leadership. The party suffered another blow on 26 August 2019, when the Supreme Court barred two other senior members, Baruch Marzel, and Ben-Zion 'Bentzi' Gopstein, from running for parliament. The Supreme Court ruled that Gopstein, leader of the racist *Lehava* organization which advocated against mixed Jewish and Muslim relationships as well as gay rights, 'systematically incites racism against the Arab public' and that he presented the 'entire Arab public as an enemy with which no contact should be made that could be interpreted as coexistence.'[11] As for Marzel, who had a history of racist remarks and numerous arrests, the court ruled that he continued to incite to racism, despite having previously showed remorse for some comments made throughout the years. The ban on Marzel and Gopstein was seen as victory among most Israeli lawmakers who saw this as proof that the Supreme Court was a vital gatekeeper, preventing openly racist politicians from entering the Knesset. As expected, the ruling only added to Jewish Power's loathing for the court, which Gopstein labeled a branch of the left-wing *Meretz* party. In the days leading up to elections on 17 September, Likud reinforced its old scare tactic, accusing Blue and White of wanting to create a left-wing government with support by the Arab parties. Blue and White in the meantime continued its attacks on Netanyahu and what they saw as a clear conflict of interest, having a potential prime minister on trial for corruption.

Aftermath

As feared by many commentators and lawmakers, the second round of elections didn't change the political map. Both Likud and Blue and White lost ground, receiving 32 and 33 seats respectively. *Yamina,* however, surprised everyone by receiving seven seats with Shaked at its helm. *Yisrael Beitenu* also grew from five to seven seats. On the left-wing of the political spectrum, the Joint Arab list received a staggering 13 seats, making it the third biggest in parliament. The Labour party, which had merged with the old centre-right-wing party *Gesher,* only got six seats, a historically bad election for the once political giant. The other left-wing party *Meretz* had merged with Israel Democratic Party, led by former Prime Minister Ehud Barak, and the Green Movement. The results were also disappointing for the hopeful left-wing merger, receiving just five seats. Lieberman and his *Yisrael Beitenu* party were once again kingmaker, a complete repeat of the previous elections in April. With everyone realizing that neither side had the necessary mandates, talks about a unity government emerged. Netanyahu called on Gantz and Blue and White to join forces to prevent another round of elections. Blue and White, however, would only consider a unity government with Likud if Netanyahu resigned as party leader. The suggestion was dismissed outright by Likud which continued to support its leader. Netanyahu, who was still considered the party leader with the most realistic chance of forming a government, was handed the mandate once again by President Rivlin. After failing to form a government, Gantz received the mandate for the first time. Netanyahu, in what appeared to be a direct attempt to prevent any of his allies from defecting to Gantz's camp, appointed Bennett as defense minister on 8 November. The New Right party, which had split from the URWP shortly after the elections, also merged with Likud, further stabilizing the Netanyahu camp. Being number two in one of the smallest factions in Knesset, Bennett had gained maximum influence considering his party's size. While Gantz was in the middle of coalition talks, Bennett was thrown into the role as defense minister during an ongoing military operation. On 12 November, Israelis woke up to a barrage of rockets fired from Gaza at southern and central cities, including Tel Aviv. The Israeli military had assassinated Baha Abu al-Ata, a senior Islamic Jihad commander in Gaza, whom they held directly responsible for previous terror attacks as well as planning new ones. Tamir Hayman, the Military Intelligence chief at the time, said Bennett wasn't the mastermind behind this since he was in the middle of being appointed defense minister while the operation was ongoing. Hayman said:

> It had already been planned and Bennett had no effect on the operation. Not at all. He had only been appointed some seven hours before and we were already in the middle of it (planning). It was one of the most efficient strikes I was involved in during my military career. Baha was a unique character. He couldn't bear that there wasn't any violence (coming from Gaza. He suffered from that. But he had a personal relationship with the leadership. So, it was a perfect storm all manifested in one person. He created problems that Hamas suffered from. The Egyptians tried to moderate between us and him, but he betrayed them more than once. That led to the final decision to take him out, because it was unbearable.

'Operation Black Belt' lasted about 48 hours, with the Israeli military killing 34 people, including 24 militants, according to Israel. In return, Islamic Jihad fired 450 rockets at Israel, of which 90% were intercepted by the Iron Dome missile defense system. Bennett boasted that the operation had been a success, a view that was shared by opposition lawmakers like Yair Lapid and Itzik Shmuli from the Labour party. But both said the government's overall policy towards Gaza wasn't effective. The ongoing Gaza conflict was yet another example of the need to solve Israel's political crisis. Gantz, meanwhile, struggled to convince any of Netanyahu's partners to join him. On 20 November, Gantz admitted he had failed in forming a new government, handing back the mandate to President Rivlin. The political drama reached a new level the day after, when Attorney General Avichai Mandelblit announced the bombshell, everyone had been waiting for. Netanyahu would be indicted for bribery, breach of trust and fraud in three different corruption cases. Mandelblit had found that there was evidence pointing to 'grave' actions allegedly being committed, which carried a 'reasonable likelihood of conviction. I call on everyone, and first and foremost the leaders of the state, you must distance yourself from discourse that threatens law enforcement officials. We're not infallible or above criticism. But we acted without fear or prejudice, for the rule of law.' Mandelblit called the 'many lies' about the prosecution 'dangerous', and that those who were behind it were 'playing with fire.'[12] As had been the case throughout the investigation process, Netanyahu launched a new vicious attack on the judicial system after Mandelblit's announcement, decrying a 'coup' attempt, orchestrated by the left-wing. Blue and White demanded Netanyahu resign, which he dismissed outright.

The indictment only added fuel to the fire in the already deeply divided nation, with Netanyahu's supporters standing firmly behind him, believing his accusations about a deep state attempt to silence their elected leader. With neither Gantz nor Netanyahu able to form a government, and with a sitting prime minister now facing trial over severe corruption charges, Israel was in the middle of an unprecedented political chaos. On 11 December, the Knesset again voted to dissolve itself, calling fresh elections for 2 March 2020.

Notes

1 Ha'aretz, 'Netanyahu blasts Gantz-Lapid alliance: They rely on parties intent on destroying Israel', *Ha'aretz*, 21 February 2019.

2 Jacob Magid, 'Jewish Home voted overwhelmingly to back merger with extremist party', *Times of Israel*, 20 February 2019.

3 Yvette J. Deane, Lahav Harko, Gil Hoffman, 'Bennett, Shaked announce new political party; Regev calls them leftists', *Jerusalem Post*, 30 December 2018.

4 Gil Hoffmann, 'Benny Gantz slams Netanyahu: Meir Kahane would be proud', *Jerusalem Post*, 12 March 2019.

5 Jacob Magid, 'Extremist Otzma Yehudit announces unity pact with Jewish Home', *Times of Israel*, 20 February 2019.

6 American Jewish Committee & AIPAC, *Twitter*, 22 February 2019.

7 Yotam Berger, 'Israel's top court bans Kahanist leader from election run, okays Arab slates, far-left candidate', *Ha'aretz*, 17 March 2019.

8 TOI Staff, 'Likud campaign tries to portray Gantz as mentally unstable', *Times of Israel*, 27 March 2019.

9 TOI Staff, 'Netanyahu derides Israel's top 2 TV news stations as "propaganda channels', *Times of Israel*, 23 November 2019.

10   TOI Staff, 'Netanyahu derides Israel's top 2 TV news stations as "propaganda channels', *Times of Israel*, 23 November 2019.

11   Jacob Magid, 'Supreme Court bans extreme-right Gopstein and Marzel from elections', *Times of Israel*, 26 August 2019.

12   Raoul Wootliff, 'AG announces Netanyahu to stand trial for bribery, fraud and breach of trust', *Times of Israel*, 21 November 2019.

8

Chaos

'Unity' government

The outrage among Israelis over an unprecedented election cycle only deepened the growing rift in the country. For the 'anyone but Bibi' camp, there was no doubt who was responsible for the political chaos. Netanyahu had singlehandedly managed to drag Israel to three elections, refusing to resign from his position as prime minister despite facing a corruption trial that could cost him up to ten years in jail if found guilty. Blue and White kept saying that a unity government with Likud could be formed tomorrow, if Netanyahu resigned. For Netanyahu's camp, Lieberman and Blue and White were to blame for refusing to form a unity government. While Lieberman had insisted that his refusal to join a Netanyahu government was based on not wanting to cave to demands of the ultra-orthodox parties, it became clear after the elections that his old boss was the real problem for him. After initially saying that Gantz wasn't ready to be prime minister, Lieberman gave his party's official backing to the Blue and White leader. The idea of a unity government was not only pushed by President Rivlin, who called on all parties to do whatever they could to stop the endless elections, but also by Netanyahu and eventually Gantz, who ended up breaking with his repeated promises not to sit with an indicted prime minister.

Israel's third consecutive election in less than a year was held as another crisis erupted. The COVID-19 pandemic was evolving day by day, throwing the world into a state of emergency. Israel had detected its first case of COVID-19 less than two weeks before elections and had begun imposing quarantine restrictions on people entering Israel. Netanyahu's position as interim prime minister gave him immense responsibility over a historic health crisis, with Israelis glued to the TV every night to get the latest news about the virus and new restrictions. In the shadow of COVID-19, Israelis cast their votes at the ballot boxes once again, only to discover that very little had changed.

Netanyahu's Likud party emerged as the biggest faction in the Knesset, with 36 seats. But Netanyahu's bloc was still short of at least three seats to form a government. Blue and White received 33 seats, also failing to get a majority behind it. Gantz, however, received the mandate from President Rivlin to form government, with Lieberman's *Yisrael Beitenu* finally backing him. But with a rapidly escalating health crisis, Gantz finally succumbed to pressure from Likud to form a unity government. It would however take several months until the structure of the government became clear.

Yaid Lapid and Moshe Ya'alon refused to follow Gantz into a government with Netanyahu, something they had promised voters from the beginning that they wouldn't do. It effectively split the alliance, with Lapid going back to heading his Yesh Atid party. Several Blue and White lawmakers supported Gantz, who cited the COVID-19 emergency and the need for political stability as a reason to capitulate to Netanyahu and Likud. Surprisingly, Labour lawmakers, who had also refused to sit with Netanyahu, joined the government as well, along with Shas, United Torah Judaism, *Gesher*, and the new *Derekh Eretz* faction, formed by Yoaz Hendel, Netanyahu's former Director of Communications and Public Diplomacy. Hendel, who split from Ya'alon's *Telem* party, insisted it was the 'right decision' to unite with the prime minister they had promised to remove from power. The far-right was in complete distress over the political bombshell. Both Shaked, Bennett and Smotrich slammed Netanyahu for creating a 'left-wing' government and giving Gantz's Blue and White party a disproportionate amount of ministry portfolios, including the justice ministry, which was essential for Shaked. But Rafi Peretz from Jewish Home broke with the *Yamina* alliance and was named Minister of Jerusalem Affairs. Shaked was particularly furious with Netanyahu's decision to ally with Blue and White as well as the Labour party. Shaked said:

> Handing over of the Defense and Justice ministries to the Left means ideological subjugation to the Left and the destruction of the reform instated in the Justice Ministry, as well as of the regularization effort (of settlements) in Judea and Samaria effort we have led in the courts in recent years. [1]

Painting Netanyahu as left-wing was a trick taken out of his own playbook, but it didn't have the same effect on the public. In fact, Netanyahu had campaigned on promising to annex Jewish settlements in the West Bank, in line with President Trump's 'Peace Plan.' The decision by Bennett, Shaked and Smotrich not to join the government was therefore based on two things; not being able to justify to their voters sitting in a government with Labour and having to accept less powerful ministerial positions. Bennett, who was the second most powerful man in the country, saw himself stripped of the defense minister post, only to hand it to Gantz. He had been given a temporary reward for years of loyalty to Netanyahu, supporting him through three elections despite his corruption allegations.

The deal that was eventually signed between the new coalition parties had one crucial detail. Gantz entered in a rotation deal with Netanyahu, which stipulated that Netanyahu would continue as prime minister for the first 18 months, whereafter Gantz would take over. Commentators as well as lawmakers opposing the deal, warned Gantz that he was a fool for believing that Netanyahu would hand him the keys and honour their agreement. Secondly, betraying the trust of a million people who voted for a party promising to get rid of Netanyahu was nothing short of unforgivable. Thirdly, an elected prime minister on trial for corruption was now a fact. The biggest humiliation was reserved for Lapid, who had allowed him to give up the co-chair of Blue and White and let Gantz, a political novice, come in from the right and build on years of hard work by *Yesh Atid*. Lapid raged at the Knesset:

> (Gantz) looked me in the eye and said we would never sit in this bad government. I believed him. Together with us over a million Blue and White voters marched from street to street and from bridge to bridge. Good, honest Israelis. People who serve in the IDF, pay their taxes, obey the law. They feel betrayed today, and justifiably so. Their votes were stolen and given as a gift to Netanyahu. The coronavirus crisis doesn't give us the right or permission to abandon our values. We promised not to sit under a prime minister with three criminal indictments. We promised not to sit in a coalition of extremists and extortionists. We said we wouldn't allow anyone to undermine Israel's democracy. And on this week of all weeks, in which the attacks on the justice system were at their worst, a prize is given to those who disobey the law. A prize to criminality. You can't crawl into a government like that and tell us you did it for the good of the country.[2]

The COVID-19 pandemic threw the new government straight into an emergency. Up until the new government had been sworn in on 17 May 2020, Netanyahu's interim government had decided on some of the harshest lockdown restrictions in the world, closing the borders entirely, banning gatherings of more than 10 people, imposing restrictions of movement, with people not being allowed to leave their home for more than 100 metres. Several exceptions were made to this rule, such as grocery shopping, medical treatment, demonstrating and praying. Fines were handed out to anyone breaking the rules of the state of emergency announced by Netanyahu on 19 March. Thousands of businesses were forced to close, schools were shut and only essential workers, such as doctors, medics, journalists, and deliverymen were allowed to move around freely. The restrictions faced harsh backlash from the public, with people openly flaunting the rules. Absurd scenes of policemen chasing people doing yoga on an empty beach were recorded, while ultra-orthodox communities were documented over and over gathered in large numbers to pray. Private and underground 'COVID' parties were held in Tel Aviv, and outdoor private events were seen held in parks across the country. The government's failure to adequately financially compensate businessowners for lost income sparked outrage, and Israelis stranded abroad were furious that they weren't allowed to come back.

As the first wave faded and the new emergency unity government was in place, the harsh restrictions continued in the second wave over the summer. On 21 July, the Knesset passed a law that allowed Israel's Shin Bet intelligence agency to track infected individuals' phones, leading to harsh criticism by civil right organizations. The initial Shin Bet tracking of infected Israelis in March had also been banned by the Supreme Court, demanding the government pass a temporary law that would protect civil liberties. As the pandemic continued to unravel, the deep conflicts in the unity government were quickly exposed. Gantz's Blue and White faction disagreed with Netanyahu's Likud party over the government's handling of COVID, demanding that the IDF and the Defense Ministry take charge in the field. In other words, Gantz wanted to have control of the practical handling of curbing COVID. Netanyahu, on the other hand, thought Gantz was playing politics, trying to block his efforts to impose new restrictions. The internal fights and loathing between Blue and White and Likud were leaked to the media, serving as a warning sign of what was to come. Netanyahu had no intention of honouring the agreement made with Gantz.

He saw him, and by extension Blue and White, as having gotten too much power in the agreement, considering they only made up 16 seats in the government. With the defense, justice and foreign ministries in their hands, Blue and White had significant leverage, causing widespread anger among Likud lawmakers who didn't receive any ministry portfolios. The most critical issue, which eventually brought down the government, was the state budget. Like most countries, Israel passes a new state budget every year, but the political chaos in Israel had left country without an approved state budget for 2020. The coalition agreement between Likud and Blue and White stipulated that a two-year budget was to be approved in the summer, to prevent Israel's state-funded institutions from being harmed during a nation-wide health emergency. But as the months dragged on, Likud refused to honour the agreement, arguing that a one-year budget was appropriate due to the uncertainty of the COVID-19 crisis.

After failing to pass the budget in August, the coalition agreed to extend the deadline to December. It became clear to everyone in the following months that Netanyahu was using the only loophole in the coalition agreement to avoid letting Gantz become prime minister: If the government failed to pass a state budget, new elections would automatically be called. Realizing that Gantz had fallen in one of Netanyahu's traps, secret meetings between Blue and White lawmakers and Lapid and Bennett were reported in the Israeli media. On 23 December, the deadline for passing the budget expired, triggering an unprecedented new round of elections in Israel, just seven months after the new government had been sworn in. Each side blamed the other for the crisis, accusing each other of neglecting coalition deals. It was, however, widely seen among Israeli political experts and commentators as a deliberate move by Netanyahu to prevent Gantz from becoming prime minister. Gantz had taken a huge risk by sitting with Netanyahu, and according to the polls, the Blue and White leader would pay a significant price, dropping to just five or six seats.

Rebellion

After one of the worst government failures in Israel's history, another round of elections was scheduled for 23 March 2021, the fourth in just two years. Despite an ongoing corruption trial, Netanyahu's Likud party was not about to turn their backs on him. The best example of that was the show of support by numerous senior Likud lawmakers who stood by Netanyahu's side when he held a press conference ahead of his first pre-hearing at the Jerusalem District court, shortly after forming his new government with Gantz. Netanyahu raged against the judicial system, repeating his accusations that he was the victim of a deep-state, left-wing conspiracy to oust him. Behind him, all wearing face masks, stood Finance Minister Yisrael Katz, Transportation Minister Miri Regev, Education Minister Yoav Gallant, Public Security Minister Amir Ohana, Intelligence Minister Eli Cohen, as well as senior Likud lawmakers Tzachi Hanegbi, Nir Barkat, and David Amsalem.

The demonstration of solidarity spoke volumes, showing exactly how much Netanyahu was still feared and admired in the Likud party. It also proved that Netanyahu had no intentions of changing his approach toward the judicial system, despite sitting in a government with parties which all put their trust in the court's ability to reach a fair verdict in his trial. Yoaz Hendel, who had been named communication minister in the short-lived government, lambasted Netanyahu's press conference at the court, calling it a 'shameful act.' The only two senior Likud lawmakers who had had enough of the radical direction the party was going in were Gideon Sa'ar and Zeev Elkin. Sa'ar had returned to politics after a five year break from 2014-19 and had challenged Netanyahu for Likud leadership in 2019, in which an overwhelming majority voted for Netanyahu. Sa'ar had been seen by many as an heir to the Likud throne after Netanyahu, having had close ties with both Sharon and Olmert.

It therefore wasn't a big surprise when he announced in early December 2020 that he would leave Likud to launch his own party, *New Hope*. But Sa'ar's speech was fiery and repeated what many former Likud lawmakers had said before him. He accused the Likud party of having turned into a 'tool for the personal interests of the person in charge, including matters relating to his criminal trial,' and that Netanyahu had fostered 'a cult of personality' around him.[3] Sa'ar's new party ran on a right-wing platform, based on the same core values of Likud. This meant that he would pull crucial right-wing voters with him. Not long after, several Likud lawmakers joined Sa'ar. Likud lawmaker Yifat Shasha-Biton would be the first to defect, soon followed by Michal Shir and Sharren Haskel from Likud. When the government collapsed on 23 December, Ze'ev Elkin, a long-time ally of Netanyahu, announced he would also join Sa'ar. In yet another fiery speech on live TV, Elkin accused Netanyahu of 'destroying Likud', repeating Sa'ar's claim that Likud had turned into a personality cult. Elkin said:

> As someone who has been observing this from up close, I am more and more concerned. My trust in you and your intentions has increasingly eroded as your personal considerations have come before those of the nation. We are heading to yet another election because you want to control who will be appointed state prosecutor and to pass laws that will protect you from the prosecution you are facing for corruption. [4]

The rebellion by four Likud lawmakers and the announcement of a new right-wing party was a severe blow to Netanyahu. Initial polls in the media projected New Hope would win 20 seats in the upcoming elections. Despite the rebellion as well as a severe economic ramification of the pandemic, Netanyahu was optimistic that he would get the crucial 61 seats in the upcoming elections. He could boast of two big victories, which were used in the election campaign to once and for all show Israeli voters the statesman he was.

In August, President Trump announced that Israel and the UAE would normalize ties under the new 'Abraham Accords', taking the Middle East by surprise. The huge achievement was followed by yet another Arab Gulf state, Bahrain, joining the agreement. The signing of the Accords took place on the White House lawn on 15 September 2020, with Netanyahu, Trump, Emirati Foreign Minister Sheikh Abdullah bin Zayed al Nahyan and Bahrain Foreign Minister Abdullatif al-Zayani sitting next to each other. The historic agreement came after decades of covert relations between Israel and several Gulf states, revealing a new Middle East order in which Israel was becoming increasingly accepted. For Netanyahu, the normalization deals came at a crucial time. His corruption trial was still dominating the news, only surpassed by the COVID-19 pandemic and his bickering with Gantz. Netanyahu used the achievement of the Accords to ramp up the image of him being the only statesman that could bring about peace with Arab neighbours, promising that more countries would normalize ties with Israel soon.

COVID-19, meanwhile, had been a disaster for the Israeli economy, bringing the unemployment rate to a record 20% in spring 2020, and causing thousands of businesses to close. But on the vaccine front, Israel had managed to strike a deal with the pharmaceutical giant Pfizer, the leading vaccine producer, that saw some of the first vaccines sent to Israel. The official vaccine rollout began just three days before the government fell in December 2020. Netanyahu claimed that his statesmanship and personal relationship with Pfizer CEO Albert Bourla made sure Israel was among the first nations to get the vaccines. Bourla later confirmed that Netanyahu managed to convince him that Israel was 'the place with the right conditions' and that he was 'impressed' with Netanyahu's 'obsession' over getting the rights to roll out Pfizer's vaccines.[5] Israel became the fastest country in the world to vaccinate its citizens, making it a the center of attention for the rest of the world, where most countries were still trying to either develop vaccines or sign deals to buy them. The tremendous success was a combination of convincing Pfizer to let Israel be the testing ground, along with a highly effective health system, that made it possible for thousands of Israelis to get vaccinated every day.

As Netanyahu was pushing the vaccine and Abraham Accord achievements in the election campaign, two political developments happened that would have crucial consequences for him. Smotrich, the far-right extremist with a long list of racist and homophobic remarks behind him, split from Bennett and Shaked's *Yamina* list to form the Religious Zionist party. The differences between Bennett, the long-time representative of religious Zionism, and Smotrich, the heir, were only growing with time. Smotrich's positions on religion, the Palestinians and gays were much more extreme. While Smotrich wanted to restore the ancient Jewish Kingdom of David, with a judicial system built on the Torah, Bennett wanted to maintain modern democracy. On the Palestinians, Smotrich spoke out in favour of segregated maternity wards for Arabs and Jews, while Bennett promoted pragmatic changes to Israel's attitudes towards its Arab citizens. Lastly, Smotrich had made numerous homophobic remarks over the years. In October of 2020, he spoke out against equal rights for gays and heterosexuals, causing Bennett to say believed in full equal rights for the gay community. According to Professor in political science at Bar Ilan University, Moshe Hellinger, Bennett was very different from Smotrich from the beginning. Professor Hellinger said:

> Bennett is what you call "religious light." You can say that he is "left-wing" when it comes to religion but very right-wing when it comes to economy and politics. A capitalist, like Smotrich. Bennett was never a messianic figure who wanted to make Israel a *halachic* (religious) state, like Smotrich. Most religious Zionists today somewhere between Bennett and Smotrich. But Bennett never intended for one second to be the leader of religious Zionism. It wasn't important to him. When he understood he couldn't be the leader of Likud because of Netanyahu, he wanted to become the leader of a big Religious Zionism party, and then one day be able to conquer Likud with Shaked. He wanted to one day be the prime minister for the biggest party in Israel.

Bennett and Shaked's journey became clear when they slowly moved away from their hardline, far-right stances. They would continue to run in the elections as the *Yamina* party, trying to appeal to both secular and religious right-wing voters. Smotrich, however, made a clear shift to the far-right again, running together with the Jewish Power party and *Noam*, another extreme, fringe, party known for its anti-LGBTQ policies. Noam was created in 2019 by a far-right extremist, Avi Maoz, who believed in enhancing 'Jewish identity' in Israeli society, banning Pride Parades, and restoring 'normal' family structures. In other words, turning back the clock for the LGBTQ community and the progress it had made in Israel in recent years. Ben-Gvir, who headed the Jewish Power party, was placed third on the list, putting him on the trajectory to enter Knesset for the first time in his career. Knowing full well that the Israeli public was still getting used to Kahanist politicians slowly making their way into Israel's political life, Netanyahu admitted that the highly controversial Ben-Gvir would indeed become a part of his coalition if he was re-elected. However, in a rare TV interview a month before elections, Netanyahu promised that Ben-Gvir wouldn't be a part of his security cabinet or become a minister. In Netanyahu's words, Ben-Gvir was 'unfit' to be a senior minister. Like many politicians before him, Netanyahu would soon break that promise. Religious Zionism swore allegiance to Netanyahu, but Bennett, who had been vocal in his criticism against Netanyahu's handling of the COVID-19 crisis and the endless, harsh restriction, was seen as a joker.

In what would become a pivotal and historic moment in Israeli politics, Bennett pledged in an interview on the right-wing, Netanyahu-friendly Channel 20 not to sit with Yair Lapid in a government after the elections. To make it even more dramatic, he signed a piece of paper on which the promise was written, showing it to the cameras. 'I won't allow Yair Lapid to be prime minister, including in a rotation (agreement.) and I will not establish a government based on the support of Mansour Abbas from the Islamic Movement,' Bennett said.[6] The reference to Mansour Abbas' United Arab List party was taken straight out of the Likud election campaign playbook, and came as a response to growing pressure on Bennett to once and for all give his unequivocal support to Netanyahu. The pledge not to sit with Lapid just two days before elections was seen as a show of support for Netanyahu, despite Bennett's refusal to promise that.

The election results on 23 March 2021 were a disaster for the Netanyahu camp. Likud dropped to just 30 seats but remained the largest party in Knesset. *Yesh Atid* soared to 17 seats, while Gantz's Blue and White party was punished for his adventure with Netanyahu, receiving just eight seats. Smotrich's Religious Zionist list received a surprising six seats, which meant that Ben-Gvir made it into Knesset, causing a huge uproar in parts of the Israeli media, which dubbed it the return of Kahanism. Netanyahu's bloc, however, only managed to get 52 seats combined, which meant that even if it convinced Bennett, whose Yamina party got seven seats, to join the bloc, they would still need to convince another party. The prospects of Netanyahu pulling this off was next to zero. Lieberman, who in the previous elections had conditioned his party joining Netanyahu on passing a law that would draft ultra-orthodox men to the army was now completely rejecting the idea of supporting a prime minister standing trial for corruption. In fact, *Yisrael Beitenu* was pushing to pass a law that would prevent any lawmaker facing indictment from forming a government, something that was directly aimed at Netanyahu. The election results also didn't give Lapid the necessary mandates to form a government, at least not if Bennett's promise not to join him were to be taken seriously. Rivlin therefore handed Netanyahu the mandate, once again, buying more time for the prime minister who was under huge pressure to resign due to his trial and failure to form a stable government.

Ethnic unrest

In the aftermath of the elections, ethnic unrest between Israeli Jews, Arabs and Palestinians was brewing. Almost every year during Ramadan, the Temple Mount, where the Al-Aqsa Mosque was located, became the focus point for clashes between Israeli security forces and Palestinians. The escalation began in April when Israeli security forces put up barriers at Damascus Gate Plaza, one of the entrances to the Old City of Jerusalem. Every year, Palestinians would gather at the plaza for Ramadan in the evening. The barriers were therefore met with widespread anger by the Palestinians, leading to violent clashes with Israeli police, who used water cannons and stun grenades to disperse the crowds. A few days later, a video of a Palestinian teen slapping a young ultra-orthodox man on the light rail in Jerusalem went viral on TikTok, leading to copy-cat attacks on other Jews. A violent attack in broad daylight on a rabbi in the mixed Jewish-Arab city of Yaffo, outside Tel Aviv, by two Arab men drew a lot of media attention and anger among lawmakers. The attack was condemned by Netanyahu, as well as Bennett and Jerusalem Affairs Minister Peretz. Attacks on Palestinians followed in the coming weeks, by extremist right-wing Jews in Jerusalem. The far-right *Lehava* organization, led by Ben-Gvir's friend and former Jewish Power party member Benzi Gopstein, organized a march through East Jerusalem, to 'restore Jewish dignity.' Chants of 'death to Arabs' were heard in the crowd, which clashed with both police, Palestinians and left-wing counter protesters. More than 100 people were injured in the far-right march. Not long after, rockets were fired from Gaza, causing Israel to retaliate with airstrikes on Hamas positions.

Watching the situation slowly get out of control in East Jerusalem, Hamas was encouraging Palestinians and Arab Israelis to rise and revolt, trying to draw direct line from what happened in the West Bank, Jerusalem and Gaza. Sporadic attacks by both Jews and Palestinians in East Jerusalem became almost daily events, while Palestinian attacks against Israelis in the West Bank also increased, leading to Israeli soldiers killing the assailants.

The situation worsened when it became clear that several Palestinian families were about to be evicted from their homes in the East Jerusalem neighborhood of *Sheikh Jarrah*, also known as *Shimon HaTzadik* for Jews. A decades old dispute over ownership of homes had gone to the Supreme Court, with Palestinian families arguing they had lived there for generations, some as far as before the State of Israel was established. The Jerusalem Municipality, however, argued they were residing there illegally, with no proper documentation proving their ownership or rights to keep building on their homes. With a looming eviction, *Sheikh Jarrah* became the new friction point with right-wing Jews and Palestinians demonstrating against each other, leading to several violent clashes. The issue became even more political when Ben-Gvir established a temporary 'office' in *Sheikh Jarrah* in a show of force in the first week of May. The stunt, which was widely reported in the media, was meant to force more Israeli police officers to the scene, with Ben-Gvir arguing that Jews felt unprotected. His old friend, Benzi Gopstein, sat next to him in the 'office', which was closed the next day. Ben-Gvir was frequently taking part in far-right demonstrations against Palestinians in *Sheikh Jarrah*.

On 7 May, over 70,000 attended the Friday prayer at the Al-Aqsa Mosque on Temple Mount, leading to Palestinians throwing rocks at Israeli police officers deployed on the site. Over 200 Palestinians and 17 Israeli police officers were injured in the clashes. Hamas kept warning Israel that the 'storming' of the Al-Aqsa Mosque by Jewish 'settlers' was a red line. So was the eviction of Palestinian families from *Sheikh Jarrah*. With the Palestinian Authority, and in particular President Abbas, increasingly unpopular among Palestinians, Hamas filled the vacuum by portraying itself as their only protector. The following day, another march by far-right Jews took place in East Jerusalem, with young Yeshiva students chanting nationalistic slogans against Palestinians. Clashes elsewhere in the city lead to over 100 Palestinians injured.

On 10 May, the situation exploded. The annual Flag March on Jerusalem Day was scheduled despite a security situation spiraling out of control in both Jerusalem and the West Bank. As right-wingers prepared to march through East Jerusalem with Israeli flags, Hamas gave Israel an ultimatum: Remove all security forces from the Temple Mount by 6:00 PM or face rockets. Shortly after six o' clock, rockets were fired at Jerusalem, setting off sirens across the city, including in Knesset, where lawmakers were rushed in to bomb shelters in the building. Hamas had finally decided to escalate the situation, drawing Israel into another war in Gaza. Not long after, Israel responded with airstrikes.

Operation 'Guardian of the Walls' was launched the following day, with Netanyahu and Gantz having to cooperate on their first real security crisis. An equally serious conflict was escalating simultaneously, which in many ways threatened Israel's internal stability. The same day as Hamas launched rockets at Jerusalem, Arab-Israeli protesters in the mixed city of Lod threw firebombs at a synagogue and Jewish homes. A Hamas flag was seen raised in the crowd while some called on the liberation of Palestine. In return, an Arab-Israeli man was killed and two injured, leading to the arrest of a Jewish suspect. In the following days, riots erupted across Israel, with Arab and Jewish Israelis attacking each other daily. Synagogues, cars and businesses were set on fire. A Jewish mob lynched an Arab driver in city of Bat Yam, pulling him out of the car and severely beating him until he was saved and sent to the hospital. In Lod, an Arab mob killed a Jewish man by stone-throwing. In the northern city of Acre, masked Arab men looted and destroyed businesses.

The mass riots continued for days, with Netanyahu declaring a state of emergency in Lod, with police struggling to get the riots under control. The riots were the worst between Jews and Arabs in over two decades and was fanned by extremists on both sides. The Arabs responsible for the attacks on Jews were not affiliated with any political groups or terrorist organization but were mostly young. On the Jewish side, there was a clear attempt by member of the far-right to fan the flames. Many were either members of the Hilltop Youth, or supporters of the *Lehava* organization and an ultranationalist group known as *La Familia*. The latter was notorious fan group of the Betar Jerusalem football club, which was known for its anti-Arab slogans and violent clashes at football games. Both *Lehava* and *La Familia* wanted to exclude Arabs from Jewish neighborhoods and saw the riots in mixed cities as a pretext to defend Jewish citizens from violent attacks by Arab Israelis. In some instances, residents of mixed cities like Acre said that far-right Jews as well as young Arab Israelis who didn't live in the city came to fan the flames. This was also reported in cities like Lod and Ramla. According to a report by Channel 13, Police Commissioner Kobi Shabtai held Jewish Power party leader Ben-Gvir as well as Lehava directly responsible for the ongoing riots. Shabtai reportedly told Netanyahu during a briefing:

The person who is responsible for this intifada is Itamar Ben-Gvir. It started with the Lehava protest at Damascus Gate. It continued with provocations in Sheikh Jarrah, and now he is moving around with Lehava activists. Yesterday police managed to calm things in Acre, when the activists showed up in a bus and caused an uproar. The police don't have the tools to deal with it. [7]

Ben-Gvir responded by calling for Shabtai to be fired, claiming that he was failing to bring the riots under control. The deep civil unrest between Jews and Arabs was unfolding as the Gaza conflict saw thousands of rockets fired at Israel, sending civilians to shelters several times per day in the southern and central part of Israel. Fighter jets pounded Gaza, targeting Hamas positions and a building where Al-Jazeera and Associate Press were residing. Israel warned everyone in the building to get out before they bombed it. The destruction of the building led to intense criticism against Israel, which argued that it had been used by Hamas, something both media outlets denied.

On 20 May, Israel and Hamas reached a ceasefire, mediated by Egypt. Over 4,300 rockets were fired at Israel, while over 260 Palestinians were killed. 13 people were killed on the Israeli side. The combination of civil riots between Jews and Arabs across Israel and war in Gaza at the same time was unprecedented. Meanwhile, a historic political upheaval was about to rock the nation.

Notes

1   Ariel Kahana, Yehuda Shlezinger, 'Yamina threaten to "topple Netanyahu" if new government is not to their liking', *Israel Hayom*, 30 March 2020.

2   Raoul Wootliff, 'Lapid: I trusted Gantz, but he stole our votes and handed them to Netanyahu', *Times of Israel*, 26 March 2020.

3   Raoul Wootliff, 'Gideon Sa'ar quits Likud, "a tool for Netanyahu's interests," to lead "New Hope"', *Times of Israel*, 8 December 2020.

4   Moran Azulay, 'Blasting PM, Likud Minister Ze'ev Elkin bolts party to join Sa'ar', *Yediot Ahronot*, 23 December 2020.

5   TOI Staff, 'Pfizer CEO hails 'obsessive' Netanyahu for calling 30 times to seal vaccine deal', *Times of Israel*, 11 March 2021.

6   Naftali Bennett interview on Channel 12, 21 March 2021.

7   TO Staff, 'Police chief said to blame far-right lawmaker Ben Gvir for 'internal intifada', *Times of Israel*, 14 May 2021.

9

Bennett

Brothers in arms

As the Israeli-Palestinian conflict was heating up, the political chaos continued with Netanyahu failing to form a government. Instead of extending Netanyahu's deadline, President Rivlin decided to hand the mandate to Lapid on 5 May 2021. For the first time in his career Lapid was officially tasked with trying to form a government. But the anti-Netanyahu bloc, or the 'change bloc' as it had become known as, was struggling to bridge their ideological differences.

The Gaza conflict made both United Arab List and *Yamina* put negotiations with Lapid on hold. But after the ceasefire was announced, Bennett publicly announced his willingness to form a unity government with Lapid and other opposition parties, while lashing out at the Netanyahu government for its handling of the security crisis. Bennett criticized Netanyahu personally, both for his handling of the COVID-19 pandemic but also for the Gaza conflict and the riots inside Israel. With a race against time, Lapid slowly made progress, signing a coalition deal with Labour first. But it quickly became clear that Lapid would have to make serious compromises to succeed in forming a government, first and foremost allowing someone else to serve as prime minister first. With Bennett being the kingmaker and standing to lose the most from entering a coalition with Arab and left-wing parties, Lapid eventually reached the conclusion that Bennett had to be prime minister first in a rotation deal, like the one made by Netanyahu and Gantz. According to the deal, Lapid would become prime minister in September 2023, and would start off as foreign minister. The drama reached its peak on 2 June when Lapid's deadline would expire. The *Yesh Atid* leader was negotiating with parties until the eleventh hour, with the rest of the country watching the news intensely to find out if he had managed to overcome what seemed to be a Herculean task. An hour before midnight Lapid informed Rivlin that he had managed to form a government. A picture was released to the media with Bennett, Lapid and United Arab List leader Mansour Abbas sitting next to each other, celebrating the political breakthrough. The announcement was hailed abroad as the most diverse government in history, but at home, Bennett's U-turn made Likud, and Netanyahu in particular, fume. The former leader of the far-right in Israel took a massive risk by breaking his election promise not to sit with Lapid, and even more so, by sitting with an Arab-Israeli party. Netanyahu raged against the new government, saying: 'We are witnessing the greatest election fraud in the history of the country, in my opinion in the history of any democracy.'[1]

While Lapid was hailed as the big compromiser, managing to bring together *Yamina*, United Arab List, *Meretz*, Labour, *Yisrael Beitenu,* New Hope and Blue and White, Bennett was seen as the one reaping the fruits. Representing a party with just seven seats, the *Yamina* leader had gained a disproportionate amount of power, but without it there would be no government. *Yamina's* seven seats secured a razor-thin majority of 62 seats, making it fragile and open to attempts by Likud to use all means necessary to destabilize it. Rumours about last-minute defectors from Bennett's party filled media reports. Likud lawmakers viciously attacked Bennett in the media, repeating Netanyahu's claim that it was tantamount to election fraud. The accusation that the new government relied on 'terror supporters' from the United Arab List were however not only inaccurate but also hypocritical. Party leader Mansour Abbas had repeatedly condemned terror attacks against Jews, most recently the attack on a synagogue in Lod during the ethnic riots in May. But he had held secret negotiations with Likud prior to agreeing to join Lapid and Bennett's government. So, while Likud attacked Bennett for joining a 'terror' supporter, the party had tried to get the Arab Israeli party to join them instead.

13 June was set as the day that lawmakers in Knesset would officially cast their votes, swearing in the new unity government led by Bennett. The atmosphere in Knesset was extremely tense. Labour and *Meretz* lawmakers were seen smiling, full of excitement to finally be part of a government again, and more importantly to be the ones helping topple Netanyahu. Others, however, were less excited. Gantz had lost significant power, going from a deal that would make him the next prime minister to handing over the leadership to Bennett and his own ally Lapid. Gideon Sa'ar's party was also uneasy about the prospects of sitting with *Meretz* and United Arab List, with whom they had next to nothing in common.

Finally, *Yamina's* lawmakers were seen wandering the hallways in Knesset with gloomy looks on their faces, having been the punching bag of their old allies. Bennett was of course the big scapegoat, but Shaked was attacked harshly, and so were the other party members, Idit Silman,

Amichai Chickli, Nir Orban and Matan Kahana. Bennett was struggling to keep the party unified in the decision, with several of them conditioning their support for the government on political demands. The first to rebel against Bennett was Chickli, who announced a month earlier that he wouldn't support the new government in the making. This effectively meant that the government only had 61 lawmakers supporting it. Chickli caused a huge headache for the party, which now had a rebel lawmaker who didn't support its leader. When Bennett finally emerged in the Knesset hallway to enter the plenum for the vote, he was surrounded by a sea of security guards and journalists. Inside the Knesset, he was heckled throughout his speech at the plenum by lawmakers from Likud, Religious Zionism and the ultra-orthodox parties, calling him a liar and a criminal. Bennett's old ally Smotrich was particularly furious, exploding in a tirade against him.

After the intense heckling against Bennett, Lapid took to the podium and said he would forgo his planned speech after witnessing how lawmakers had treated the incoming prime minister. Lapid said he asked forgiveness from his 86-year-old mother whom he had invited to Knesset, saying they were both ashamed of the opposition lawmakers for their behaviour. Netanyahu on his part mocked Bennett throughout his farewell speech, repeating his accusation that Israel was witnessing the greatest election fraud in the country's history, and that the public wouldn't forget it. Iran, Netanyahu continued, was 'celebrating' the fact that Israel now had a 'dangerous' government, and that Bennett had no 'global standing' or 'credibility'.[2]

The other party leaders from Netanyahu's bloc repeated the claim of election fraud. Smotrich was particularly enraged, calling it a 'government of hatred and boycotts' the only glue of which 'is jealousy and hatred,' and disdain for the Torah. 'A government of the desecration of God's name' which relies on 'terror supporters' won't be forgiven, Smotrich railed.[3] After numerous speeches, the Knesset finally cast its votes in what would become a historic moment. The government was approved with 60 votes for and 59 against after United Arab List lawmaker Saaed Al-Harumi decided to abstain. Cheers were heard in Knesset as it was announced that a new government had officially been sworn in. For the first time in its history, Israel had a government with an Arab Israeli party and a prime minister who was wearing a kippah at the same time. But cheers of joy would, however, soon be replaced with intense internal bickering and an unprecedented smear campaign against the government.

Trouble in paradise

The toppling of Netanyahu by his old protégé and close ally was seen as the ultimate betrayal by Likud. The very idea of not having Netanyahu as prime minister anymore was unthinkable, which is why he was still greeted as prime minister by several of his allies when he met with them in Knesset, something that was ridiculed in the media.

While many political observers declared the Netanyahu era over, predicting his inevitable retirement, the Likud leader refused to resign as party leader. Instead, he took on the role as opposition leader, which he had been twice before, promising to destroy the fragile government.

The 'government of change' started out with a lot of hope and worries at the same time. With just 60 seats it would be extremely difficult to pass new laws and to make big decisions. The only way to keep the fragile government alive was to steer clear from making any decisions on sensitive issues, such as the Palestinian conflict. Several party leaders and coalition lawmakers also had to swallow their pride. Gantz had saved face by being appointed defense minister and Sa'ar was named justice minister. Shaked, who had campaigned on promising to finish her 'judicial revolution' had to compromise and got the interior ministry portfolio. Lieberman had asked for the finance ministry, which he received, while *Meretz* leader Nitzan Horowitz was appointed health minister, a powerful position given the COVID-19 crisis still wasn't completely under control. Labour party leader Merav Michaeli was given the transportation portfolio, while her colleague, Omer Bar-Lev received a notoriously difficult role as public security minister. United Arab List had managed to get a promise of 30 billion shekels ($8 billion) earmarked for a five-year development plan for infrastructure projects in badly neglected Arab communities across Israel. This would make it possible for him to justify to his constituents why he chose to enter a government with right-wing parties. Abbas was seen as a black sheep by the Joint Arab List, who despised him for entering the government. At the same time, Likud was pounding the new government for 'selling' the country's Negev desert to 'terror supporters' (Abbas). Likud's strategy was simple; don't cooperate with the government on a single issue and put enough pressure on *Yamina's* lawmakers with the intention of either defecting to Likud or resign from the coalition. Netanyahu would criticize every decision made by Bennett, no matter what it was.

When the new government signed a deal in July 2021 that would allow neighboring Jordan, one of Israel's most important allies in the region, to buy water from Israel, Netanyahu drew an absurd conclusion that it was tantamount to selling oil to Iran. Jordan, he argued, sold oil to Iraq, which he said was effectively controlled by Iran. Therefore, selling water to Jordan was the same as giving Iran oil. Of course, Israel had made several agreements with Jordan over the years under Netanyahu. One example was $10 billion gas deal signed by an Israeli gas consortium and Jordan in 2016, putting Israel on the trajectory of becoming the biggest supplier of gas to the kingdom. The agreement was praised by Energy Minister Yuval Steinitz as historic. Netanyahu's accusations about the water agreement with Jordan was therefore clear spin aimed making the public believe that Bennett was a danger to Israel's security. Bennett, on his part, had set out to turn a new leaf in the diplomatic relations with Jordan, which had suffered in recent years.

In 2019, relations between the two neighbours reached an all-time low, according to King Abdullah II, and would only worsen with Netanyahu's promises to annex the West Bank. As Netanyahu focused on ridiculing and criticizing the government's decision, the pressure campaign against *Yamina* lawmakers began heating up. Shaked and Nir Orbach had already faced immense pressure, with hundreds of right-wing voters protesting outside their private homes after Lapid had announced he was able to form a government headed by Bennett in early June. Smotrich joined the protesters, which were encouraged by Likud, calling on Shaked to come out and face her voters. Chants of 'shame' were heard, and demonstrators held signs with Orbach and Idit Silman's faces on them, urging them not to join a left-wing government. Other lawmakers were also subject of demonstrations outside their homes, including Bennett and *Meretz's* Tamar Zandberg. *Yisrael Beitenu* leader Lieberman received death threats, and so did Zandberg, after a false media campaign claimed that she was sponsoring a bill that would criminalize attempts by *Chabad* activists to approach unaccompanied minors on streets and outside schools. Bennett had also received death threats, causing Shin Bet to provide him with personal security.

The intelligence agency warned that there had been an uptick in incitement against Shaked and Lapid, ordering police and Knesset security to give extra protection to Shaked in particular. Both Orbach and Silman were given extra security by the Knesset Guard in early June after harassment intensified from right-wing extremist activists. Permanent security guards were deployed outside Shaked and Bennett's homes. As the government was sworn in and began its work, the harassment against *Yamina* lawmakers continued, with Silman saying her family were attacked and threatened daily. 'My friends, I wish to tell you this: it is not I who is under investigation, but those who incite against me on and off social media 24/7, Silman said.[4] The vicious attacks on Bennett and the rest of his party were not limited to Likud and Smotrich's Religious Zionism party. The ultra-orthodox were furious that Bennett had 'betrayed' the Netanyahu bloc. Their real concern was that they had been part of almost every coalition for decades, yielding disproportionate amount of power with their often-crucial seats they brought to the government. This was particularly the case under Netanyahu, apart from his short-lived experiments with Gantz in 2020 and Lapid and Livni in 2013. For the first time in decades, they faced a government who didn't have their core interests at heart. On the contrary, several parties in the new government were fed up with the ultra-orthodox community's special treatment, such as being exempted from the army and a sky-high unemployment rate compared to the rest of the population. In addition, despite only constituting roughly 10% of the population, the ultra-orthodox had immense power over other societal structures, such as marriage, transportation and religion.

Now, their arch enemies Lieberman, Lapid, and *Meretz* were in power, all because of Bennett, without whom there would be no government. Their fury against him was designed to undermine his religiosity and the 'danger' he constituted to the Jewishness of Israel. Shas party leader Arieh Dery, who had been convicted twice and served jail time for corruption, said Bennett's government would 'destroy the Jewish character' of the state. Senior lawmaker from United Torah Judaism, Moshe Gafni, called Bennett 'wicked', while the party's leader, Yaakov Litzman, went even further: 'What's the difference between him and a gentile? He wears a kippah. I urge him to remove his kippah. It's a great chutzpah that he wears a kippah. Let everyone understand that he's Reform.'[5] The attacks aimed at Bennett, who became the ultimate scapegoat for the Netanyahu bloc, were directed at all levels of his leadership and personality. While Bennett, and Lapid for that matter, were trying to stabilize the government and ignore the daily attacks, the big differences between the parties and their ideologies were beginning to show.

The first showdown came when the Citizenship Law expired, which barred Palestinians married to Israelis from residing permanently in Israel and prevent them from acquiring citizenship. The law had been extended annually by all Israeli governments since 2003, most of which had been headed by Netanyahu. But vowing to make the new government's life as miserable as possible, the entire Netanyahu bloc voted against, while two lawmakers from the United Arab List abstained, ending the vote in a 59-59 tie. The proposed amendment to the law, spearheaded by interior minister

Shaked, had minor changes, such as extending the law for six months instead of a year, while some 1,600 Palestinians who had lived in Israel for a considerable amount of time would be offered non-residency status. The compromise was reached with UAL ahead of the vote, and had been in line with her predecessor, Dery.

The defeat exposed exactly how vulnerable the government was, and how tight a ship Netanyahu was steering. Shaked slammed the 'reckless conduct of Likud and Smotrich', calling the sight of Likud, Religious Zionism and the Joint Arab List all celebrating together 'madness.' Likud defended its decision to vote against a law it had itself had extended year after year, accusing it of being a 'corrupt deal sewn together in the dark of night between Bennett, Lapid and Shaked, United Arab List and Meretz,' and that it had been 'crushed thanks to the determined effort ran by the opposition led by Netanyahu.'[6] It would take almost nine months before Shaked managed to find a compromise with opposition lawmakers who could support the extension of the law, which for right-wing lawmakers was vital for Israel's national security. For the left-wing and Arab parties, the law was yet another sign that Israel would do anything it could to prevent Palestinians and Israelis from engaging with each other.

Violence

One of the main issues the government was trying to avoid was the Palestinian conflict and settlements in the West Bank. Under Netanyahu, the settlers had experienced increasing political support since 2015, numbering nearly 500,000 in 2021, across some 130 settlements. For them, however, it was not enough. There was still a long list of illegal outposts that hadn't been legalized, and some were demolished by the military over and over.

The only real solution for the settlement movement was an annexation of the West Bank, with unlimited building permits. Bennett inherited a situation in the West Bank that had become reminiscent of the Wild West, with settlers attacking Palestinians and Israeli soldiers. In autumn 2021, efforts were made to build another illegal outpost a few hundred meters from the ruins of *Migron*, other outposts which existed until 2012 when it was evacuated per order by the Supreme Court. The new outpost, *Ramat Migron*, was built by hardcore settlers, some of which were associated with the 'Hilltop Youth.' The military, which was under the control of Defense Minister Gantz, demolished the outposts in November, leading to clashes with the settlers. Five suspects were arrested. Earlier in the day, Israeli security forces had been attacked by 20 masked settlers in the West Bank after they had demolished another illegal outpost known as *Geulat Zion*. The 'residents' of *Ramat Migron* had no intention of leaving their new home and continued to return to the illegal site, rebuilding their shacks. The new government had also inherited a different headache in the form of an illegal outpost, *Evyatar*, located deep in the northern part of the Palestinian controlled West Bank. *Evyatar* was erected in May 2021 in response to a Palestinian terrorist attack which killed of 19-year-old Yehuda Guetta, a yeshiva student in the nearby illegal settlement of *Itamar*.

Evyatar quickly became a flashpoint for Palestinians who demonstrated nearby, leading to several clashes with settlers and Israeli soldiers. *Evyatar* was another test for the new government. Bennett, a previous leader of the Yesha settler Council in the West Bank, was a strong believer in the right for Jews to settle everywhere in the West Bank. And so was the rest of his *Yamina* party, as well as *Yisrael Beitenu* and Gideon Sa'ar's New Hope party. But *Meretz*, Labour, United Arab List and *Yesh Atid* were vehemently opposed to allowing illegal outposts to exist. Eventually, the settlers of *Evyatar* reached a compromise with the government which would see them leave the site voluntarily with the promise of building a yeshiva there in the future. But in early February 2022, shortly before Avichai Mandelblit finished his term as attorney general, he authorized that a settlement could be established on the site where *Evyatar* had been erected. Lapid sent a strong-worded letter to Bennett, warning that legalizing the outpost could have serious diplomatic consequences for Israel and that he hadn't been included in discussions on the issue. Labour and *Meretz* also fumed over the apparent plans to legalize *Evyatar*. *Meretz* said it was the last thing the country needed right now, with one the party's lawmakers, Mossi Raz, threatening to topple the government if it meant stopping the retroactive legalization. Raz also accused the government of being the 'most right-wing in the history of Israel' when it came to the occupied territories.[7] The issue of *Evyatar* and the illegal outposts in the West Bank was a clear example of how deeply divided the government was on fundamental issues.

Yamina did everything it could to portray the government as right-wing, while *Meretz*, Labour and United Arab List had to pull in the other direction so as not to appear to be complicit in some right-wing agenda. As the debate over *Evyatar* continued, the government's Achilles heel was finally hit. On 22 March, an Israeli Arab citizen killed four other Israelis in a terror attack in the city of Beersheba, using his car and a knife to kill the victims in two separate locations. He was eventually killed by an Israeli bus driver and another armed Israeli civilian. The horror of the attack in broad daylight committed by an Arab Israeli citizen became even more chilling when it was revealed that the terrorist was affiliated with Islamic State, and that he had previously served jailtime for affiliating with the terror group. The terrorist attack was highly unusual for two reasons; it was committed by an Israeli Arab citizen, and he was affiliated with Islamic State. Less than a week later, another terror attack was carried out by Israeli Arab citizens who shot and killed two Israelis and injured six others when they opened fire on civilians in the city of Hadera. Both were killed by nearby officers who rushed to the scene of the attack. The seriousness of the two attacks could not be overstated. Islamic State was not considered an active group inside Israel. It posed a huge challenge for the Shin Bet intelligence agency which doesn't have the same authority to surveil Israeli citizens the same way it can with Palestinians in the West Bank for example. The situation became even more difficult for the government because the attack in Hadera happened as Foreign Minister Yair Lapid was hosting his counterparts from Egypt, Morocco, UAE, Bahrain and the U.S. in what was dubbed the 'Negev Summit' (It took place in Israel's Negev desert). In other words, as Israel was building on its newfound friendships in the Arab world, Israeli citizens affiliated with Islamic State brutally murdered civilians on the streets of Hadera.

The following day, yet another terror attack hit Israel, this time in the ultra-orthodox city of Bnei Brak just outside Tel Aviv. A Palestinian man from the town of Ya'bad, not far from Jenin in the northern West Bank, shot and killed five people before he was killed himself. Harrowing video footage showed how he gunned down random civilians with a rifle, one of whom was executed while sitting in his car. The attack claimed the lives of four Jews and one Arab Israeli Christian. On 7 April, a Palestinian man from Jenin killed three people in central Tel Aviv, shooting civilians who were having drinks at a bar on one of the busiest streets in Israel. The entire city was turned into a warzone, with people asked to stay indoor while some 1,000 soldiers, special forces, and police hunted the Palestinian man. The manhunt took about nine hours until he was found in Yaffo where special forces shot and killed him on the spot. The opposition, led by Netanyahu, used every terror attack as ammunition for its relentless attacks on the 'dangerous' government which was supported by an Islamic party (*Ra'am*). Itamar Ben-Gvir, the leader of the extremist Jewish Power party, was particularly cynical in his exploitation of the terror attacks, doing what Netanyahu did in the mid-1990's when suicide bombings rocked Israel. Netanyahu showed up on the scenes of the terror attack, denouncing the government and its failure to crack down on terror.

Some 27 years later, Ben-Gvir did the exact same. After the terror attack in Hadera, Public Security Minister Omer Bar-Lev came to the scene and gave interviews. In the middle of a live interview with Israeli TV, Ben-Gvir interrupted and started screaming at Bar-Lev, saying he should be 'ashamed' of himself, that he should resign and that 'they took the biggest left-winger and made him public security minister.' The rest of the opposition joined the daily attacks on the government. Netanyahu said in April 2022:

> When terrorism smells weakness, it raises its head. And when it encounters power, it bows its head. It is no coincidence that the last decade, in which we led the country, was the best security decade in the history of Israel, because in our neighborhood there is no place for the weak.

Knowing fully that Israelis demanded action in response to the string of terror attacks, the military launched 'Operation Break the Wave' to clamp down on Palestinian terrorists in the West Bank. Army raids became an almost daily occurrence for months, which ended up killing over 144 Palestinians in 2022, making it the deadliest year in the West Bank since 2004, according to the human rights group B'Tselem. According to the Israeli army, most of those who were killed were either armed or directly involved in terror attacks against Israelis.

While the Bennett-Lapid government was facing an immense security crisis, *Yamina* lawmaker Idit Silman who had been harassed and attacked ever since joining the government, finally succumbed to the opposition's pressure. On 6 April she dropped a bombshell when she announced her resignation from the government, saying she would 'return' to her right-wing home. Netanyahu, whose Likud party had assailed Silman for months, welcomed her 'courageous move.'[8] The opposition had finally opened the first crack in the government which no longer had a 61-seat majority. Smelling blood, they continued attacking the government at every chance possible, over the continuation of Palestinian terror attacks. To make matters even more challenging for the government, the Muslim holiday of Ramadan opened for a different yet familiar flashpoint, namely the Al-Aqsa Mosque compound. The Jewish high holiday of Passover collided with the Ramadan, bringing hundreds of Jewish visitors to the Temple Mount. Anger at Israeli over its military raids and Jewish visitors on the Temple Mount sparked intense clashes between Palestinians and Israeli security forces. The issue of the Temple Mount brought the government one step closer to a collapse, exposing the deep ideological differences between the left and right-ring coalition partners. The Arab and Islamic *Ra'am* party could not sit idly by as Israeli security forces entered the Al-Aqsa Mosque, third holiest place for Muslims, to arrest Palestinians, although they had thrown stones at Israeli police. Footage of Israeli police forces using stun grenades and beating Palestinians on the Temple Mount went viral, causing Muslim countries to condemn Israel. Hamas and Islamic Jihad were as usual fanning the flames, but so was the Israeli opposition.

Smotrich repeated the claim that the government depended on 'enemies of Israel', referring to *Ra'am*, and that it posed an existential threat to Jews. *Ra'am*, on its part, decided to suspend its membership of the coalition, seeing no other alternative if they were to save face among their Arab voters in Israel. While party leader Mansour Abbas was trying to solve the crisis in the government over the Al-Aqsa riots, where hundreds of Palestinians had been injured, lawmakers in his own party were less optimistic about staying in the coalition. Bennett ultimately decided to close the Temple Mount for Jewish visitors and tourists for the final days of Ramadan to avoid further clashes between Israelis and Palestinians at the holy site. The year before, Israel had been dragged into a war with Hamas when similar scenes unfolded at the Temple Mount. The decision was, however, in line with longstanding Israeli policy. In fact, the Temple Mount had been closed to Jews every year during the final days of Ramadan since 2013.

As expected, Bennett's decision immediately drew harsh accusations about a 'surrender to terror' by opposition lawmakers. Jewish Power party leader Ben-Gvir called it a 'victory for Hamas, for terrorism, for the riots of our enemies', while accusing Bennett of 'handing a reward to the enemy'. The harsh condemnation was echoed by Religious Zionism leader Smotrich, who blasted his old colleague, calling it a 'security and political blunder that is tantamount to the Arab lie that the Jews are to blame for the current escalation'. Bennett, on his part, pointed out (rightly so) that he was only continuing Netanyahu's policy. 'The "shock" that gripped the Likud and Smotrich is completely fake, and its motives are purely political. The decision on the Temple Mount will be made on the basis of security considerations and recommendations of the defense establishment like every year. Last year, Netanyahu closed the Temple Mount for 19 days under Hamas pressure.'[9] The attacks by the opposition were completely in line with the overall populistic approach to every decision made by the government. On 7 May, Netanyahu once again repeated his false claim that the government 'relied on terror supporters (United Arab List)' and that Hamas therefore saw it as 'weak'. The constant attacks and false claims about the nature of the UAL party was meant to play on fear in the public, as well as make people forget that Likud had negotiated with UAL in the last election to get its support for a government led by Netanyahu.

While the intense clashes on the Temple Mount almost brought down the government, it was a different issue that ultimately became the last straw. On 13 June, yet another *Yamina* lawmaker defected from the coalition. Nir Orbach said he could no longer be a part of a coalition where 'extremist anti-Zionist elements', such as Mazen Ghanaim from Ra'am and Ghaida Rinawie Zoabi from *Meretz* (both Arab lawmakers) held Israel 'hostage'.[10] Part of Orbach's frustration (and many other right-wing lawmakers) stemmed from the coalitions failure to pass a bill that would extend regulations applying Israeli law to settlers in the West Bank. The vote failed to pass with 52 voting for and 58 against, with several Ghanaim and Zoabi voting against. The opposition, which was in favour of not only extending the regulations but to annex the West Bank settlements entirely, also voted against the bill, showing once again that it would do whatever it took to topple the government, even if it meant not serving the interests of its voters. With Orbach out of the coalition, Bennett was now effectively running a government with 59 lawmakers, a situation that he knew wasn't sustainable. A week after Orbach resigned from the coalition, Bennett and Lapid announced they would dissolve the government and call for new elections. According to the rotation agreement between the two, Lapid would take over as prime minister in the interim period until new elections were held. Yair Golan, Meretz lawmaker and deputy minister of economy in Bennett's government, said:

Naftali Bennett did a terrible job building his party. It was a very strange collection of unknown figures. No one ever heard about Nir Orbach, Idit Silman and Amichai Chikli. I don't consider Bennett an ideologue. He's a populist. He learned from Netanyahu. He's not an extreme right-winger but just wants to gain more power. What happened to Bennett had also happened to Sharon. He also came from the right-wing with all this talk about our origins and renewing biblical times. All these terrible things that aren't fitted to modern life. For Bennett it was a way to get more power but the minute he did he wasn't able to switch, like Sharon. He didn't understand that now he had a true responsibility because he isn't a true leader. He did nothing, and treated the position as prime minister like it was a technical bureaucratic position, instead of what it really is, which is leading the Jewish people. Sharon did that. Therefore, he decided about whether to head for annexation or separation (from the Palestinian territories). And he made the right decision.

On 30 June, 92 lawmakers voted in favour of dissolving Knesset, setting elections for 1 November. Netanyahu used the moment to once again mock and ridicule the outgoing government, saying 'they tried and failed. This is what happens when you bring together the fake-right and the far-left.'[11] The old claim that parties like *Yamina* and *Yisrael Beitenu*, and to some extent Blue and White, weren't right-wing would slowly but surely seep into Israeli consciousness as a fact, however wildly inaccurate it was. Prominent Israeli journalists would buy into this claim, that the anti-Netanyahu bloc was left-wing, which did tremendous damage to the political debate in Israel, with voters buying into it. Netanyahu had succeeded, against all odds, to remain opposition leader, fight off anyone who dared try to remove him from the Likud leadership, and finally topple the most diverse government in Israel's history within a year. Those who had written him off a year ago were about to get a reality check and a lecture in Israeli politics.

Notes

1   Jeffrey Heller, 'Netanyahu alleges Israeli election fraud, accuses rival of duplicity', *Reuters*, 6 June 2021.
2   TOI staff, 'World reacts as Bennett, Lapid form new government, oust Netanyahu after 12 yrs', *Times of Israel*, 13 June 2021.
3   TOI staff, 'World reacts as Bennett, Lapid form new government, oust Netanyahu after 12 yrs', *Times of Israel*, 13 June 2021.
4   Moran Azulay, Coalition whip's assault claim raises doubts after refusing to provide details', *Yediot Ahronot*, 7 November 2021.
5   TOI staff, 'Deri says Jewish state is 'in danger'; Gafni brands Bennett "wicked"', *Times of Israel*, 8 June 2021.
6   Michael Hauser Tov, 'In Blow to Bennett, Knesset Votes Down Extending Citizenship Law', *Ha'aretz*, 5 July 2021.
7   TOI Staff, Labor, Meretz warn authorizing illegal outpost Evyatar threatens coalition', *Times of Israel*, 2 February 2022.
8   TOI Staff, 'Bennett's government in crisis as whip Silman quits, stripping coalition of majority', Times of Israel, 6 April 2022.
9   Itamar Eichner, 'Israeli police to close Temple Mount to Jews for final days of Ramadan', *Yediot Ahronot*, 20 April 2022.
10 TOI Staff, 'Yamina MK Nir Orbach quits coalition; PM admits it could collapse 'in a week or two'', *Times of Israel*, 13 June 2022.
11 Michael Hauser Tov, Noa Shpigel, 'Israeli Lawmakers Dissolve Knesset, Elections Set for November 1', *Ha'aretz*, 30 June 2022.

10

Rise of the far-right

Bennett-Lapid legacy

Few prime ministers in Israel's history have been exposed to the same level of threats, harassment, smear and lies than Naftali Bennett. From the beginning, Bennett was labeled a traitor by both Likud and Religious Zionism supporters, a term that was extremely controversial in Israel because it was used by extreme right-wingers against Prime Minister Rabin, who was ultimately assassinated.

Shin Bet chief Nadav Argaman held a rare press conference shortly before Bennett was inaugurated as prime minister, warning that the levels of incitement could lead to physical violence. Argaman fell short of mentioning Bennett as the possible victim of physical violence, but it was clear to everyone that he was referring to the overload of online incitement against the incoming prime minister. The incitement against Bennett was also aimed at sowing doubt about his Jewishness. In an online sermon, seen by some 700,000 people, Rabbi Ronen Shaulov claimed that Bennett's mother Myrna had undergone a Reform conversion, that Bennett was 'worse than a dog' and that he had 'sold the country' to non-Jews.[1] The claim was of course false, but it helped spreading fake information about him. It was just one of many examples of people spreading lies about Bennett online, causing him to file several lawsuits when he finished his term as prime minister. Other Israeli politicians and journalists who had been subject to intense online harassment by Netanyahu supporters, referred to the phenomenon as 'the poison machine.' Over the years the term had become almost mainstream for Netanyahu's biggest critics, using it to describe campaigns orchestrated by the Likud party against rival politicians.

Bennett and his *Yamina* party allies felt the full force of the 'machine', which eventually caused Silman and Orbach to give in to the massive pressure put on them. When Lapid took over as prime minister, Bennett virtually disappeared from the public scene, announcing later he wouldn't run in the upcoming elections. The anger among the religious Zionist movement, and the right-wingers who had voted for him, stemmed from the obvious fact that he broke an essential election promise not to sit with Lapid. They indeed felt betrayed, and rightly so. But his leadership could in no way be characterized as 'left-wing.'

The military campaign to crack down on terrorists in the West Bank was relentless, hunting down wanted terrorists on an almost daily basis in the spring of 2022. When Al-Jazeera journalist Shireen Abu Akleh was killed while covering an army raid in Jenin against Palestinian terrorist, Bennett quickly denied that the army had any responsibility, but rather pointed fingers at the Palestinians who had fired indiscriminately against Israeli soldiers. Despite eyewitnesses reporting immediately after that Abu Akleh had indeed been hit by an Israeli soldier, both the army and the government continued to deny that it was responsible. Only after the U.S. said it had found that Israel was likely behind the killing, albeit unintentionally, the army followed up with a similar conclusion after months-long investigations. When Abu Akleh was laid to rest, Israeli police in East Jerusalem beat those carrying her coffin at the funeral procession, which was caught on live TV. The atmosphere was extremely heated, since Abu Akleh had become a symbol and icon for the Palestinians. Police argued that bottles were thrown at them at the funeral procession, which led to their violent attacks. Although police conduct is entirely in the hands of the commissioner and his subordinates, there was seemingly no intention by the government to try and lower the tension and allow the funeral to proceed peacefully. Police conduct on the Temple Mount was similarly strict, not showing any sign of a 'left-wing' government playing into the hands of Palestinian extremists. Bennett had repeatedly said there would be zero tolerance for 'provocateurs' on Temple Mount. The government's policies vis-à-vis the settlements were also inherently right-wing, even more so than the Netanyahu governments. According to the human rights organization Peace Now, six new illegal outposts were built during the Bennett-Lapid government, which also issued tenders for constructing 1,500 housing units in settlements, marking an annual increase of 15% compared to the Netanyahu governments from 2012-2020. The number of Palestinian homes that were demolished also increased 35% compared to previous Netanyahu governments. According to the human rights organization B'Tselem, settler violence rose 28% in 2021, something Bennett dismissed as 'insignificant.' Overall, the Bennett-Lapid government, despite its inclusion of left-wing and an Arab party, led a right-wing policy in the West Bank and East Jerusalem. This continued under Lapid, who took over as prime minister in the period leading up to elections on 1 November.

The IDF arrested a senior Islamic Jihad commander in the West Bank in early August and decided to close off the entire area adjacent to the Gaza Strip in anticipation of rocket attacks. After days of an unprecedented lockdown in parts of the Gaza border area, Lapid gave the order to launch a military operation in Gaza, assassinating dozens of Islamic Jihad commanders. According to the army, the group was preparing an immediate terror attack across the Gaza border, which led to the decision to launch a pre-emptive strike. As expected, Islamic Jihad launched some 1,100 rockets at Israel over the course of 66 hours, until a ceasefire was reached. 46 Palestinians were killed, most of whom Israel said were members of Islamic Jihad. 15 children were also killed, some in Israeli airstrikes and others in failed rocket launches by Islamic Jihad. Lapid, as well as Defense Minister Gantz, were applauded by Israeli commentators for the 'successes' of the Gaza operation, which was short and didn't claim any Israeli lives. While it was difficult for the opposition to criticize Lapid for his handling of the Gaza conflict, a different topic became a central theme in Netanyahu's election campaign.

Israel was advancing a negotiation with Lebanon to settle a dispute over maritime borders, which for years had prevented both sides from extracting gas in certain areas of the sea. As it became clear that the two arch enemies were making significant progress, the Netanyahu camp raged against Lapid and the government for conducting negotiations on matters of national security during an election campaign. Netanyahu and Likud accused Lapid of 'surrendering' sovereign Israeli territory to Hezbollah, providing the terrorist group with billions of dollars in future gas revenue. What Netanyahu and Likud failed to admit was that it had engaged in the very same negotiations in previous governments. Back then, the U.S. had also acted as the mediator. When asked about whether there was any truth to the claims made by Netanyahu, U.S. ambassador to Israel, Tom Nides, replied that it was 'ridiculous.' In fact, Netanyahu 'also supported a very similar deal a few years ago,' Nides added.[2] It didn't stop the opposition from repeating the absurd claims daily in the media, insisting that the gas deal should be brought before the Knesset for a vote. After months of uncertainty, Israel finally signed the maritime border agreement with Lebanon on 27 October, less than a week before elections.

Fifth time is the charm

The legacy of the Bennett-Lapid government was tainted by the internal bickering and animosity between coalition parties, and an incredibly successful campaign by the opposition to frame every political decision as a failure. Yoaz Hendel, who kept his position as communication minister after he entered the Bennett-Lapid government, said the opposition succeeded in portraying the coalition as a 'Muslim Brotherhood working against Israel. And people bought it.' Itamar Ben-Gvir had simultaneously managed to turn every terror attack into a media circus for his own political gain. His messages were spread on social media, receiving hundreds of thousands of views, while the Israeli mainstream media gave him increasingly more airtime. He managed to woo young voters with a populist rhetoric, promising security and stability in Israel and a harsh crackdown on terrorism. When he arrived at a high school outside Tel Aviv in September to participate in a mock election, Ben-Gvir was received like a rock star by enthusiastic students who gathered around him to get selfies and shake his hand. While Ben-Gvir took the stage to answer questions from students, demonstrators had gathered outside the school to demand that the controversial far-right leader be boycotted from speaking.

Meanwhile Ben-Gvir's supporters also held a demonstration in a show of support, which led to dozens of police officers having to physically divide the two camps. The camp that demonstrated against Ben-Gvir's participation in the mock election warned that Jewish Power would turn Israel into a fascist theocracy on par with Iran, while Ben-Gvir's supporters claimed that the left-wing were 'supporters of terror', echoing the false and dangerous claim by the opposition. The highly unusual scene on that September morning in 2022 illustrated just how contentious the elections were and how much was at stake.

The Jewish Power party made a tactically important decision by merging with Religious Zionism, headed by Betzalel Smotrich. The fringe, anti-LGBTQ *Noam* party, also became part of the merger. As before, Netanyahu played an instrumental part in brokering the merger, seeing this as his only chance of winning the election. Less than two weeks before elections, Netanyahu celebrated his 73rd birthday at the Likud headquarters in Tel Aviv, giving interviews to American and Jewish media. Looking more confident than ever, Netanyahu highlighted the issues he would prioritize if he won the election. Stopping Iran's nuclear program and expanding the Abraham Accords were the two focus points, with the crown jewel being a peace deal with Saudi Arabia. He did, however, admit that annexation of the West Bank would once again be a priority. Acknowledging, however, that it would 'probably not' happen on President Biden's watch, Netanyahu said:

Would I do it (annex) unilaterally? No, I said that right from the start. I would not, because I would like to do it with the understanding and support of the United States. We were on the verge of getting it. I think that if I'm re-elected, I will get it. I have plans on how to get it. [3]

The grand master of Israeli politics didn't shy away from lighting up a cigar in a nearby room after the interviews while journalists were packing up their things. It was a clear sign that he had no intentions whatsoever of hiding his love for cigars despite the intense attention that habit had been given in the media due to the corruption cases against him, alleging that he received cigars and champagne from billionaires in return for political favours. While Netanyahu was running a tight campaign, not leaving anything to chances and preventing voter loss, the outgoing government was half asleep. Lapid was growing more popular in Israel during his reign as both foreign and prime minister. But the many votes he was stealing came mainly from the centre and left-wing parties.

Meretz had warned against this for weeks leading up to the elections, when it became clear that it was once again fighting to get enough votes to cross the electoral threshold. To prevent a loss of votes and to make sure it would enter Knesset, *Meretz* called on Labour to merge ahead of elections. The merger was even encouraged by Lapid, who saw the writing on the wall, but Labour party leader Merav Michaeli dismissed the proposal, saying previous mergers had ended in failures. Another looming failure among the Arab Israeli parties to bridge their gaps also risked wasting valuable votes. The radical party *Balad* failed to reach an agreement with the two other Arab parties, *Hadash* and *Ta'al,* that would see them running together in the Arab Joint List. Polls had shown that *Balad* was in the same boat as *Meretz,* failing to get enough votes to enter Knesset. As the first exit polls emerged on 1 November, it became evident neither *Meretz* nor *Balad* would pass the electoral threshold, thereby wasting incredibly valuable votes. Throughout the night it became clear that Netanyahu had managed to make a historic comeback, securing 64 seats for his coalition, partly since *Meretz* and *Balad* didn't make it. The other reason was that the Religious Zionism list received astonishingly 14 seats, making it the third biggest faction in Knesset after Likud's 32 seats and *Yesh Atid's* 24 seats. The political earthquake rocked Israel to its core. The most extreme government in Israel's history was about to be formed. It would quickly find itself immersed in more scandals than any other government in Israel's history.

Ben-Gvir and Smotrich

Few incidents in Israeli politics can be compared to the meteoric rise of Itamar Ben-Gvir. In the span of just two years, Ben-Gvir went from been considered a fringe, almost ridiculous politician who wasn't taken seriously, to becoming one of the most influential ministers in Israel. 27 years after inciting against Prime Minister Rabin on live TV, Ben-Gvir was now positioning himself as the next public security minister, a role he had demanded to be given during his election campaign. With a record of eight indictments, including inciting to racism and supporting a terror group (*Kach*), Ben-Gvir was about to become the most controversial and extremist politicians to ever hold be named minister. Living in the West Bank settlement of Kiriyat Arba near Hebron, Ben-Gvir was a well-known figure in Israel due to his aggressive behavior toward Palestinians, as well as verbal attacks against police, Arab Israeli lawmakers and Israeli human rights activists. Ben-Gvir's representation of Jewish extremists in courts over the years had given him notoriety in the Israeli media, as well as close ties to the 'hilltop youth.'

His radical views on Palestinians became abundantly clear after a TV show was made about him in 2016. The show painted a clear picture of the lawyer devoting his life to defend Jewish extremists in court. When the presenter of the show realized that Ben-Gvir had a picture of Baruch Goldstein hanging on his wall (the Jewish terrorist who slaughtered 29 Palestinians in Hebron in 1994) he pleaded with him to take it down so they could continue filming. Ben-Gvir refused, and so did his wife, who said 'we aren't ashamed of it.' It wasn't any different than for an Arab Israeli lawmaker like Ahamd Tibi to have a picture of Yasser Arafat hanging on the wall, Ben-Gvir argued. The show also highlighted his close connections to Michael Ben-Ari and Baruch Marzel, two of the most extreme right-wingers in the Israeli settlement movement. When he finally entered the Israeli political scene, Ben-Gvir quickly tapped into the underlying animosity against Palestinians and Arab Israelis among certain right-wingers in Israel, using populist slogans to gain a following. Imposing the death penalty for Palestinian terrorists, deporting Arab Israeli lawmakers like Ahmad Tibi and Ayman Odeh, giving soldiers and police officers immunity, and 'restoring' security in Israel were among his core election promises. The civil war-like situations in mixed Jewish and Arab cities in May of 2021, as well as the string of terror attacks during the Bennett-Lapid government played right into Ben-Gvir's hands. He represented a new far-right stream in Israel, which differed in many ways from Smotrich and Religious Zionism. Assaf Shapira, PhD in Political Science from the Hebrew University of Jerusalem, said.

> The far-right secular stream has mostly disappeared. Today we have Jewish Power and Religious Zionism, which are two different streams. Jewish Power is based on Kach (Kahane's party) which isn't purely religious. They also have more secular figures, like Zvika Fogel. They are ultra-nationalists and populists, and their voters aren't necessarily religious either. You can clearly see it in the areas they chose to focus on in the last election: more personal security, public order, fight against Arab crime, and less focus on the settlements. It's a combination of xenophobia and racism. It's much more similar to far-right parties in Europe. It's a much less religious party than Religious Zionism, which is a far-right version of the National Religious Party. Ben-Gvir and Smotrich know that Netanyahu is much weaker than in the past, and they came to this government with the intention to change Israel's policies.

The prospects of having Ben-Gvir as the new minister in charge of Israeli Police sparked an outcry in the Israeli mainstream media. The fact that he continued to surround himself with former far-right extremists and 'hilltop youth' gave even more reason to worry. The best example was Chanamel Dorfmann who had a long history with law enforcement, having been arrested numerous times by the Shin Bet during his time as a radical member of the 'hilltop youth.' He accused Israeli Police of being racist and the most 'antisemitic police in the world.' In an absurd turn of events, Dorfmann would become Ben-Gvir's chief of staff when the Jewish Power party leader was appointed Minister of National Security. According to a report by Ha'aretz Daily, Dorfmann even participated in interviews of police officers seeking promotions.[4]

Ben-Gvir also continued to surround himself with Gopstein, who had been barred from running for Knesset on the grounds of systematically inciting racism against Arab Israelis and Palestinians. Gopstein was now roaming the hallways of Knesset freely, entering the Jewish Home party faction's meeting room as he saw fit. But while Ben-Gvir was largely seen as the most controversial figure in the new government by Israeli and international media alike, Smotrich posed a far bigger danger, according to Dvir Kariv, who had experience with him during his time as agent in Shin Bet's 'Jewish Division.' According to Kariv, Ben-Gvir wasn't enough of a 'high-profile' figure for the Shin Bet to deal with him.

Kariv said:

> Smotrich was in custody more than three weeks. In other words,
> Smotrich is more extreme than Ben-Gvir. In the media they think
> it's the opposite. Kahane followers (like Ben-Gvir) cause a lot of
> trouble, but they don't commit a lot of terror attacks. Hilltop Youth
> do. Therefore, it's mostly the Police that deals with the Kahanists and
> Shin Bet deals with hilltop youth. Hilltop is more dangerous.
> Smotrich thinks the (Jewish division) should be closed, so Shin Bet
> has a big problem.

Smotrich represented a much more religious and messianic version of the
far-right, seeing the Palestinians as an obstacle for 'Greater Israel.' Unlike
Ben-Gvir, whose political ideology is far less sophisticated and offers no
solution to the Israeli-Palestinian conflict, Smotrich had articulated a
thorough political manifesto in 2017, in which he laid out the actions
needed to be taken to create a Jewish state 'from the river to the sea.' In
other words, a Jewish state encompassing the entire West Bank, East
Jerusalem and Gaza, all under Israeli sovereignty.

Aggressive settlement construction was an essential key to finally get
rid of the Palestinian 'illusion' of getting their own state one day. The
Palestinians, or Arabs as he referred to them as, would not get the right to
vote in Israeli elections but would have semi-autonomous municipal
governmental regions. Eventually, he argued, Jordan would become part of
a regional agreement, which would allow Arabs to vote in Jordanian
elections. At a final stage of this process, Arabs would be allowed to get an
Israeli citizenship, provided they serve in the army and declare full loyalty
for the state of Israel. For those not willing to let go of their aspirations of
a national home, emigrating to other Arab countries would be an option,
the manifesto explained. His vision of Jewish supremacy was of course
rooted in religion, with Jews being chosen by God to live in Israel. Another
crucial part of Smotrich's view on the Israel-Palestine conflict was the
Temple Mount. After yet another Palestinian terror attack had claimed the
lives of three Israelis in the West Bank in 2017, Smotrich, then a member
of Knesset for the Jewish Home party, said an appropriate response to terror
would be to 'set up a synagogue on the Temple Mount today, this morning.'
He told Arutz Sheva news:

> If someone thinks that through terrorism, violence, and the massacre
> of a family he will push our sovereignty back, then - if I am the Prime

Minister - this morning I would close the Temple Mount to Arab prayer and establish a Synagogue for Jews. And if the terrorism continues I would close the mount to Arabs and there will be only Jews there. [5]

This was perhaps one of his most dangerous ideas. The only thing every security, intelligence and political expert in Israel could possibly agree on would be that erecting a synagogue on the Temple Mount would be tantamount to declaring war on the entire Muslim world. A catastrophe which Israel probably wouldn't survive. Smotrich's fundamentalist views on the future of Israel, combined with his homophobia and outright racist remarks against Palestinians represented a stream in Israeli society that had gradually grown in recent years, and could no longer be considered fringe. His views became more and more mainstream and would be echoed frequently by fellow lawmakers in the Knesset and in the media.

Expanded powers

After the elections, the Religious Zionist list split into three separate parties again, with Religious Zionism having seven seats, Jewish Power six seats and *Noam* one seat. Despite only representing seven and six seats respectively, both Smotrich and Ben-Gvir went into coalition negotiations from a position of strength. They knew this government was Netanyahu's only chance of staying in power, and ultimately help him cancel his trial. He therefore couldn't afford to alienate them.

Ben-Gvir's demand to be named public security minister was almost certain, but Smotrich aimed even higher. He wanted to be defense minister, the second most powerful position in the country. What should have been an easy task for Netanyahu became a massive headache, with coalition partners all smelling weakness and issuing ultimatums for their joining the government. But the reason why the negotiations dragged on for much longer than expected was that all the coalition partners insisted on having detailed deals signed with Likud, fearing Netanyahu would do what he did best; secure power and then renege on promises.

Shortly before elections on 1 November, an audio recording was leaked to the Israeli media in which Smotrich was heard slamming Netanyahu. 'If I wanted to take two (Knesset) seats from Bibi I should have attacked him head-on. He's a liar and a son-of-a-liar. He didn't want to go with the United Arab List? He most definitely did. I'm the only one preventing a disaster, and I would have gotten two Knesset seats,' Smotrich said. The recording was not only embarrassing to Netanyahu, it also revealed that even his closes allies on the far-right didn't trust him for a second. Ben-Gvir also had his doubts about Netanyahu's true intentions after he famously said in the previous election that the Jewish Power party leader would never be a minister in his government. The fact that Netanyahu did everything he could to avoid being seen next to Ben-Gvir and have any photos of the two circulating in the media made the far-right leader suspicious about how much he could trust him.

After nearly two months of coalition talks, Netanyahu finally presented his new government. The makeup of Netanyahu's new government handed immense powers to his coalition partners, in particular Jewish Power and Religious Zionism. Ben-Gvir had gotten his demand and was named national security minister (the public security portfolio changed name), while Smotrich was named finance minister. Both were given a seat at the powerful security cabinet, where matters of national security were discussed and decided on. In addition to being the finance minister, Smotrich was given a role in the defense ministry, overseeing the two key bodies that deal with civil life in the West Bank, namely Coordinator of Activities in the Territories (COGAT) and the Civil Administration. Both bodies normally fell under the command of the defense minister, a role which Netanyahu gave to Likud lawmaker Yoav Gallant. The decision to divide the defense minister role in two, giving a radical settler like Smotrich responsibility for crucial aspects of civil life in the West Bank, was met with fierce criticism by former IDF generals as well opposition lawmakers. Gallant was also furious, according to Israeli media, which reported that he refused to let anyone come between him and the army.

The outgoing IDF chief of staff, Aviv Kochavi, also smelling disaster, gave a series of interviews to Israeli media at the end of his term, in which he stressed the importance of keeping the command structure intact. 'The IDF chief reports to one minister, the minister of defense, and I have no doubt that this will continue,' Kochavi told Channel 12.[6] Smotrich had previously responded to media reports indicating that Kochavi was fiercely against handing him any responsibilities in the West Bank, accusing the outgoing army chief of seeking a political career. Smotrich went as far as suggesting the 'cooling off period' for army chiefs before entering politics should be extended from three to ten years. In an unprecedented jab at the outgoing army chief, Smotrich said:

> If Kohavi wanted to understand and not just attack with populism
> in preparation for his entry into the political field, he could have

talked to me and understood that the goal is not to harm the IDF's chain of command but to remove the Civil Administration from the IDF and make it civilian. The IDF will deal with security and a civilian system will manage civilian life. Good for the citizens and good for the IDF. Kohavi is confused and forgot that Israel is a country that has an army and not an army that has a country. The responsibilities were transferred to me by law and I am convinced that his successor and the rest of the IDF commanders will act in accordance with the law.[7]

Outgoing Defense Minister Benny Gantz was particularly harsh in his criticism of Smotrich's expanded powers, saying he was 'worried about the splitting up of the Defense Ministry and about the consequences of the actions of extremists in the government, which could have strategic ramifications,' and that he felt a 'real concern for Israel's security, now reliant on the whims of experience-lacking extremists.' The Palestinians, meanwhile, as well as rights groups and left-wing Israeli politicians were concerned that Smotrich's new powers would mean a de-facto annexation of West Bank settlements. The far-right leader had been working for years to significantly expand and annex settlements and was against evacuating any illegal outposts. But it wasn't just Smotrich who had expanded powers spilling over to security areas. Ben-Gvir had managed to negotiate a deal that would give him direct control with Israeli Border Police, which operate in the West Bank.

Again, the outgoing IDF chief of Staff, Aviv Kochavi, expressed his firm position on the matter. 'The work that the Border Police is doing in Judea and Samaria is excellent and I hope that the situation remains just as it is today. The chain of authority needs to be preserved,' Kochavi said, adding that the 'people who think aggressive open-fire rules are the recipe for security are mistaken. It would produce the absolute opposite.'[8] The latter remark was directly aimed at Ben-Gvir who had campaigned on wanting to relax the rules of engagement for soldiers. Even before taking office both Smotrich and Ben-Gvir had been in direct confrontation with the army chief. The rift was seen as deeply damaging to the IDF's relationship with the government.

Annexation

The issue of annexing West Bank settlements had officially been shelved ever since Netanyahu hastily declared his intention to move forward with it shortly after the Trump 'peace plan' had been announced at the White House in 2020. But with Religious Zionism, *Noam* and Jewish Power making up vital parts of Netanyahu's new government, annexation quickly became a priority again. Something Netanyahu had also admitted just two weeks before elections. Religious Zionism's coalition deal with Likud not only declared that the settlements should be annexed, but that some 70 illegal outposts should be legalized and connected to water and infrastructure. A budget of $450 million would be allocated to building new roads in connecting settlements, while the 2005 Disengagement Plan, promoted by former Prime Minister Sharon, would be repealed. The plan, which evacuated Jewish settlements in Gaza, also evacuated four illegal outposts built in the northern West Bank, causing widespread anger in the settlement community at the time. The illegal outpost of *Homesh* would be erected and legalized, according to the coalition deal. 'The Jewish people have an exclusive and indisputable right to all areas of the Land of Israel. The government will promote and develop settlements in all parts of the Land of Israel in the Galilee, Negev, Golan, Judea and Samaria,' one of the key principles of the government stipulated.[9]

The principle was in line with the thinking of the far-right, that the land belonged to Jews, never mind the non-Jewish minorities making up big parts of the population. For the Palestinians, it was just proof of what they had been saying for years, namely that Israeli governments for decades had pushed for Jewish supremacy in areas where they lived as well. With voices in the government beginning to talk about retaking Gaza, the idea of 'Greater Israel' was being pushed aggressively forward. In the first six months, the government advanced 12,855 settler housing units in the West Bank, the highest number in two decades.

Homophobia

For years, Israel, and in particular Tel Aviv, had been seen as the 'gay Mecca' of the Middle East. Hundreds of thousands of people took part in the annual Pride Parade in Tel Aviv, while thousands joined the Pride in Jerusalem. But with openly homophobic ministers and lawmakers in the new government, the prospects of rolling back some of the community's civil rights had become a real fear. Before the government was even sworn in, a pandoras box of homophobia had opened. The power drunk and newly elected far-right lawmakers saw their election victory as an excuse to verbally attack the LGBT community. Avi Maoz, the leader of the anti-LGBT *Noam* party, signed a coalition deal with Netanyahu that made him deputy minister in the prime minister's office in charge of a newly established Jewish identity authority. Maoz would also be given control over the Education Ministry's external programming, causing an outcry among teachers across Israel. Maoz's homophobic and ultra conservative views were well known and repeated during the intense period of coalition talks. Maoz said:

> The Pride Parade in Jerusalem needs to be canceled, first of all. I will make sure to cancel it. It is a disgrace. I am quite straightforward about this. Do you know how much those marches harm holy Jerusalem, its public space? You want to demonstrate — demonstrate. But a parade of promiscuous abomination in public?,[10]

The *Noam* party leader also vowed to end the 'radical, progressive brainwashing' in the Education Ministry, as well as the canceling the role of gender advisor to the IDF chief of staff, claiming it was the 'most important thing for Israel's security, more than anything else.' Teachers, principals and mayors in local municipalities across Israel quickly reacted to the agreement between Likud and *Noam*, vowing to undermine his efforts to impose radical ideas in school curriculum. It was later revealed by the newspaper *Yediot Ahronot* that *Noam* had drawn up a list in 2019 of gay TV, radio and print journalists in news and entertainment, apparently to mark the party's enemies. It was, however, not clear what the purpose of the document was. The list of dozens of journalists from the biggest media in Israel, such as Channel 12 and 13, KAN Public Broadcaster and *Yediot Ahronot*, also included photos of 'extreme left-wing women' working in NGO's. The document also described what it said was a takeover of the justice and education ministries by left-wing organizations.

This McCarthy style document was widely covered in the media, adding to the already big pile of controversies in the government. Maoz was, however, far from being the only lawmaker drawing attention for his wildly homophobic remarks. Religious Zionism had made a deal with Netanyahu's Likud party that would change Israel's discrimination law, which forbids discrimination against citizens based on sexuality, gender and race. For Religious Zionism, led by a deeply homophobic party leader, changing the law to allow for discrimination against the LGBT community was important. Religious Zionism lawmaker, Simcha Rhotman, who would later be named chair of the powerful Knesset Constitution, Law and Justice committee, admitted on several occasions that the changes to the discrimination law would allow for doctors and business owners to refuse service to patients and costumers if it contradicted their religious beliefs.

In other words, ultra-orthodox doctors and business owners would be allowed to discriminate against women and gays. Although Netanyahu kept reiterating that he wouldn't allow any discrimination against the LGBT community, the coalition agreement between Likud and Religious Zionism was clear. In fact, Rhotman went as far as admitting outright that the changes to the discrimination law was based on the case known as Masterpiece Cakeshop vs Colorado Civil Rights Commission which ended up with a ruling by the U.S. Supreme Court allowing a business owner to refuse service to a gay couple. Contradicting himself, Rhotman did, however, not interpret it as a carte blanche to target the Israeli LGBT community. Rhotman said:

> It's not true and it's definitely not the situation in question. The idea behind the law is Cake Master vs Colorado, and to try and legislate something similar in Israel. Of course some people saw this as discrimination against gays but the Supreme Court said it wasn't.

But according to him, the issue of the LGBT community was not the central focus of the law. The government wanted to make sure people can exercise their religious freedom, which Rhotman said wasn't the case currently. The LGBT community in Israel quickly saw the red flags and took to the streets to demonstrate against the new government and what it saw as a direct threat to its rights. The homophobia peaked when Likud lawmaker, Amir Ohana, was chosen as the next Knesset Speaker, once again making history by becoming the first openly gay person to hold that office in Israel's history. At the swearing in ceremony, ultra-orthodox lawmakers as well as Maoz were seen with their heads on the table in front of them or looking away, while another lawmaker, Yitzhak Pindrus, simply left the plenum. Pindrus later told KAN Public Broadcaster that he left because it was his 'right to feel uncomfortable when Amir Ohana talks about his family.' Powerful rabbis also lashed out at Ohana after he was sworn in. 'This whole thing with the abominations — today they're glorified. For shame. Such a disgrace. Woe to the ears that hear of such things. It is unbearable. They appoint them to roles that are considered lofty. They have lost all of their shame,' Jerusalem's Sephardic chief rabbi, Shlomo Amar said. Another influential rabbi with close ties to lawmakers, Meir Mazuz, claimed that Ohana was 'infected with a disease.' Mazuz said:

> There is a time when everyone will be asked: Are you part of the Pride Parade or part of the humility parade? You should distance

yourself from it. You see people walking and bragging (about) the Pride Parade in Jerusalem. Close the windows and tell your children: 'This is a parade of animals, you have no business looking at it. These are animals walking on two legs. What can we do about them?.[11]

Shas party leader Arieh Dery was quoted by the ultra-orthodox news site, *Kikar Hashabbat Haredi,* as saying that Netanyahu had tricked him by installing Ohana as Knesset Speaker. 'We erred in our conduct in the plenum. I headed out immediately after the speech, I can't understand the Haredi MKs who went to hug him after that address,' Dery was quoted as saying.[12] Meanwhile fellow lawmaker from Dery's Shas party, Nissim Zeev, suggested that Ohana should 'form a kosher family and marry a woman.'

Zeev told Radio 103FM:

> In what country in the world is there a gay (parliament) speaker? There is no hate here, but there is a deviation from the path of the Torah. This must be protested. Amir Ohana can serve in any role, but not as Knesset speaker — sensitivity should be shown. He is definitely a respected person, but he isn't a role model. [13]

Ohana was again subject to homophobic slur by the government a few months later after he brought his partner to official state ceremonies. Noam party leader Avi Maoz said:

> During an official ceremony by Israel and its official representatives to remember the holy Holocaust victims, and during state ceremonies on Memorial Day and Independence Day, they introduce in front of everyone "the Knesset spokesperson and his (male) partner" as if it were an accepted, authentic Jewish norm. I was filled with shame and pain down my soul. [14]

The most vile and extreme comment perhaps came from ultra-orthodox lawmaker Pindrus, who declared in an interview with Channel 12 that homosexuality is the 'most dangerous thing to the State of Israel — more than Islamic State, more than Hezbollah, more than Hamas. Not the economy. This is the most dangerous thing for the State of Israel. That is why... I need to not only prevent the Pride parade, but in general to prevent this movement.'[15]

While Netanyahu repeatedly had to clarify that his Likud party in no way condoned homophobic attacks on its party members or Israelis in general, the hateful remarks were reported in the mainstream media in Israel and abroad, painting a picture of an increasingly intolerant, religious and messianic Israel.

Religious extremism

While Netanyahu managed to keep the most powerful ministries for Likud, namely defense and justice, Religious Zionism had received the Finance Ministry, a role in the Defense Ministry, the Ministry of Aliyah and Integration, and Ministry of National Missions. Jewish Power, whose aim was to 'restore security' in Israel gained control over the National Security Ministry, and the Ministry for Development of the Negev and the Galilee.

The ultra-orthodox Shas party succeeded in securing equally important ministries for itself, controlling the Ministries of Interior, Health, Education, Labour, Social Affairs and Social Services as well as Religious Affairs. In addition, Arieh Dery was named vice prime minister with a seat at the security cabinet. United Torah Judaism, with the new and inexperienced Yitzhak Goldknopf as party leader, was got less influential roles. Goldknopf was named minister of housing and construction, while his party obtained control over the Ministry of Jerusalem Affairs and Jewish Tradition.

The ultra-orthodox parties did, however, strike coalition deals that gave them billions of dollars in financial support for their communities, as well highly controversial promises of increasing religious influence. Shas and United Torah Judaism's coalitions deal with Likud included a variety of benefits for the ultra-orthodox community. Going forward, local municipalities were now ordered to help fund all ultra-orthodox educational institutions, including private kindergartens and religious schools that didn't teach core curriculum. Although ultra-orthodox schools had been required by law to teach a minimum of for example math and English, it had been widely documented for years in Israeli media that many didn't, leaving children without a proper education. The coalition deals also stipulated that a law exempting ultra-orthodox from the army would once and for all be passed, after years of squabble over the issue and despite the Supreme Court ruling that the arrangement was unconstitutional.

Other agreements in the coalition deals revealed an intention increase the power of the ultra-orthodox, such as giving the Chief Rabbinate full control with *kashrut* certification system, which is vital for businesses seeking to get the kosher rubber stamp. Other parts of the coalition deals aimed at enabling gender-segregated public events and increasing the stipends for yeshiva students. The intentions to significantly strengthen

Israel's religious character were widely criticized by women's rights groups as well as opposition parties. Both *Yesh Atid* and *Yisrael Beitenu*, the two biggest opponents of the ultra-orthodox parties, accused Netanyahu of creating a religious state on par with Iran. Yair Lapid raged:

> At a time when brave women in Iran are fighting for their rights in Israel, Smotrich and his ultra-Orthodox nationalists are trying to place women behind barriers and legalize separating men from women. Where is Likud? Why are they being silent? This isn't Iran.[16]

But the criticism of the far-reaching demands by the ultra-orthodox and far-right parties weren't limited to Israel. Other proposals caused a massive rift with Diaspora Jews, such as the intention to review and possibly to cancel the 'grandchild clause' which allowed individuals with just one Jewish grandparent to immigrate to Israel under the Law of Return. The cancelation of the clause was seen as getting closer to a complete purification of immigration. According to the ultra-orthodox tradition, only a person born to a Jewish mother can be considered Jewish. The intention to cancel the 'grandchild clause' as well as amend the Law of Return in general was backed up by both Jewish Power and Religious Zionism. 'Only a Jew who converted in accordance with Jewish law (Halacha) would be eligible under the Law of Return,' Ben-Gvir said, referring to another proposal to prevent Reform converts to immigrate to Israel.[17]

According to Religious Zionism lawmaker Simcha Rhotman the changes would primarily affect those immigrating from former Soviet Union countries. 'Most of the Olim (immigrants) from there are non-Jews and some of them don't even want to be Jews. And they make Aliyah to Israel because they get benefits. A lot of them get the benefits and go back or leave for other countries,' Rhotman claimed. The issue over the Law of Return only scratched the surface of a deeper division looming between the ultra-orthodox and far-right parties in Israel and Diaspora Jews. It opened a can of worms, bringing the question of Jewish identity to the forefront of a clash between the incoming government and world Jewry. The Sephardic Chief Rabbi of Israel, Yitzhak Yosef, warned that Israel 'is an Orthodox state, not a Reform one,' accusing Reform Judaism of 'causing assimilation abroad.' The flood of spiteful remarks against Reform Jews, and the proposals to limit Jewish immigration to Israel based on religion caused a huge backlash from Diaspora Jews. Rabbi Laura Janner-Klausner of Bromley Reform Synagogue in England called Ben-Gvir's demands 'just one corrosive, toxic and depleting element of a slew of foul policies that will undermine the very nature of Jewish Peoplehood. It is disturbing, disgusting and demeaning.' Her criticism was echoed by Rabbi Deborah Blausten from the Finchley Reform Synagogue in the UK, who warned that the rhetoric and demands coming from the far right and ultra-Orthodox were inflicting personal and emotional damage on Diaspora Jews. 'For Israel, at this moment, to turn around to Jews around the world and say "your Jewishness isn't valid" is like a kick in the teeth. It's a horrible thing to be told.'[18] The head of Israel Religious Action Center, Orly Erez Likhovski, also lashed out at the new government's insensitive and condescending remarks about Reform Jews. Likhovski said:

> The demands to cancel recognition of Reform conversions and to alter the Law of Return are dangerous demands that will mean the State of Israel will stop being the country of the entire Jewish people and will instead become an Orthodox-Haredi Jewish state. These steps will cause an irreparable rift with Diaspora Jewry, and we hope that the prime minister-elect will not accept them. [19]

In addition to the long list of Jewish organizations as well as Reform and Conservative Rabbis in the Diaspora, the powerful and highly respected Jewish Agency took a clear side in the toxic debate about Jewishness. In an unprecedented letter to Netanyahu the agency said:

> It is our duty to share with you our deep concern regarding voices in the government on issues that could undermine the long-standing status quo on religious affairs that could affect the Diaspora. Any change in the delicate and sensitive status quo on issues such as the Law of Return or conversion could threaten to unravel the ties between us and keep us away from each other. [20]

While the ultra-orthodox parties had been parts of left-wing governments for decades until the 1990's, a significant shift happened under Netanyahu's rule. *Shas*, under Arieh Dery, was an ally of Yitzhak Rabin and supported the Oslo Accords, despite most of their voters being against it. But over the years it changed significantly, especially after the second *Intifada*. According to Dr. Gilead Malach, Director of the Ultra-Orthodox in Israel Program at the Israel Democracy Institute, *Shas* almost began to compete with Likud over who was most right-wing. The message to the voters, especially in the election cycles that began in 2019, was that 'they would get the religious and the right-wing element. This was their propaganda,' Dr. Malach said.

Racism

One of the things that became clear as the new Knesset was sworn in was the increasing racism heard at the Knesset. Ben-Gvir already had a long history of racist remarks behind him, having also been formally indicted on inciting racism in 2008. During his election campaigns, the Jewish Power party leader would repeatedly call on the deportation of 'disloyal' Arab Israelis. But two people were of specific interest to him; the Arab Israeli lawmakers Ayman Odeh and Ahmad Tibi. Ben-Gvir repeatedly called fort Odeh and Tibi to be deported to Syria, or some other Arab country. According to Tibi, the racism spouted by Ben-Gvir has helped normalize that kind of rhetoric among lawmakers. 'He said "Amhad Tibi you are my project", Tibi recalled Ben-Gvir telling him. 'I am used to it. There were ministers who attacked me (in the past). I'm not sure, however, I should be relaxed about this. The atmosphere in the corridors has changed in this Knesset term. You see more and more hilltop youth, not only in the government but also the parliamentary assistants, assistants to the ministers,' Tibi said. In Ben-Gvir's eyes, both Tibi and Odeh were nothing short of terrorists due to their views on the occupation and harsh criticism of Israel's treatment of Palestinians. Tibi would use the word 'martyrs' to describe Palestinians killed by the Israeli army despite Israel insisting they were terrorists. Odeh went as far as visiting a member of Hamas who was on a hunger strike in a hospital in Israel to protest his administrative detention in 2021. Ben-Gvir showed up at the hospital and exploded at Odeh, calling him a terrorist. The two ended up physically scuffling at the hospital. But Ben-Gvir was far from being the only lawmaker in Knesset using racist slur and rhetoric against Palestinians and Arab lawmakers.

Almog Cohen, lawmaker from the Jewish Power party, filmed a TikTok video inside the Knesset, making animal calling sounds at Arab lawmakers, telling them to 'shut up.' 'When you talk to them in their language, they understand you. You need to talk to them like a sheep. I'm not telling him to be quiet in Hebrew because he doesn't speak Hebrew,' Cohen was heard saying in the video as he filmed Arab lawmakers. 'That's a doctor. I wouldn't let him treat my dog,' Cohen said when he filmed Ahmad Tibi, who is also a trained gynecologist. While only apologizing for lashing out in the same video at a female lawmaker Merav Ben-Ari from Yesh Atid, Cohen doubled down on his racist slur at the Arab lawmakers, saying 'they're traitors. It might have been inappropriate because they're not worthy of being sheep, they're not humans. I will make their lives miserable.'[21] Shas party leader Arieh Dery was seen smiling and laughing in the video as Cohen made his racist remarks while Likud lawmaker May Golan encouraged him to shout the word 'out' in Arabic at a female lawmaker. While the media put Cohen under harsh scrutiny, most government officials were silent. During a debate in the Knesset House Committee over legislation that would revoke citizenship of terrorists receiving funds from the Palestinian Authority, newly elected Likud lawmaker Hanoch Milwidsky said he 'preferred' Jewish murderers over Arab murderers while claiming, incorrectly, that there currently aren't and never has been any Jewish terrorists. His remarks were made at Ahmad Tibi who engaged in the heated debate. His statements, which were backed by fellow coalition lawmaker Limor Son Har-Melech from the Jewish Power party, received little attention despite their inflammatory and borderline racist nature. They were, however, in line with the new government's view on Jews and Palestinians, reflecting the increasing willingness to openly say what had been known for years, namely that Jewish blood was more valuable than Arab or Palestinian blood. It also reflected the growing view that there is no such things as 'Jewish terrorism', despite a long, historic and proven record of that very phenomenon. Finance Minister Smotrich took this view one step further when he declared in speech during a visit to Paris that 'there is no such thing as Palestinians because there is no such thing as the Palestinian people.' Smotrich made the remarks at a podium where a map of 'Greater Israel' appeared, showing borders that include territory in modern day Jordan. 'Do you know who are the Palestinians? I'm Palestinian,' Smotrich said, mentioning his family which had lived in what was then Palestine for centuries. He continued:

> The Palestinian people are an invention of less than 100 years ago. Is there a Palestinian history or culture? No. There were Arabs in the Middle East who arrived in the Land of Israel at the same time as the Jewish immigration and the beginning of Zionism. After 2,000 years of exile, the people of Israel were returning home, and there were Arabs around [us] who do not like it. So what do they do? They invent a fictitious people in the Land of Israel and claim fictitious rights in the Land of Israel just to fight the Zionist movement. This is the historical truth. This is the biblical truth. The Arabs in the Land of Israel need to hear this truth. This truth should be heard here in the Élysée Palace. [22]

As expected, his remarks drew widespread condemnation. Jordan's foreign ministry called it a continuation of 'extremist, racist actions' by Smotrich, causing the Israeli foreign ministry to quickly clarify that Israel was indeed committed to the 1994 peace treaty with Jordan. Palestinian Prime Minister Mohammad Shtayyeh called Smotrich's remarks 'conclusive evidence of the extremist, racist Zionist ideology that governs the parties of the current Israeli government', while the EU condemned his comments as 'unacceptable, wrong, and dangerous.'[23] Egypt, the U.S., France, and Morocco also issued statements denouncing the finance minister.

The racist remarks were not however limited to lawmakers and ministers in the Knesset. In April, a phone conversation between National Security Minister Ben-Gvir and Police Commissioner Kobi Shabtai was leaked to the media. Ben-Gvir and Shabtai were talking about the continuing rise of crime and murder among Arab Israelis. Shabtai was heard saying 'Mr. Minister, there is nothing that can be done. They kill each other. That is their nature. That is the mentality of the Arabs.' The commissioner fumed at Ben-Gvir for leaking the conversation, alleging that his words were taken out of context. 'In any other country, a racist commissioner like Shabtai would be fired in an instant. Shabtai, Resign!' Ayman Odeh said following the leak, while UAL party leader Abbas demanded Shabtai apologize or resign. [24]

Notes

1   TOI staff, 'Bennett sues rabbi for false claims his parents weren't Jewish', *Times of Israel*, 6 December 2022.

2   Jotam Confino, 'US ambassador to Israel on allegations that Israel ceded to Hezbollah over Lebanon gas deal: 'Ridiculous'', *The Jewish Telegraphic Agency*, 6 October 2022.

3   Jotam Confino, ''More of a wild card'': What a Netanyahu comeback could mean for US-Israeli relations, *USA TODAY*, 26 October 2022.

4   Josh Breiner, 'Ben-Gvir's Ex-hilltop Youth Chief-of-staff Interviews for Top Police Positions', *Haaretz*, 19 May 2023.

5   Eliran Aharon, 'MK: Build synagogue on Temple Mount', *Arutz Sheva News*, 24 July 2017.

6   TOI Staff, 'Army chief spurns Smotrich's W. Bank powers: IDF reports only to defense minister', *Times of Israel*, 13 January 2023.

7   TOI Staff, 'Army chief spurns Smotrich's W. Bank powers: IDF reports only to defense minister', *Times of Israel*, 13 January 2023.

8   TOI Staff, 'Army chief spurns Smotrich's W. Bank powers: IDF reports only to defense minister', *Times of Israel*, 13 January 2023.

9   Ha'aretz, 'Netanyahu's Government, the Most Right-wing in Israel's History, Takes Office', *Haaretz*, 28 December 2022.

10 TOI Staff, 'Anti-LGBT incoming Jewish identity czar Avi Maoz vows to nix Jerusalem Pride Parade', *Times of Israel*, 1 December 2022.

11 Michael Bachner, 'Top rabbi calls gay Knesset speaker Ohana 'infected,' blames him for Meron disaster', Times of Israel, 1 January 2023.

12 TOI Staff, 'Likud MK urges colleagues to defend new Knesset speaker from homophobic attacks', *Times of Israel*, 2 January 2023.

13 TOI Staff, 'Likud MK urges colleagues to defend new Knesset speaker from homophobic attacks', *Times of Israel*, 2 January 2023.

14 Noa Shpigel, 'Israeli Far-right MK "Shamed and Hurt" by Gay Lawmaker's Appearance With Husband at Ceremonies', *Ha'aretz*, 28 April 2023.

15 Michael Bachner, 'Coalition MK: LGBTQ community poses greater threat to Israel than Hezbollah or Hamas', *Times of Israel*, 21 June 2023.

16 Judah Ari Gross, 'Orthodox parties demand legalization of gender-segregated public events', *Times of Israel*, 20 November 2022.

17 Jotam Confino, 'Outrage at far-right plan to ban aliyah for non-Orthodox converts', *Jewish News*, 16 November 2022.

18 Jotam Confino, 'Outrage at far-right plan to ban aliyah for non-Orthodox converts', *Jewish News*, 16 November 2022.

19 Judah Ari Gross, 'Ben Gvir calls for revoking state recognition of non-Orthodox conversions', *Times of Israel*, 13 November 2022.

20 Jotam Confino, 'Jewish Agency to Netanyahu: "Concern" about Law of Return and religious status quo', *Jewish News*, 4 January 2023.

21 TOI Staff, '"They're inhuman": Far-right MK likens Arab party MKs to sheep, refuses to apologize', *Times of Israel*, 21 February 2023.

22 TOI Staff, 'Smotrich says there's no Palestinian people, declares his family "real Palestinians"', *Times of Israel*, 20 March 2023.

23 Associated Press, '"No such thing" as Palestinian people, top Israeli minister says', *Associated Press*, 21 March 2023.

24 TOI Staff, '"They kill each other": Israel Police chief says it is Arabs' "nature" to murder', *Times of Israel*, 4 April 2023.

11

Coup d'état

'Judicial reforms'

The new government led by Netanyahu had campaigned on a variety of different issues, with each party emphasizing something different. Common for all of them were that having an Arab-Israeli party in the government was unacceptable, and that replacing the 'left-wing' government which had 'surrendered to terror' was of utmost importance for Israel's security. At no point, however, had it been made clear to the public that the most important issue for the government was an overhaul of the judicial system.

Netanyahu had stressed in several interviews prior to the elections that his main priorities were to curb Iran's nuclear program and expand the Abraham Accords, more precisely strike a peace deal with Saudi Arabia. Likud and the far-right parties had mentioned their intentions to change limit the Supreme Court's power and change the judicial system in Israel, but it was never made clear to the public that it would be an immediate and overarching goal for the government to radically change Israel's democracy.

On January 4, less than a week after Netanyahu's new government had been sworn in, Justice Minister Yariv Levin held a televised speech that would go down in history as a breaking point in Israel's history. Levin began his speech by referring to a quote by former Prime Minister and Likud founder Menachem Begin, who allegedly said 'there are judges in Jerusalem.' Despite there being no proof of Begin saying those words, the quote became iconic over the years and would be referred to repeatedly by Israeli politicians in connection to the rule of law. 'But there is also a Knesset and a cabinet. The constitutional revolution and the growing intervention of the judicial system in cabinet decisions and Knesset legislation have dragged the trust in the judiciary down to a dangerous low, leading to a loss of governance and severe damage to democracy. We go to the polls (and vote), but time after time, people whom we have not elected decide for us,' Levin said, referring to former Supreme Court President Aharon Barak's constitutional revolution in the mid 1990's.

Levin then went on to present the government's new judicial reforms. The 'override clause' would prevent the Supreme Court from striking down legislation passed in Knesset, by allowing a simple majority in parliament overriding court rulings. The second part of the reform changed the structure of the Judicial Appointments Committee, effectively giving the government control with appointing new Supreme Court judges. The committee consisted of three Supreme Court judges, the justice minister and a cabinet minister, two Knesset members, and two representatives from Israel's Bar Association. According to the government's plan, the representatives from the Bar Association would be replaced with 'public representatives' chosen by the government. The third part of the reforms would cancel the 'reasonableness standard' used by the Supreme Court to determine the legality of government decisions and appointed ministers.

Although rarely used, the government specifically included the cancelation of this standard as it expected that the Supreme Court would deem the appointment of Shas party leader Arieh Dery as Health and Interior minister unreasonable and thereby order Netanyahu to remove him from the positions (the court did exactly this later that month). Dery had resigned from the Knesset in a plea deal with the court a year earlier after being indicted yet again on tax fraud charges, with the promise of leaving public life. Finally, the reforms would change the status of the legal advisors so that their advice would no longer be legally binding. Each change, Levin said, would 'restore the balance' of the judicial system, and thereby 'strengthen' the democracy. But the radical changes proposed by Levin and the government were transparent to anyone with the slightest knowledge of Israel's judicial system. Without a constitution, the Supreme Court was the only institution that protected human and civil rights. The reforms would not only politicize the court by allowing the government to appoint its judges and thereby destroy its independence, it would also effectively annul its powers by allowing a simple majority to override its decisions.

That combination would make the government all powerful, removing any significant checks and balances known in classic democracies with separations of powers. The opposition, as well as the media and virtually every important sector in Israel's civil society understood this immediately after Levin's speech. The opposition and media were the first to react. 'What Yariv Levin presented today is not a legal reform, it is a letter of intimidation. They threaten to destroy the entire constitutional structure of the State of Israel,' Opposition Leader Yair Lapid raged. Benny Gantz called it a 'political coup' while right-wing lawmakers like Gideon Sa'ar, who had previously been critical of the court's power, said 'there is no doubt that Menachem Begin would have rejected each of the sections of the plan to change the regime in Israel,' in a reference to the former prime minister and founder of Likud.[1]

The Israeli media (not including the Netanyahu friendly Channel 14) gave a similar verdict, warning about the dramatic consequences the overhaul would have on democracy. Netanyahu, as expected, echoed Levin's claim that the judicial system was in dire need of reforms, and the ones suggested by the government would strengthen democracy, not weaken it. Netanyahu claimed that his ongoing corruption trial was not related to the overhaul, although Levin would later admit that the three indictments had 'really contributed to the very wide public understanding that there are failures in the system that must be fixed. There is no doubt that they contributed a lot,' Levin said less than two weeks after presenting the reforms.[2] After much anticipation, Supreme Court President Esther Hayut finally broke her silence, 12 days after Levin's speech. She would become the most senior figure in Israel to publicly speak out against the overhaul in a speech that would go over in history as an unprecedented attack on a government. 'This is a plan to crush the justice system. It is designed to deal a fatal blow to the independence of the judiciary and silence it,' Hayut said in a speech held in Haifa.

> If the reforms were implemented, the 75th anniversary of Israel's independence will be remembered as the year in which the country's democratic identity was dealt a fatal blow. Anyone who claims that the majority who elected their representatives to the Knesset were giving them a "blank check" to do as they please, takes the name of democracy in vain. One of the most important functions of a court in a democratic country is to provide effective protection for human and civil rights in the country. It is the guarantee that the rule of the majority does not turn into the tyranny of the majority. The planned override clause allows the Knesset, with the support of the government, to enact laws that would harm these rights without hindrance. In fact, what we are talking about is overriding the human rights of each and every individual in Israeli society.[3]

As expected, Levin fired back at Hayut immediately, accusing her of acting like a politician and for using the same rhetoric as the 'Black Flag' movement (which had organized protests against Netanyahu following his indictment), aiming to 'set the streets on fire.'

In the meantime, the first mass rally against the reforms had taken place in Tel Aviv on 14 January, drawing some 80,000 people. The rally was attended by a long list of opposition lawmakers as well as former high-level officials, such as Prime Minister Ehud Barak and Foreign Minister Tzipi Livni, both of whom would be among the most vocal and active critics against the reforms in the months to come. The list of highly influential public figures and organizations who all echoed to varies degrees the intense criticism hurled at the government grew day by day.

The high-tech sector was among the first to speak out against the overhaul, warning that a country without an independent judiciary would scare off foreign investors. Turkey was a clear example of that, with its economy plummeting after President Erdogan gradually seized more and more power. Then came former intelligence and military chiefs, who all warned that the overhaul would jeopardize Israel's security. Top economists, academics, medical staff, teachers, and Diaspora Jews followed. Never in Israel's history had a government been subject to such intense criticism, spanning across the political spectrum. Hayut was backed by former Supreme Court Presidents and judges, the Bar Association, and former attorney generals. Eighteen former Supreme Court presidents and judges signed a letter which warned that the government's reforms were a 'serious threat' to the legal system as well as to the very nature of Israel's 'regime and way of life.' The harshest warning was perhaps the one issued by former Attorney General Avichai Mandelblit who said what most people who criticized the reforms were thinking, namely that they were meant to stop Netanyahu's trial. 'My evaluation and opinion are that he (Netanyahu) wants to lead to a situation in which the trial will not reach its end in a proper way,' Mandelblit told Channel 12, adding that the deep societal divisions over the reforms could 'end in violence, someone will pay the price in blood.'[4]

Mass protests

As the movement against the reforms began to evolve shortly after Levin's speech, the demonstrations grew exponentially from week to week. What began in Tel Aviv had now spread to other cities like Jerusalem and Haifa at the end of January. For the first time since the protests began, more than 100,000 gathered in Habima Square in central Tel Aviv, marking the biggest demonstration so far. Slowly but surely, the demonstrations took on a life of their own, with slogans, signs, and speeches. The chant 'democracy' (yelled in Hebrew) would become synonym with the protests, while signs depicting Netanyahu as a dictator were seen everywhere. Words like 'fascism' and 'dictatorship' were seen everywhere on signs held by angry protesters. One comparison was made repeatedly by demonstrators. Israel was on its way to become a country like Hungary, which was considered an illiberal democracy with no oversight of parliament. The chants 'This isn't Hungary' and 'Bibi, Sarah, this isn't Hungary' (it rhymes in Hebrew) were chanted by thousands of people at the same time. Netanyahu was also depicted alongside Hungary's Prime Minister Victor Orban on signs at demonstrations. The far-right regime of Hungary was often brought up as an example during heated media debates, with experts arguing that the reforms would put Israel in the same category. Orban and his Fidesz party had since 2010 amended Hungary's constitution, weaking the constitutional court's ability to strike down laws in parliament, while appointing political allies as judges. Experts in Hungarian law warned in interviews to Israeli media as well as a conference held by Israel's Democracy Institute that the government's reforms were similar to what had Orban had done to cement his grip on power and weaken the country's democracy. The difference, some said, was that the public was too slow to realize what had happened, unlike in Israel, where mass protests were growing week by week. Netanyahu's close friendship with Orban only made critics of the reforms all the more worried that he was slowly copying him in an attempt to change Israel's regime.

Despite the mass protests growing in numbers and spreading to all corners of Israel with each week passing, the government had no intention of removing the reforms from its agenda. It was no longer possible to dismiss the protests, which began in Tel Aviv, as a bunch of 'left-wing' demonstrators who were against Netanyahu no matter what he did. All elements of Israeli society were represented on the streets, ranging from young left-wing activists to older people who belonged to the right-wing camp. Religious and secular people were also demonstrating side by side. And the public profile people who began to get involved in the demonstrations also included former right-wing and Likud lawmakers, such as Dan Meridor, Limor Livnat, and Moshe Ya'alon.

After weeks of demonstrations held in different locations across Israel, organizers encouraged people to demonstrate outside the Knesset on what they called 'Black Monday.' The demonstration was set to take place on 13 February, as the Constitution, Law and Justice Committee was scheduled to approve the approve the first bill in the reform, which would change the composition of the committee selecting judges. A chaotic committee hearing ended with opposition lawmakers screaming 'shame' at chairman Simcha Rhotman, with some jumping on the table. Several were removed forcibly from the hearing by Knesset ushers. Outside the Knesset, over 100,000 Israelis had gathered, some with their kids who had taken a day off school. 'We are not here just to pay taxes and send our children to the army.

We will not shut ourselves in our houses when they try to turn the State of Israel into a dark dictatorship and silence us,' Lapid told the massive, cheering crowd from a stage erected outside the Knesset.

As the mass rally in Jerusalem continued to draw people, a large demonstration took place in Tel Aviv, while university and high school students demonstrated at their schools in several locations across the country. Despite the growing pressure on the government, protesters were still dismissed as 'left-wing anarchists' by Netanyahu, as well as Ben-Gvir, who had been propelled into a national crisis in which he was responsible for national security. Netanyahu repeatedly accused the opposition of fanning the flames and causing 'anarchy' in the streets by encouraging people to demonstrate. The anarchy they referred to involved the blocking of highways in Israel by protesters. Their aim was to make Israel came to a halt by literally stopping traffic, usually on the Ayalon Highway which connected Tel Aviv to the rest of Israel.

Week after week, increasing numbers of protestors would challenge the police in blocking Ayalon. As Ben-Gvir visited the Police Headquarter in Tel Aviv in early March ahead of one of the mass demonstrations, police began cracking down more harshly on protestors whom they considered responsible for vandalism or disorder. Policemen on horses were deployed to the streets of Tel Aviv to disperse large crowds. Stun grenades were also thrown for the first time by a policeman into a crowd, severely injuring one person's ear. Dozens of people were arrested across Israel in other demonstrations. Ben-Gvir's arrival at the HQ in Tel Aviv was seen as a direct attempt to interfere with police conduct, pressuring officers to be more aggressive. Ben-Gvir was furious with Police Commissioner Kobi Shabtai and in particular Tel Aviv District Commander Ami Eshed for being too lenient with the protestors and failing to prevent Ayalon Highway from being blocked week after week.

On 8 March, Eshed was fired from his position by Shabtai. Israeli media reported that Shabtai told Attorney General Gali Baharav-Miara that Ben-Gvir had forced him to fire Eshed. The removal sparked an outcry among opposition lawmakers and former security officials, who saw it as politically motivated and a personal vendetta against Eshed, who was generally liked and respected in the Tel Aviv District. Just two days later, Baharav-Miara ordered an immediate freeze of Eshed's removal, raising severe concern about the legality of the process. The attorney general's move infuriated Ben-Gvir, who called on Baharav-Miara to be fired, claiming she had been acting as a 'de facto opposition leader' due to her blocking several highly questionable orders by Ben-Gvir since he assumed office. The attorney general had stopped Ben-Gvir from imposing a lockdown over an entire neighbourhood in East Jerusalem following a deadly terror attack in January. Ben-Gvir, however, wasn't the only one fuming over the attorney general, the police and the growing mass protests. Netanyahu's son, Yair, had in seen recent years been considered yielding immense influence over his father's decisions and in the Likud party in general. The day before Eshed was fired from his position, Yair accused police in Tel Aviv of 'cooperating with anarchists', claiming their behavior was part of a 'full-blown rebellion of the higher-ranking command.' While some of the more rhetorically aggressive government officials usually resorted to using the words 'anarchists' and 'privileged' about the hundreds of thousands of protestors, Yair Netanyahu took it one step further, as he rarely faced any consequences for outrageous and false accusations. He told Galey Israel radio:

> The process which the Israeli left is undergoing... is one-to-one comparable to the 1930s in Germany. What happened in the 1930s in Germany? Paid thugs carried out political terror in the streets. No murder by the way, no one was murdered. Political terror via intimidation, via violence, via disruption of public order, and intimidation of citizens. They created chaos and then their party rose undemocratically... 'They are the ones who are calling for a dictatorship, they are the ones who are marching Israel towards fascism. They are the ones who use the same methods as the blackshirts in Italy, it is unpleasant to say, [also] the SA in Germany.[5]

Yair also accused the Shin Bet intelligence agency of staging a 'coup' against his father, after a pro-Netanyahu journalist reported a false story about alleged Shin Bet officials, leaking information to the media about Netanyahu while they were working as his drivers.

'The Shin Bet is involved in a coup against the prime minister! Investigative committee now! These people need to stand trial and be sent to prison for many years,' Yair tweeted, only to delete it later.[6] The highly inflammatory and false accusations by Yair were, however, not condemned by his father.

Cherry picking

As the protests grew stronger and louder, Israel's closes allies began voicing their concern about the overhaul. U.S. Secretary of State Antony Blinken was among the first foreign officials to publicly comment on the judicial crisis.

During a visit to Israel in late January, Blinken gave what was interpreted as an unprecedented lecture in democracy at a press conference with Netanyahu. After repeating the usual diplomatic language about the U.S. and Israel having unbreakable ties and shared values, Blinken stressed the need to protect human rights, minorities and the rule of law, urging Netanyahu to build a consensus around the judicial reforms. He also gave a thinly veiled compliment to the mass protests, saying Israel's vibrant democracy had been at display lately. Blinken then took time to meet with civil society organizations in Israel, telling them that they (civil society in general) served as a 'North Star, keeping government's focused and honest when it comes to making sure that we're adhering to the principles we all espouse.' It was highly unusual for a U.S. Secretary of State to make time to visit with Israeli civil society leaders, but his message to Netanyahu was even more striking.

As expected, coalition members from the far-right parties weren't happy being lectured in democracy by their closest ally. Religious Zionism lawmaker Orit Strock lashed out at Blinken, saying:

> I understand that you decided to give our prime minister a lesson in democracy. Well, democracy is first of all the duty of a country to determine its course according to the votes of its citizens, each of which is given equal weight, without foreign involvement. Demonstrations, however legitimate they may be, are not equivalent to a ballot. [7]

Not long after, U.S. ambassador to Israel, Tom Nides, also drew anger from ministers and coalition members after he said he had told Netanyahu to 'pump the brakes' and 'slow down', urging him to find a consensus with the opposition. Diaspora Affairs Minister Amichai Chickli (Likud) fired back at Nides, telling him to 'put on the brakes yourself and mind your own business. You aren't sovereign here, to get involved in the matter of judicial reform. We will be happy to discuss foreign and security matters with you - but respect our democracy.'[8] Biden also got personally involved when he urged Netanyahu to 'walk away' from the judicial overhaul, while stressing that Netanyahu wasn't invited to the White House anytime soon. 'Like many strong supporters of Israel, I'm very concerned ... They cannot continue down this road, and I've sort of made that clear,' Biden told reporters in North Carolina in late March.[9]

But the U.S. wasn't the only close ally urging Netanyahu to reach a consensus. French President Macron, UK Prime Minister Sunak and German Chancellor Scholz all repeated the same message to varies degrees, some more bold than others. Each time, Netanyahu had to reassure his counterparts that Israel would indeed remain a democracy, something no Israeli leader in the history of the country had to do on any of their visits abroad. The Israeli media lambasted Netanyahu each time he was lectured in democracy in a new European capital, while the opposition used it as ammunition against the government. Time and time again, Netanyahu tried explaining the rationale behind the overhaul. Being compared to Hungary, Poland and Turkey wasn't a good look for his new government, neither abroad nor at home.

Netanyahu's central argument was that the balance of power in the judicial system had been skewed over the years, giving extraordinary powers to the Supreme Court. Many Israelis agreed on this. Even opposition parties were in favour of some sort of judicial reform, but not on the scale proposed by the government. When defending the reforms, Netanyahu, and to a wide extent Simcha Rhotman who was at the forefront of the legal battle inside the Knesset, tried to compare Israel to other Western nations where Supreme Court judges were picked by the government, or where it didn't have power to strike down laws. It was a smart, yet wildly misleading line of arguing to compare Israel's judicial system to its closest allies, such as the U.S. and Canada.

The term 'cherry picking' was the appropriate way to describe the comparisons. The two biggest flaws in the arguments were that both the U.S. and Canada have a constitution with civil rights enshrined, unlike Israel. Canada does, however, have an 'override clause' but with specific constraints. To remove any doubt about the unfair comparison, former Canadian Justice Minister Irwin Cutler said that 'the override in Canada is within a Charter of Rights and Freedoms' and that Canada has 'two Houses of Parliament — the House of Commons and the Senate. There's a whole series of protections with regard to the override.' Cutler's argument was backed by former Canadian Ambassador to Israel, Vivian Bercovici, who said 'any suggestion that Canadian parliamentary democracy operates in the manner suggested by Rothman – an unfettered exercise of majority power – is false,' referring to Rhotman who had repeated similar false claims in the media about judicial systems in Canada, New Zealand and the UK to justify the government's reforms.[10]

But the biggest blow to Netanyahu's attempt to compare other Western countries to Israel came from an old ally, Harvard Law professor Alan Dershowitz, who called the reforms a 'terrible mistake.' Dershowitz, one of Israel's biggest supporters abroad, argued that Israel had a better democracy than most, 'precisely because the Supreme Court has enforced basic minority rights even when a temporary majority has sought to violate them.'[11] The Supreme Court, he said, is among the best and most highly regarded in the world and serves as an 'Iron Dome' against criticism hurled at Israel in the international system. But he also picked Netanyahu's comparison to the U.S. apart. The U.S. system on appointing judges, which Netanyahu cited repeatedly as an inspiration for the reforms, has been an 'absolute disaster,' Dershowitz said. 'It's turned the entire Supreme Court into a political institution, and the appointment proves it has become very politicized… the Supreme Court has lost credibility… If you want to borrow successes, fine, but please don't borrow the failures of the U.S.,' Dershowitz said.[12] The Harvard Law professor also said if he lived in Israel, he would join the protests.

Michael Oren, former Israeli ambassador to the U.S. and lawmaker in Netanyahu's coalition from 2015-2019, also warned about the dangers of the reforms. 'This is a gutting of the legal system. It can't be defended as a way to preserve judicial review because it basically eviscerates it (judicial review),' Oren said. The comparisons between Israel and Western countries fell on deaf ears, both abroad and inside Israel. Most Israelis understood the dangers of the overhaul. In fact, every poll conducted in the months after Levin's presentation on 4 January revealed that most Israelis were against the government's reforms. A survey conducted by Israel's Democracy Institute found that 63% believed that the current structure of the Judicial Appointments Committee should be kept, while 66% supported the Supreme Court's power to strike down laws which ran counter to the Basic Laws. It served as a reminder that although Netanyahu had won the election democratically, he didn't have most Israelis behind him when it came to radically altering the judicial system.

Economic fallout

Israel's high-tech sector is in many ways the country's unicorn and pride. Since 2019, over $50 billion from abroad had been invested in Israeli startups. As of 2023, some 40,000 people were employed in high-tech, constituting 11% of the workforce and amounting to 25% of the nation's income tax. Not surprisingly, the sector was among the first to speak out vocally against the judicial overhaul. Numerous companies even encouraged its employees to take to the streets to protest, giving them days off from work. The sector also planned collective protests on weekdays. Their main argument was that crushing the Supreme Court's independence and weakening it to a point where it would serve as nothing but a symbol, would deter foreign investors. And since the vast majority of the money invested in the high-tech sector comes from abroad, the overhaul would cause irreparable damage to Israel's economy. Three weeks after Levin's speech, two companies announced they would withdraw their money from Israel. The CEO of Papaya Global, an international payroll company valued at $3.7 billion in 2021, cited the overhaul as the reason for their decision to withdraw all the firm's money from Israel. 'Just like in Brazil, Venezuela and Hungary, no leading investor or financial institute will let his billions stay in a country with a crumbling democracy. Let's say this loud and clear: Startup Nation without a democracy cannot stand,' Eynat Guez, a co-founder and CEO of Papaya Global, said.[13] Another company, VC funds Disruptive and Disruptive AI, informed their investors that they would also withdraw their money from Israel. Other major companies like Wiz, the American Israeli cybersecurity startup, also warned it would withdraw its funds from Israel if the reforms were passed. 'The high-tech sector needs stability, needs the rules of the game to be clear, needs a certainty that...they will have the court to go to. This sector...would take their brains...their ideas, their entrepreneurship, and there will be a red carpet laid out for them in some countries,' explained Karnit Flug, former Bank of Israel Governor.[14]

But the high-tech sector wasn't the only ones in uproar over the economic implications of the overhaul. Hundreds of leading Israeli economists published a letter to Netanyahu, warning that the 'concentration of vast political power in the hands of the ruling group without strong checks and balances could cripple the country's economy.' Among the signatories were Nobel Prize winner Prof. Daniel Kahneman, Prof. Eugene Kandel, a former Netanyahu economic adviser and National Economic Council head, and Prof. Omer Moav, a former adviser to the finance minister. Not long after, 56 world-renowned international economists (including 11 Nobel laureates) echoed their Israeli colleagues in a letter to Netanyahu. The letter said:

> The governing coalition in Israel is considering an array of legislative acts that would weaken the independence of the judiciary and its power to constrain governmental actions. Numerous Israeli economists, in an open letter that some of us joined, expressed concerns that such a reform would adversely affect the Israeli economy by weakening the rule of law and thereby moving Israel in the direction of Hungary and Poland. Although we significantly vary in our views on public policy and on the challenges facing Israeli society, we all share these concerns. A strong and independent

judiciary is a critical part of a system of checks and balances. Undermining it would be detrimental not only to democracy but also to economic prosperity and growth.

While two former Bank of Israel Governors, Karnit Flug and Jacob Frenkel had already warned that the overhaul would deal a severe blow to Israel's economy, the current Governor Amir Yaron initially warned Netanyahu in private, staying out of the intense public discourse. But as the reforms kept advancing, Yaron finally spoke out publicly in an interview with CNN in mid-March. He warned:

> Right now, the changes in the judicial reform could weaken some of this (Bank of Israel) independence. Moreover, the process itself is hasty and does not have a wide agreement in the public. We have seen some high-tech leaders and industry leaders telling us that maybe first investments won't come in, and some are even talking that they might take their business elsewhere. In the long run, the implication might be, basically, brain drain, etc., and this is why this should be handled with care. This has huge implications, and this is why it's imperative that we maintain the strength and independence of this institution, and this is done in a way that has a wide acceptance in the public and it's a transparent process.[15]

Yaron, who was already warning about the dangers to the bank's independence, hit the nail on the head. When he raised the interest rates once again in February to 4.25%, the highest since 2008, Foreign Minister Eli Cohen (Likud) called on Finance Minister Smotrich to intervene to 'stop' the rate hikes. 'Due to the moderation of inflation, there was no justification in hiking the rate today, which continues the mistreatment of mortgage takers,' he said.[16] Cohen's unprecedented meddling with the Bank of Israel's work drew headlines in the most important financial journals of the world. Smotrich rebuffed Cohen's statement as 'populism', and both him and Netanyahu promised to ensure the independence of the bank. But the damage was already done. One of the most senior officials in the government revealed exactly how some in the party viewed the bank. When Yaron raised the interest rates again in April to 4.5%, Communication Minister Shlomo Karhi ridiculed the Governor, thanking him for the 'magnificent holiday gift he gave to the citizens of Israel. With such opaqueness, on the eve of Passover, perhaps it is possible to put a robot in the position of governor, who will make decisions on interest rate increases based on an objective algorithm, disconnected from the people.'[17]

The warnings and outcry from the most highly regarded economists, businessmen, and Bank of Israel came amid sky-high inflation and interest rates. But the Shekel (Israeli currency) was also taking a hard beating following the announcement of the government's judicial overhaul. By 20 March, the Shekel had weakened against the dollar to the lowest level in four years. And in early April, the Bank of Israel forecast predicted that Israel, in a worst-case scenario, could lose 2.8%, or $14 billion, of its economic output annually because of the overhaul. But despite the massive warning signs, the government kept advancing the reforms. Netanyahu insisted that the economy would benefit from the reforms, ignoring the deepening economic crisis and every advice and assessment by the most revered economists in the world.

'Go to hell'

It didn't take long for Israel's security apparatus to get deeply involved in the controversies surrounding the government's judicial reforms. Previous high-level security officials began criticizing the government harshly. Former Prime Minister Barak, the most decorated soldier in Israel's history, was among the first to warn about the slippery slope toward a dictatorship. Former Defense Minister and IDF chief Moshe Ya'alon became one of the leaders of the movement, speaking at numerous times at demonstrations across the country. Ya'alon thought, like Barak, that Netanyahu was taking the country in the most dangerous direction in the country's history, ultimately aiming for a dictatorship. All living former intelligence chiefs would later, in separate letters, speak out against the judicial reforms and the dangers the deep societal rifts posed to the country's security and cohesion. Many of the former chiefs had been outspoken critics of Netanyahu for years, so it didn't come as a surprise when Barak, Ya'alon, former IDF chief Dan Halutz, former Shin Bet chiefs Nadav Argaman, Yuval Diskin, Carmi Gilon and Yaacov Perry as well as former Mossad chief Tamir Pardo and former National Security Adviser Uzi Arad warned in a public letter that the judicial reforms were tantamount to a coup d'état. Hundreds of former Mossad employees, including former Mossad chiefs, Pardo, Efraim Halevy, Danny Yatom and Nahum Admoni, and Shabtai Shavit, signed a similar letter. The letter said:

> As those who have fought and acted for decades against our enemies in the region and around the world to protect the supreme interests of the state and the security of its citizens, we are horrified by the

accelerated and uncontrolled legislative process that undermines the foundations of Israel as a Jewish and democratic state, that tears Israeli society apart from within and threatens its security (and) social and economic resilience.

Netanyahu and the government didn't care much about any of their warnings, seeing them as belonging to the left-wing elicits camp. If anything, they were part of the problem. But the few high-level intel and security officials who had remained on good terms with Netanyahu shared their colleagues' concerns, removing any doubt about the seriousness of the issue. Former Mossad chief Yossi Cohen (widely seen as one of Netanyahu's closest allies and a future candidate for prime minister) as well as 12 former national security advisors, warned that the social and political conflict was 'endangering national resilience' and that only a broad compromise on the reforms would solve the issue.

It was, however, not the warning from the most senior security officials in Israel that would cause the biggest blow to Netanyahu. In February, the first reserve officers and soldiers in Israel's reserve unit threatened to stop volunteering for reserve duty if the reforms weren't halted. 'If the so-called 'legal reform' legislation passes in its entirety, without consultation and in the absence of broad consensus, we will not continue to volunteer for reserve service for a country that has unilaterally changed the basic contract with its citizens,' hundreds of officers from the prestigious 8200 intelligence unit said. The unprecedented warning started an avalanche among other units in the Israeli reserve. Hundreds of pilots in the Israeli Air Force would follow suit, causing the biggest concern yet for the military. Pilots were the backbone of the IDF and were among the most used and important units when it came to attacking Israel's enemies, whether it be against Hamas and Islamic Jihad in Gaza, or Iranian affiliated proxies in Lebanon, Syria, or Iraq. 'Brothers in Arms', a protest group consisting of reserve soldiers and officers from a variety of units, including the elite *Sayeret Matkal* unit, backed up the intelligence and pilot reserves, warning that 'tens of thousands' would stop volunteering for duty if the overhaul wasn't stopped. The reservists shared similar concerns as the vast majority of Israelis, only their situation was rooted in the security, first and foremost. Without an independent judiciary, soldiers would find themselves answering only to the government, fearing they could be asked to carry out orders that would have otherwise been challenged by the Supreme Court. But not only that, the lack of an independent judiciary would also mean that combat soldiers and pilots engaged in wars could be subject to arrests abroad, accused of committing war crimes. This scenario had been avoided precisely because the international system relied on the Israeli Supreme Court to hold soldiers responsible for their actions. Although soldiers weren't prosecuted for war crimes in wars against Hamas in Gaza, for example, cases like Elor Azaria (who executed a Palestinian terrorist after he had already been disarmed and shot) proved to some extent that the courts did punish reckless behavior. Every security official in Israel knew this. It therefore wasn't a surprise that former IDF and Shin Bet chiefs were in uproar over the government's reforms. Everyone from Barak, Ya'alon, Diskin, Perry to Benny Gantz, a former IDF chief, could theoretically be met with arrest warrants abroad if the Supreme Court lost its independence. Ya'alon said:

> During my decades of military service, I never saw such reckless behavior as that of the accused Netanyahu now. The accused has been warned thousands of times that his obsessive plot to turn Israel into a dictatorship represents an immediate, existential threat to Israel's security. Those issuing the warnings were all the defense, legal, science and economic experts, who made it clear to him that his plot is a critical blow to the IDF and its spirit. Netanyahu pushed to center stage messianic, racist elements who seek to set the region ablaze with messianic fire. The want a fascist, racist, homophobic, messianic and corrupt dictatorship. [18]

The upheaval among the Israeli reservists only added to the already highly intense national debate over which society Israel was going to be. While many applauded the soldiers for drawing a red line as to how far they were willing to go to serve their country, others opposed them. Both Opposition Leader Lapid and National Unity Party leader Gantz recognized the painful situation they were in but called on the soldiers to continue serving no matter what. The government, as expected, was furious with the soldiers. Netanyahu said it threatened Israel's existence and that he expected the IDF chief and heads of branches of the security services to 'aggressively combat the refusal to serve. There is no place for refusal to serve in the public discourse. A state that wishes to exist can't tolerate such phenomena and we will not tolerate it as well.'[19] Netanyahu's claim had been less absurd if it wasn't for the fact most of his coalition partners from the ultra-orthodox and far-right religious parties hadn't served in the army. The issue over ultra-orthodox men and women being exempted from army duty had been a highly contentious issue for years, bringing down Netanyahu's government once before. It was just one of many thorny issues in Israeli society that had caused deep divisions over the years. His harsh words rang even more hollow among the hundreds of thousands of Israelis who had served in the army but were now on the trajectory to having those same extremist lawmakers radically change Israel's democratic character. Netanyahu, however, was moderate in his tone compared to other members of his government who criticized the soldiers refusing to serve. Communication Minister Shlomo Karhi (Likud) told the soldiers that 'the people of Israel will manage without you, and you can go to hell.'[20] Karhi's insensitive and highly provocative remark sparked an outcry among the reservists, with some of them showing up in front of his house to verbally confront him. As the debate about the refusal to serve continued to ravage, the IDF foresaw the security ramifications and relayed it to Defense Minister Gallant.

Pogrom and terror

At the same time as the government announced its judicial reforms, the Israeli-Palestinian conflict was heating up. The IDF continued its campaign to crack down on terror suspects in the West Bank initiated under the Bennett-Lapid government. On 26 January, the IDF killed 10 Palestinians in Jenin during an army raid to eliminate an Islamic Jihad squad that posed as a 'ticking time bomb.' Both Islamic Jihad members as well as civilians were killed during the exchange of fire. In response, six rockets were fired from Gaza at Israel, leading to a measured response from the IDF, which carried out a few targeted bombings of military sites. Ben-Gvir, who had promised during his election campaign that each rocket from Gaza would be met with 50 airstrikes from Israel if he were a member of the government, realized his hands were tied. The day after the lethal IDF raid, a 21-year-old Palestinian man shot and killed seven people near a synagogue in East Jerusalem after they had finished Shabbat prayer. The terror attack was the deadliest in over 15 years. As expected, both Netanyahu and Ben-Gvir showed up at the scene shortly after, where they were met with frustration from residents and relatives of the victims. Ben-Gvir, who had raged against his predecessor, Omer Bar-Lev at every single attack during his time, found himself in the exact same situation, having to explain why this happened on his watch. Ben-Gvir's response was to arm more civilians as well as seal off the home of the terrorist's family immediately. The day after, a 13-year-old Palestinian boy shot and wounded a father and his son in a terror attack in East Jerusalem. Israeli Police were on high alert across the city in anticipation of more attacks. And more attacks would indeed hit Israel in the coming months.

In February 2023, an Israeli delegation traveled to Aqaba in Jordan to meet with representatives from Egypt, Jordan, the Palestinian Authority, and the U.S. Netanyahu decided to send National Security Advisor Tzachi Hanegbi and Shin Bet chief Ronen Bar to represent Israel. The purpose of the security summit, as it was called, was to lower the flames of between Israelis and Palestinians. Two deadly raids in Jenin and Nablus and a string of terror attacks had already left over 60 Palestinians and 11 Israelis killed in less than two months. The meeting, however, was not coordinated with Netanyahu's Likud coalition partners, who were staunchly opposed to any contact with the Palestinians. As the meeting was about to start, a Palestinian man shot and killed two Israeli brothers sitting in a car on a road near the Palestinian town of Huwara in the West Bank. They were caught in a traffic jam when the Palestinian man opened fire, killing both. The killing of two young boys, aged 21 and 19, at the same time as an Israeli delegation was meeting with the Palestinian Authority was an ultimate humiliation for the far-right parties in Netanyahu's government. Finance Minister Smotrich demanded that the Israeli delegation return from the 'superfluous' summit immediately. Likud lawmaker Danny Danon issued a similar demand. Not long after the summit ended, a press release from the White House stated that all parties present at the summit had agreed to several commitments, which included an Israeli commitment to stop discussion of any new settlement units for four months and to stop authorization of any outposts for six months. The statement caused instant outrage among Netanyahu's coalition partners. Smotrich quickly dismissed the agreement, saying there wouldn't be a halt to settlement construction for even one day. National Security Minister Itamar Ben-Gvir mockingly vowed that 'what happens in Aqaba stays in Aqaba.' It was hardly surprising that the two biggest supporters of unlimited settlement expansion refused to comply with what had been agreed upon in a high-level diplomatic summit. But the subsequent denial by both Netanyahu and Hanegbi of the agreement was unprecedented. It made Washington, as well as the rest of the participants of the summit, look ridiculous.

As the diplomatic faux pax was unfolding, a different crisis was about to explode in the government's face. Incitement from civilians and officials exploded on social media, reaching the highest echelons of Israel's political establishment. Smotrich was caught liking a tweet by the deputy head of the Samaria Regional Council, Davidi Ben Zion, which said:

Here in Huwara, the blood of our children, the residents of Samaria, who were murdered here an hour ago, has been spilled on the road. The village of Hawara should be erased today. Enough with the talk of construction and strengthening the settlement, the deterrence that was lost should be returned immediately and there is no room for mercy.

The writing was on the wall and was a clear indicator exactly what was going to happen just hours later. After a storm of criticism hurled at Ben Zion, the tweet was deleted but the cat was out of the bag. Settlers in the West Bank began organizing a march to revenge the killing of the two Israelis.

The march was announced on social media and was set to begin at 6:00 PM at Tapuach Junction and would continue toward the town of Huwara where the brothers had been killed. Despite the announcement of the march, with precise details of an impending revenge rampage, the Israeli military didn't prevent it from taking place. At precisely 6:00 PM, the march began. Chants of 'revenge' was heard in the crowd, which grew bigger as they neared the entrance of Huwara. Hundreds of angry settlers entered the city, some masked and armed. Rocks were thrown at closed businesses while homes and cars were set on fire. Large flames were suddenly seen all over the city, causing nine Palestinian families to evacuate their homes after they were set on fire while they were inside. As the flames grew bigger, the entire city of Huwara looked like it was on fire from the outside. Meanwhile, the Israeli military failed to stop the attacks, which it later described as outright terror. According to Josh Breiner, an Israeli journalist from the Israeli newspaper *Ha'aretz* who was on the ground that night, the army did nothing to stop the march from reaching its destination, nor did it stop the attacks. It took almost six hours from the march began at 6:00 PM until the mob was dispersed.

In the meantime, Jewish Power party lawmaker Limor Son Har-Melech tweeted a photo of herself at the entrance to Huwara, saying she had come to show support for the 'protestors' whose pain she felt over the terror attack earlier in the day. It took several hours before Netanyahu issued a statement, calling on people not to 'take the law into their own hands' and let the IDF find the terrorist who had killed the two Israeli brothers. Smotrich repeated Netanyahu's call, but his previous show of support for 'erasing' Huwara made his sudden U-turn unconvincing. The widescale terror attacks were quickly labeled as nothing short of terror and a pogrom by the IDF. The Commanding Officer of the IDF Central Command, Maj. Gen. Yehuda Fuchs, said:

The responsibility for what is happening in Huwara lies with the IDF Central Command, it lies with me. No matter the reason – I bear the consequences. This event in Huwara is a pogrom that was done by outlaws. We did not prepare for that amount of people and the way they arrived, to the extent and intensity of the violence they demonstrated and the organization they carried out. This is a bad incident that was not meant to happen, and I was meant to have prevented it. It is a shameful incident of outlaws who acted neither with the values I grew up with nor those of the state of Israel nor those of Judaism.

The use of the word pogrom by the IDF and the admittance of a severe failure to prevent it from happing was highly unusual and illustrated the seriousness of what had happened. Israeli journalists on the ground, as well Opposition Leader Yair Lapid and Labour leader Merav Michaeli also used the word pogrom to describe the attacks. None of the coalition lawmakers, however, would use neither terrorism nor pogrom to describe what happened. At most, they condemned it. One lawmaker outright supported the terror attacks. Zvika Fogel, lawmaker from Jewish Power party and chairman of the Knesset National Security Committee, said he looked 'favourably upon' the attacks in Huwara.

Fogel said:

> I want to restore security for the residents of the State of Israel. How do we do that? We stop using the word "proportionality." We stop with our objection to collective punishment (just) because it doesn't fly with all sorts of courts. We take the gloves off. Yesterday, a terrorist came from Huwara. A closed, burnt Huwara — that's what I want to see. That's the only way to achieve deterrence. After a murder like yesterday's, we need burning villages when the IDF doesn't act.[21]

Lapid and Michaeli immediately called for Fogel to be jailed for inciting to terror. A few days later the attorney general approved opening an investigation into Fogel and whether he incited to terror. At the same time, Smotrich doubled down on his initial show of support for a tweet that called on Huwara to be eradicated. When asked about why he had liked it, Smotrich replied: 'Because I think that Huwara needs to be wiped out, but the State of Israel needs to do it, most certainly not private citizens.'[22] The comment was immediately condemned by opposition lawmakers, most notably by Lapid who said Smotrich's comment was incitement to war crime. The U.S. also issued an unprecedented harsh statement condemning Smotrich, demanding that Netanyahu and other Israeli officials condemn it. State Department spokesperson Ned Price said:

> I want to be very clear about this. These comments were irresponsible. They were repugnant. They were disgusting. And just as we condemn Palestinian incitement to violence, we condemn these provocative remarks that also amounts to incitement to violence. We call on Prime Minister Netanyahu and other senior Israeli officials to publicly and clearly reject and disavow these comments, we condemn, as we have consistently terrorism and extremism, and all of its forms and we continue to urge that there'll be equal measures of accountability for extremist actions, regardless of the background of the perpetrators, or the victims. [23]

A few days later Smotrich walked back his comment, saying it had been a 'slip of the tongue' and that he made it in a 'storm of emotions.' The clarification was welcomed by Netanyahu who called Smotrich's comments about Huwara 'inappropriate.' It did little, however, to convince anyone that the far-right minister had in any way changed his mind about how to deal with Huwara. For those who had followed Smotrich for years, this was just a continuation of wildly racist and violent remarks made about Palestinians.

Michael Oren, former Israeli ambassador to the U.S. and later member of Knesset for Kulanu party, warned that about the damage this kind of rhetoric from far-right ministers could have on U.S.-Israel relations. 'If Smotrich and Ben-Gvir continue to run amok in the Judea and Samaria (West Bank) and support the burning of villages, it could lead to far more severe tensions (between Israel and the U.S.),' Oren said. As the debate about Huwara the IDF's failure to stop it raged, some 400 Israelis decided to drive to the Palestinian town to show support for the victims of the pogrom. But when the busses and cars carrying the demonstrators arrived at the road leading to the town, the IDF and Border Police blocked the road for them. This didn't stop the demonstrators, who decided to park their vehicles and continue by foot. A massive line of people started walking on the side of the road towards Huwara, chanting 'end the occupation' and waving Israeli flags. The unprecedented sight was welcomed by every Palestinian car that drove by, honking and cheering the Israeli protestors on. 'Well done' yelled one Palestinian man in Hebrew out the window, while others showed the peace sign with their fingers. The many settlers who drove by, however, were enraged by the sight of Israelis showing support for the Palestinians. Several of them slowed down on the road to harass the demonstrators, yelling 'terrorists' and 'traitors' at them. This continued until the final stretch of the road where the IDF had put up a roadblock, telling the demonstrators that they weren't allowed to continue. The argument was that they had suddenly declared the area a closed military zone, providing no proof to the Israelis who asked to see documentation. Meanwhile, settlers were allowed to drive through the checkpoint. The 400 Israelis began chanting 'where were you in Huwara' at the Israeli soldiers, as they attempted to bypass the blockade. This led to physical confrontations with soldiers pushing demonstrators to the ground, including the former speaker of the Knesset, Avraham Burg, who had joined the protest. Several shock grenades were thrown into the crowd as the soldiers kept pushing the demonstrators back. After a few hours, the 400 Israelis gave up, and started walking back, even more frustrated than when they arrived.

It was later documented that while the IDF was preventing Israelis from entering Huwara, a mob of settlers went on another rampage in a nearby village of Burin, throwing rocks at houses and destroying olive trees on private Palestinian land. Videos showed how Israeli soldiers were standing next to the soldiers, watching it all unfold. It illustrated just how powerful the settlers had become in the West Bank and how the pogrom carried out in Huwara on the IDF's watch wasn't just a one-off incident. In fact, numerous incidents of Israeli soldiers watching settlers attacking Palestinians had been documented by rights groups over the years. And with a finance minister, as well as other far-right lawmakers making violent remarks about Huwara, it was hardly surprising that they felt they finally had political as well as military protection to do as they wanted in the West Bank. Some of the hard-core setters who confronted the Israeli demonstrators outside Huwara even repeated Smotrich and Fogel's remarks, yelling 'let Huwara burn' and 'wipe out Huwara.' Dvir Kariv, former Shin Bet agent in the 'Jewish Division', had almost prophetically predicted exactly this scenario a few months before the pogrom in Huwara. Kariv said:

> Our biggest fear is that they (violent settlers) will feel that people like Smotrich and Ben-Gvir have their backs, and that they can do what they want. The only ones who can stop this are Smotrich and Ben-Gvir. If they tell them that if they will do those things (violent attacks against Palestinians), they will be arrested, then they (settlers) won't do it. If Smotrich and Ben-Gvir don't do this, then the settlers will continue (the violent attacks).

For some, the army's handling of Huwara was hardly surprising. Nadav Weiman had both taken part in protecting settlers who were doing illegal activities in the West Bank when he served as a sniper in the elite unit known as *Sayeret Nahal*. But it was later, when he joined the NGO 'Breaking The Silence' that he experienced settler violence on his own body. Weiman, who takes groups of people from Israel and abroad on educational trips in the West Bank, said he has been assaulted by several hard-core settlers, including Benzi Gopstein, who today roams the hallways of the Knesset due to his close connections to the Jewish Power party. Weiman said:

> The first time I really experienced settler violence from one of the "big guys" was Benzi Gopstein in 2014. We did a big tour to Hebron, like eight buses. He came and wanted to stop it. He pushed and pushed me while there were numerous police officers watching. But everybody is afraid of him. They tried to stop him, but he pushed them. If I had done what he did to them they would have arrested me and sprayed tear gas. When they tried to arrest him, he refused and started hugging an electricity pole. They eventually got him off. A few moments later, a female settler tried to stop us from entering the area. She ripped my shirt, threw water on me and slapped me in my face. I stood next to a police officer who told me "Nadav, move on. Stop with the provocations. In 2017 I helped B'Tselem with field research, filming the construction of a new settlement. Baruch Marzel and a couple of other well-known settlers came and started kicking us on our shins, to avoid it being filmed. Then they called the police, telling them we were infiltrating the settlement. And we got removed. In another incident, Ben-Gvir came and threw eggs on our bus during a tour. He also came with people from Lehava (far-right group) when I did a tour in Hebron an pushed me to the ground. But in Hebron, the key figure is Ofer Ohana. He is a paramedic and is known as the "father of the soldiers" in Hebron. He is the guy who attacked me the most times. He is the archetype of the settler who uses young soldiers for his political goals. He beat me up a couple of times. I was with German parliamentarians in Hebron when he called them Nazis. And while I filmed him, he came toward me and punched me through the phone. It was golden evidence. I pressed charged but the case was closed because of "lack of evidence." I told the police that I gave them the video and they said, "we didn't get any video." I gave the video to them again and I'm still waiting. It happened five years ago.

Following the pogrom in Huwara, the IDF came under intense criticism in the Israeli media and among former senior security officials. How could the IDF fail to deal with the mob of violent settlers, who had even announced their revenge march on social media? According to Yair Golan, who was deputy IDF chief of staff from 2014-2018, the failure didn't stem from some deep conspiracy, but from a systemic change the military had undergone under Netanyahu. Golan said:

> Until 2009, the settlers understood that there was a dispute in the Israeli society and the government about the destiny of the West Bank. For them it was a sign that we were all the time walking on a rocking ground. But after 2009, and especially after Netanyahu became more and more dependent on the far-right, they perceived their power as something much bigger than they had ever seen before. So, they became more aggressive, and the military, under the command of Netanyahu, tended to stand aside on the events (settler violence) and let the police deal with it. But the police in the West Bank is very weak. So, a direct (new) policy isn't necessarily articulated. It's a common understanding of people in prominent positions. And I think that's what happened. It was more like "we in the military understand what we should and shouldn't do." I confronted them brutally about this. The years between 2009-2015 were quiet, therefore (the new policy) was reasonable. There weren't so many incidents, so we didn't need to much military in the West Bank. So, let's leave the dirty job of dealing with the settlers to the police. Those kinds of periods are very dangerous for Israel and its policies in the West Bank. There is no public discussion now about what to do with the West Bank. It seems the reason for this is that there is no solution. It's really about a sort of self-imposed ignorance.

Two settlers suspected of taking part in the pogrom were later arrested by police and put in administrative detention, an order that was signed off by Defense Minister Yoav Gallant. Ben-Gvir, who had previously made a career as a lawyer representing Jews suspected of terror, raged against Gallant's decision. 'Precisely in the days when the heroics (Jewish residents) in Judea and Samaria (West Bank) are suffering from murderous terrorism, the defense minister chooses to use administrative detention orders against two Jews, one of them a minor, while he chooses a "containment" policy vis-à-vis the terrorists, and this is regrettable,' Ben-Gvir said.[24] This reaction showed exactly how Ben-Gvir hadn't forgotten his constituents, and that he was still fighting their cause, no longer as a lawyer but a powerful minister in Israel's security cabinet. Jewish Power was against administrative detention, but only for Jews. It didn't bother the party that over 1,000 Palestinians were held back in administrative detention at the same time. Months after the Jewish terror suspects had been arrested by the Shin Bet they had still not been charged. According to former Shin Agent Dvir Kariv, the 'hilltop youth' and Jewish extremists in general were particularly difficult to handle. 'They don't speak in jail. If they don't speak, you don't have any evidence,' Kariv said.

Palestinian terror attacks against Israelis also continued at the same pace, escalating with two separate attacks on Passover evening. A mother and her two daughters were killed in by two Hamas affiliated terrorists in the West Bank in the morning on 7 April while an Arab Israeli man rammed his car into a group of pedestrians on Tel Aviv's promenade later that evening, killing an Italian tourist. This came as intense clashes between Israeli and Palestinians on the Al Aqsa compound caused Hamas to fire rockets from both Gaza and Lebanon, the latter being a highly unusual incident. Rockets from Gaza had become an almost routine response by Hamas and Islamic Jihad whenever Israeli police beat Palestinians on the Al Aqsa compound, or if a particularly deadly army raid had taken place. But the border with Lebanon had been largely quiet since the war in 2006. The barrage of rockets fired in broad daylight from Lebanon proved that Hamas was testing Netanyahu's new government, which had thrown Israeli into historic turmoil. Other enemies of Israel, such as Hezbollah in Lebanon and Iran were beginning to predict that the crisis in Israel marked the beginning of the end of the country. Israel retaliated by hitting both Hamas and Hezbollah positions in Lebanon, as well as Gaza. The following day, rockets were fired from Syria as well, causing Israel to retaliate there. But it was the over 100 rockets fired from Gaza at southern Israel in early May which came in response to a member of Islamic Jihad dying from hunger strike in an Israeli prison that caused the deepest rift over security in Netanyahu's coalition.

Netanyahu decided, again, to respond in a measured way. Instead of assassinating Hamas and Islamic Jihad leaders, like his coalition partners had demanded in the months prior after similar rocket attacks, Netanyahu decided, along with Defense Minister Gallant and the IDF, to hit Hamas and Islamic Jihad's military positions. Orit Strock, lawmaker from Religious Zionism party, accused the government of 'continuing the policy of the previous government (Bennett-Lapid)' arguing that Gaza 'does not pay a price for Hamas' terror.'[25] Likud lawmaker Danny Danon also criticized the government for failing to deter Hamas and Islamic Jihad. Danon warned that bombing 'empty positions' was tantamount to inviting the next round of fighting. But it was Ben-Gvir who reacted strongest to the 'feeble' response.

The first four months of the government had been a disaster for Ben-Gvir's Jewish Power party when it came to delivering on its core promises, namely 'restoring' security in Israel. Israelis living near the Gaza border had been bombarded with rockets on numerous occasions on their watch, only to see Israel responding by attacking military positions in Gaza. Ben-Gvir, who was a member of the security cabinet, was particularly furious that he hadn't been consulted about the response. After hearing how residents in the south fumed at the government, Jewish Power announced it wouldn't attend the upcoming votes at the Knesset and instead conduct a 'special' faction meeting in the city of Sderot, right next to the Gaza border. Likud responded to move by saying that Netanyahu, Gallant, the IDF and security agencies are the ones who handle the 'sensitive and complex security incidents that Israel is dealing with. The prime minister is the one who decides who is a relevant participant in the discussions. If this is unacceptable to Minister Ben Gvir he does not have to remain in the government.' Ben-Gvir quickly fired back, saying that if Netanyahu didn't want Jewish Home in the coalition he could go ahead and fire them. 'If you don't want a real right-wing government, you are welcome to send us home,' Ben-Gvir said.[26]

A week later, Netanyahu and Gallant gave the approval for the IDF to launch 'Operation Shield and Arrow' against Islamic Jihad in Gaza. Whether the heavy pressure from his militant coalition members and the growing calls by citizens in southern Israel to crack down on Islamic Jihad influenced Netanyahu remains unknown to the public. But on that Tuesday morning on 8 May, some 40 Israeli fighter jets and helicopters embarked on a mission to assassinate three senior Islamic Jihad commanders, each responsible for different kinds of terror activities against Israelis. Within minutes, all three had been killed in airstrikes. At least 10 civilians were also killed in the strikes, including women and children. Knowing that Islamic Jihad would almost certainly respond, the IDF instructed residents near the Gaza border to either stay near bomb shelters or to leave the area altogether if possible. Thousands of Israelis left their homes, while roads and schools closed. It took over 24 hours for Islamic Jihad to respond. On Wednesday, at 1:30, a barrage of rockets was fired at southern Israel, followed by rockets at central Israel, including Tel Aviv. Netanyahu said he had decided to resume targeted killings of Islamic

Jihad leaders in Gaza in response to the continuous attacks launched at Israel. While both his coalition partners as well the opposition gave him the full support for the surprise attack, the fighting continued for a total of five days, sending over 1400 rockets at Israel, killing an 80-year-old Israeli woman and a Palestinian worker from Gaza. Israel continued to assassinate Islamic Jihad commanders, eliminating six high ranking members and another 15 militants. A total of 33 Palestinians were killed. IDF struck over 700 targets belonging to Islamic Jihad, including rocket launchers and weapon manufacturing facilities. As usual, Egypt mediated the ceasefire between the two parties, after condemning Israel for launching the campaign. The question of legality, however, was almost completely removed from the debate inside Israel. There was a broad consensus that Israel was absolutely justified in launching the campaign, despite knowing the full risks of civilian casualties. The 'collateral damage' was considered fair, since Islamic Jihad was hiding among civilians. But the Israeli media, whose role was to hold the government and IDF responsible for its actions, barely mentioned the killing of civilians, let alone criticize it. Why was this campaign so important? What did it achieve? A similar campaign against Islamic Jihad was launched by Yair Lapid just eight months earlier, killings dozens of the terror group's commanders. And before that, Israel fought in two different conflicts against Hamas in 2021 and Islamic Jihad in 2019. In other words, a total of four military campaigns in Gaza in four years.

While Hamas stayed out of the two Gaza conflicts in 2022 and 2023, the targeted killings seemed to rile Islamic Jihad up even more. Hamas had also not stopped firing rockets after the 2021 war. It might have stayed out of the conflicts with Islamic Jihad, but it fired numerous rockets at Israel on different occasions, including from Lebanon for the first time in many years. The broad support Netanyahu enjoyed for launching the campaign illustrated exactly how inherently right-wing most Israelis were when it came to justifying attacks in Gaza. Others, including Smotrich and his party colleague Orit Strock, echoed a prediction made by National Security Council Director Tzachi Hanegbi who in 2020 warned that Israel would eventually have to invade and re-occupy Gaza. It didn't' take long after the Gaza conflict before violence in the West Bank would spiral out of control again.

The worldwide attention the Huwara pogrom received did not deter violent settlers from committing more attacks against in the following weeks and months. Quite the contrary. In late June, two Hamas members killed four Israelis at a restaurant and a gas station near the settlement of

Eli in the West Bank. In response, settlers embarked on yet another revenge rampage that would last five days. On 20 June, a few hours after the attack, dozens of settlers set fire to cars, fields and private property in several Palestinian villages near Nablus. Instead of calming down the settlers seeking revenge, Netanyahu and Smotrich announced an immediate advancement of planning for 1,000 settlement units in Eli, as a response to the attack. Meanwhile, Likud lawmaker Tali Gotliv called on the government to impose collective punishment on Palestinians (illegal under international law) while Ben-Gvir demanded the government 'return to targeted assassinations from the air, to bring down buildings, to erect roadblocks, to expel terrorists, and to finish passing the death penalty for terrorists' law.'[27] That same night, hundreds of settlers marched to the illegal and abandoned outpost of Evyatar. Settler leaders as well as far-right lawmaker Zvi Sukkot from Religious Zionism joined the march, demanding to re-establish an immediate physical presence at the illegal outpost. Despite it being a closed military zone where Israeli citizens were prohibited from visiting, the military refrained from stopping the settlers. The following day, Ben-Gvir arrived at the outpost where he encouraged settlers to 'run for the hilltops and settle them. We are behind you.'[28] The message couldn't be clearer; settlers now had a minister in the security cabinet instructing them to illegally grab Palestinian owned land, receiving full political backing.

Once again, Netanyahu had to issue a statement, calling Ben-Gvir's words 'unacceptable.' In the meantime, some 200 settlers continued their revenge in broad daylight, setting fire to over 60 cars and 30 homes ablaze in the Palestinian town of Turmus Ayya. For Dvir Kariv, the explanation was clear as to why Jews would continue to commit terror attacks. 'To prevent terror, you need to hit the motivation (making sure) they won't get any backing in their community for doing this.' The vague reactions by the most far-right lawmakers, and to some extent the approval of 'burning down Huwara' was exactly the kind of backing that motivated the radicals. For five consecutive days, settlers, some of whom were armed, attacked Palestinian towns. A mosque was attacked, and Qurans destroyed by masked settlers in the town of Urif. Once again, the IDF admitted that it failed to prevent the dozens of attacks. Human Rights Group Yesh Din reported that, similar to the pogrom in Huwara, Israeli soldiers were present at one of the scenes were settlers ran amok. The army issued another extremely critical statement as the attacks continued to terrorize Palestinians. Falling short of using the term pogrom to describe the attacks, as it did in Huwara, the IDF, Shin Bet and Police chiefs issued a joint statement, making it perfectly clear the seriousness of the situation. 'In recent days, violent attacks have been carried out by Israelis in Judea and Samaria against innocent Palestinians. These attacks contradict every moral and Jewish value; they constitute, in every way, nationalist terrorism, and we are obliged to fight them,' the statement read. Meanwhile, Netanyahu made do with another vague worded statement, saying that his government wouldn't allow 'disturbances' in the West Bank.

The complete inconsistency between the army and prime minister's description of the attacks revealed how deep the problem had become. But to make matters even worse, far-right ministers and coalition lawmakers began attacking the IDF, Shin Bet and Police for referring to the widespread settler attacks as 'terror.' Smotrich, who ironically enough was a minister in the defense ministry, claimed that the 'attempt to create an equivalency between murderous Arab terror and (Israeli) civilian counteractions, however serious they may be, is morally wrong and dangerous on a practical level.' Likud lawmaker, Danny Danon, also criticized the security establishment, saying 'serious violence of a handful of settlers does not come close to the murderous Palestinian terrorism.' But the harshest attack against the security echelon came from National Missions Minister, Orit Strock, from the Religious Zionism party. Strock, who for decades had been known for her extreme positions, once again made headlines when she compared the IDF to Wagner Group, the notorious Russian paramilitary organisation. 'They (IDF, Shin Bet, Police) issued a message about Jewish nationalist terrorism. Who do you think you are? The Wagner Group? Who are you to issue such a message under the government's nose? Are they going to preach to us?,' Strock said.[29]

It had become abundantly clear at this point that the army was no longer in control of settler violence in the West Bank, nor should it dare criticize it. The far-right ministers considered the army nothing more than a tool in their hands that should be unleashed against Palestinians, while closing its eyes to bloodthirsty Jewish extremists looking to take over the West Bank. The Jewish terror attacks in Huwara and later across the northern and central West Bank in June, marked the first time that large-scale 'price tag' attacks were committed with approval from leading government ministers. And despite its verbal condemnation of the Jewish terror attacks, the IDF proved incompetent at best, and complicit at worst. The changes in the IDF that began years earlier, as described by former Deputy IDF Chief Yair Golan, had now reached a point where the ideology of the settlement enterprise had paralyzed the commanding structure. Few Jewish terrorist were arrested after widespread attacks, which only led to vicious attacks by far-right lawmakers and ministers against the IDF for daring to lay their hands on settlers. For Netanyahu, arguably one of the most experienced and knowledgeable people on Israel's security, political survival simply trumped his willingness to put a stop to the 'price tag' attacks.

Notes

1   Jeremy Sharon, 'Justice minister unveils plan to shackle the High Court, overhaul Israel's judiciary', Times of Israel, 4 January 2023.

2   TOI Staff, 'Netanyahu trial boosted backing for judicial overhaul push, justice minister says', *Times of Israel*, 16 January 2023.

3   Jeremy Sharon, 'In fiery speech, Hayut says judicial shakeup plan "fatal blow to Israeli democracy"', *Times of Israel*, 16 January 2023.

4   Jerusalem Post staff, Mandelblit: Judicial reform is meant to stop Netanyahu's trial', *Jerusalem Post*, 10 February 2023.

5   TOI Staff, 'Yair Netanyahu compares anti-overhaul protesters to Nazi Brownshirts', *Times of Israel*, 18 March, 2023.

6   Ha'aretz, 'Netanyahu's Son Accuses Shin Bet of 'Coup' Against Prime Minister', *Ha'aretz*, 20 february 2023.

7   TOI Staff, 'Far-right minister slams Blinken: Netanyahu doesn't need "lesson in democracy"', *Times of Israel*, 31 January 2023.

8   Ha'aretz, '"Mind Your Own Business": Israeli Diaspora Minister Rebuffs U.S. Ambassador's Rare Comments on Judicial Overhaul', *Ha'aretz*, 19 February 2023.

9   Staff and agencies, 'Israel's Netanyahu rejects Biden's call to 'walk away' from judicial overhaul', *The Guardian*, 29 March 2023.

10 Sam Sokol, 'British Legal Experts Pan Coalition's Comparison of Judicial Coup to "Westminster System"', *Ha'aretz*, 20 February 2023.

11 Alan Dershowitz, 'Dershowitz: Bibi left out the most important part', *The Jerusalem Post*, 23 March 2023.

12 Ha'aretz Weekly, 'Bibi Was Right Before. He's Wrong Now': Why Alan Dershowitz Fears Israel's Judicial Overhaul', *Ha'aretz*, 26 January 2023.

13 Philissa Cramer, '2 Israeli tech firms to pull funds out of the country, citing risk posed by Netanyahu government', *The Jewish Telegraphic Agency*, 26 January 2023.

14 Steven Scheer, 'Analysis: Israel's tech sector reels from SVB collapse, proposed judicial reform', *Reuters*, 3 April 2023.

15 Richard Quest, 'Bank of Israel governor concerned about judicial reform', *CNN*, 15 March 2023.

16 Oren Dori, 'Foreign Minister wants to curb Bank of Israel independence', *Globes*, 21 February 2023.

17　Sharon Wrobel, 'Bank of Israel hikes rate to 4.5%, warns judicial shakeup could badly harm economy', *Times of Israel*, 3 April 2023.

18　Globes correspondent, 'Protests against judicial reform continue despite security situation', *Globes*, 9 April 2023.

19　Tia Goldenberg, 'Netanyahu urges military chief to contain reservist protest', *Associated Press*, 19 March 2023.

20　TOI Staff, '"Go to hell," Likud minister tells IDF reservists protesting judicial overhaul', *Times of Israel*, 7 March 2023.

21　Michael Bachner, '"We need burning villages": Coalition lawmaker backs unprecedented settler rampage', *Times of Israel*, 27 February 2023.

22　Tohav Lazaroff, 'US: Smotrich's comment about wiping out Huwara is disgusting', *Jerusalem Post*, 1 March 2023.

23　Ben Samuels, 'U.S. Condemns Smotrich's "Repugnant, Disgusting" Call for Israel to Wipe Out Palestinian Village', *Ha'aretz*, 1 March 2023.

24　Hagar Shezaf, 'Court Shortens Detention Without Trial for Israeli Settler Involved in Hawara Rampage', *Ha'aretz*, 6 March 2023.

25　Jotam Confino, 'Shaky Gaza ceasefire kicks in after Israeli airstrikes, 104 rockets fired in 24 hours', *Jewish News*, 3 May 2023.

26　Jeremy Sharon, 'Likud: If Ben Gvir doesn't like how Netanyahu runs government, he can leave', *Times of Israel*, 3 May 2023.

27　Jotam Confino, 'Settlers embark on another West Bank rampage in response to deadly terror attack', *Jewish News*, 21 June 2023.

28　TOI Staff, 'Contradicting Ben Gvir, Netanyahu says illegal West Bank land grabs 'unacceptable', *Times of Israel*, 25 June 2023.

29　Jotam Confino, '"Terrorism": IDF, Shin Bet condemn revenge rampage in West Bank', *Jewish News*, 26 June 2023.

12

Civil war

'Pause'

The pressure on Netanyahu peaked when Defense Minister Gallant became the first government minister to publicly call for a halt to the judicial reforms until after the high holidays in April. Gallant, who had been informed by the defense echelon about the looming security consequences caused by the deep unrest in Israel, held a televised speech to the nation in which he relayed those exact concerns. 'The growing rift in our society is penetrating the IDF and security agencies. This poses a clear, immediate, and tangible threat to the security of the state. I will not lend my hand to this,' Gallant said on 25 March while Netanyahu was on a state visit to London.

The second most powerful man in Israel took a huge gamble going against Netanyahu's official line, which was to keep advancing the reforms. Gallant paved the way for other Likud officials from the old guard who weren't supportive of the radical reforms. Yuli Edelstein and David Bitan, who were among the most experienced and longest serving Likud members, backed Gallant and called for a broad consensus to be reached. But the radicals in Likud, who at this point outnumbered the old guard who still believed in some of the core elements of the party's ideology, raged against Gallant. 'The State of Israel is at a historic crossroads between democracy and dictatorship, and its defense minister chose dictatorship,' said Communication Minister Shlomo Karhi. Likud lawmaker Tally Gotliv accused Gallant of 'weakness and subservience' while coalition whip Ofir Katz of Likud said that whoever voted against the reforms 'has ended his career in the Likud.'[1]

Few, however, predicted just how furious Gallant would make his boss. 24 hours after calling on the reforms to be halted, Netanyahu's office issued a short statement, saying the prime minister had decided to fire the defense minister (Netanyahu would re-instate Gallant just two weeks later). The statement sent shockwaves through Israel. For the first time in Israel's history, a defense minister had been fired for literally doing his job; relaying the facts given to him by his subordinates in the defense echelon.

Netanyahu's decision sparked immediate mass protests in Tel Aviv late at night, with thousands taking to the streets and blocking Ayalon Highway until about four in the morning. A huge bonfire was lit in the middle of the highway, with thousands of Israelis chanting anti-government slogans. It was the straw that broke the camel's back. The following day, mass protests took place across Israel, and *Histadruth,* the General Organization of Workers in Israel, announced a general strike. Ben-Gurion airport staff also went on strike, causing an immediate halt to all flights. Kindergarten, shops and malls threatened to do the same. For the first time since Justice Minister Levin presented the government's reforms, the entire country had come to a standstill.

Netanyahu had gambled with one thing that seemed to unite most Israelis: security. Not having a defense minister was unimaginable for a country that was on constant high alert, fighting enemies in several areas at the same time. That same evening, on 26 March, Netanyahu held a speech to the nation in which he succumbed to the pressure and begrudgingly announced a halt to the judicial reforms. The media focused on the parts of Netanyahu's speech that revolved around the pause and the 'need for dialogue' between the government and the opposition. But he also repeated his claim that 'extremists' in the protest movement were trying to tear the nation apart and that a reform to 'restore the balance' in the judicial system would be passed, one way or another. While some hailed it as a victory, others saw it as a clever smokescreen by Netanyahu who was trying to deflate the protest movement and buying time. President Isaac Herzog, who himself had criticized the reforms harshly and warned about the risk of a civil war, was now being catapulted into an unprecedented mediator role in one of the country's biggest crises ever.

In the coming months, Herzog would conduct marathon talks between representatives from the government and some opposition parties. Yesh Atid, National Unity Party, and the three Arab parties, United Arab List and *Hadash-Ta'al,* engaged in the initial talks while Netanyahu's old archrival, Avigdor Lieberman, refused to participate. His *Yisrael Beitenu* party had no doubt that it was all a scheme, cleverly orchestrated by Netanyahu. As the negotiations began the protests continued, albeit not several times a week and not as intensely as in the months prior to the pause of the reforms. It did, however, become clear the disagreements between the government and opposition were too big for a broad compromise to be reached.

The Arab parties and Labour eventually left the negotiations, leaving just *Yesh Atid* and National Unity party at the table. At the same time, the most radical and far-right elements of the government were furious with Netanyahu for giving in to the protest movement's pressure, promising their voters that the reforms would eventually pass, with or without a consensus. Meanwhile, the far-right was organizing a huge rally in support of the government to take place in Jerusalem on 27 April. An estimated 150,000 people showed up at the rally, raging against the 'left-wing' and calling on the government to pass the judicial reforms. Levin, Smotrich, Ben-Gvir, and Rhotman all spoke at the event, repeating their claims that they had won the election fair and square and therefore had every right to radically alter the judicial system, with or without the opposition's support. Levin once again attacked the Supreme Court in a vicious and populist way, accusing it of 'not protecting (the public) from rapists and releasing them.'[2] His comments drew immediate criticism from the opposition, accusing Levin of 'false' and 'inflammatory' remarks aimed at further deepening the rift in Israel while undermining the negotiations at the President's Residence in Jerusalem.

As usual, Netanyahu was silent. His criticism continued to be aimed at the 'extremist' protest movement, and what he considered unhinged incitement against him. In the four months of protests there had indeed been several incidents of incitement against Netanyahu, with some protestors warning that he would suffer the same fate as Romanian dictator Nicolae Ceausescu, who was executed by a firing squad after his reign. A similar outrageous statement was made, but this time from a Likud lawmaker against Ehud Barak, after the former prime minister called on the protest movement to intensity the protests and move into a civil uprising and civil disobedience to put an end to the government's judicial reforms. Likud lawmaker, Nissim Vaturi, referred to Barak as 'human waste' after his call for civil disobedience, saying 'in other countries, such a person would be up for hanging, but Israel is a democratic country so a prison term of at least 20 years.'[3] The Likud party itself had also filed a complaint with police over Barak's comments. Minister of Heritage, Amichai Eliyahu, from the Jewish Power party, went as far as claiming that Barak's call for civil disobedience was 'worse' than former Israeli President Moshe Katsav's rape of a woman, a crime he was convicted of.[4] Likud lawmaker Boaz Bismuth, the former editor-in-chief of pro-Netanyahu *Israel Hayom* newspaper, made a ludicrous claim that Barak was more dangerous than Hezbollah's leader, Hassan Nasrallah. The difference between a random civilian protester inciting against Netanyahu and a government minister as well as lawmakers from a ruling party inciting against Barak of course need no further explanation. But perhaps the most ironic part of the government's 'outrage' over Barak's call for civil disobedience stemmed from the fact that Menachem Begin, the founding father of Likud, had done the exact same.

In 1952, Begin held a fiery speech at a mass demonstration in Jerusalem in which he called for civil disobedience, including tax evasion, in response to the Reparations Agreement between Israel and West Germany. In fact, he implied that the government, led by Ben-Gurion, should be violently overthrown. 'When you fired at me with cannon, I gave the order; "No! (don't return fire). Today I will give the order, "Yes!"', Begin raged from a balcony in Zion Square, referring to Ben-Gurion's order for Israeli soldiers to open fire at the Altalena ship on the shores of Tel Aviv, which was carrying weapons for Begin's *Irgun* organization. After Begin's speech, thousands of demonstrators marched towards the Knesset, ending in violent riots and mass arrests. As a result, Begin was barred from Knesset for several months for his role in inciting the riots. Astonishingly, Likud of 2023, wanted to jail a former prime minister for a fraction of what their party's own founder had done 70 years earlier. One can only imagine if Barak had held a similar speech in Jerusalem, calling for a violent overthrow of Netanyahu's government resulting in a march on the Knesset.

A historian at heart and extremely well read, Netanyahu was undoubtedly familiar with this infamous incident in Israeli history. It's hard to say whether Nissim Vaturi would have liked to see Begin hanged alongside Barak, or if he (once again) resorted to cheap populism. 27 years after Yitzhak Rabin was labeled a traitor by the right-wing camp, led by Netanyahu, similar accusations were now made against him. 'Bibi, the traitor' would occasionally be chanted by demonstrators. At one incident, 'Bibi is a traitor' was spraypainted on the Ayalon highway. The incitement, however, did not come close to the hatred and threats aimed at Rabin, who was ultimately assassinated by a right-wing extremist. A few signs at demonstrations likened Netanyahu's rule to that of Nazi Germany. But large crowds didn't chant 'death to Netanyahu' or depict him in an SS uniform, like the extreme right-wingers did with Rabin. As for the physical and verbal assaults, it was almost exclusively committed by right-wingers against protestors across Israel. Several were pepper sprayed, while others pushed and kicked. Some used their cars to aggressively push through demonstrations while cursing the protestors. TV journalists were also harassed verbally, and some attacked physically by right-wingers while doing their job in the field. Channel 13, one of the mainstream TV networks Netanyahu frequently compared to the Arabic TV channel Al Jazeera and which he labelled 'propaganda', was attacked at least twice in the field while doing their job. In late March, a Channel 13 reporter was hospitalized with a broken rib after being assaulted by members of the racist and violent far-right *La Familia* group in Jerusalem. Members of the group also went on a rampage in Jerusalem following a protest, beating and harassing random Arab citizens. In May, a Channel 13 reporter was verbally harassed, and pepper sprayed by a right-wing extremist on the promenade in Tel Aviv. 'Worse than Al-Jazeera' the man said, repeating Netanyahu, and in particular his son Yair as well as other right-wing lawmakers' absurd claim that the channel was an anti-Israel media on par with Al-Jazeera.

Despite a sharp rise in attacks against journalists by right-wing extremists, Justice Minister Levin fanned the flames in late June when he launched a verbal attack against Channel 12 and 13 from the Knesset podium, accusing their journalists of being 'propagandists who make propaganda, which has nothing to do with journalistic work.' Levin also claimed that the media atmosphere in Israel was 'worse than what exists in totalitarian countries.'[5] His attack on Israeli media and journalists came in response to a bill put forward by *Yesh Atid* lawmaker Idan Roll, which would harshen punishment for assaulting journalists. The seriousness of Levin's false claims against journalists, and his refusal to back Roll's bill illustrated how extreme the right-wing had become in their hatred toward Israel's media establishment. The rhetoric was of course taken right out of Netanyahu's old playbook and wasn't new or surprising. But the context was very serious; signaling a carte blanche to further assaults on 'propagandist' who were out to topple a democratically elected government. Despite the existence of at least two blatantly pro-Netanyahu media (*Israel HaYom* and Channel 14, formerly Channel 20), the right-wing, and in particular Likud, loathed the Israeli media landscape. Communication Minister Shlomo Karhi went as far as making it his personal goal to close KAN Public Broadcaster, the TV funded radio and TV channel, which had also been critical of Netanyahu's governments.

Protests 2

Nearly three months after Netanyahu announced a halt to the judicial reforms and the beginning of negotiations between the government and opposition, a political drama erupted in the Knesset that would re-ignite the immense chaos. On 14 June, lawmakers voted on who would be the two new Knesset representatives on the powerful Judicial Appointments Committee. The structure of the committee, which appoints Supreme Court judges, was a key area of the judicial system that the government wanted to radically change by making sure its representatives made up a majority. In other words, the government wanted to have full control with appointing Supreme Court judges. But since the reforms had been halted, the structure continued to function in its original form. The vote was therefore seen as a crucial test to Netanyahu's government.

It quickly became clear that Netanyahu had lost control over parts of his government. His original plan was to have all coalition candidates withdraw from the election and thereby postpone the vote. However, Likud lawmaker Tali Gotliv refused to withdraw her candidacy, despite her slim chances of being elected. With the opposition putting forward one candidate, *Yesh Atid* lawmaker Karine Elharar, and Gotliv also announcing she would run, the vote could go ahead. Gotliv's rebellion was bad news for Netanyahu and the coalition, which knew that chances of her being elected to the committee were slim. But even worse, several lawmakers from the coalition broke ranks and ended up voting in favour of Elharar, securing the opposition a crucial seat at the powerful table. Gotliv, on the other hand, suffered an embarrassing loss, receiving only 15 votes. But with one seat still vacant, another vote would have to be held within a month before the committee could convene and begin its task of appointing judges. This caused both *Yesh Atid* and the National Unity Party to announce an immediate suspension of negotiations with the government at the President's residence.

The breakdown of negotiations gave Netanyahu and his coalition an excuse to relaunch the judicial reforms. It confirmed what they had been saying for months: the opposition wasn't interested in reaching any consensus. For Gantz and Lapid, the coalition's failure to agree on a candidate for the committee was another deliberate attempt to stall the process of appointing judges. A few days later, Netanyahu announced that the coalition would advance the reforms again. Simcha Rhotman, the lawmaker from Religious Zionism who was often referred to as one of the architects of the judicial overhaul, began preparing one of the laws in the reforms known as the 'reasonableness bill.' The goal of the bill was to block the Supreme Court from striking down government decisions and appointments of ministers which it deemed 'unreasonable.' This specific clause, which gave the Supreme Court great powers and judicial oversight over the government, had been used in January against Netanyahu's appointment of Shas party leader Arieh Dery as Health and Interior Minister. A year earlier, Dery was once again convicted of tax evasion, but took a plea deal with the court in which he promised to retire from public life. This, along with his long history of criminal offenses, made his appointment as minister in Netanyahu's government 'unreasonable in the extreme', according to the court. The verdict from Supreme Court President Esther Hayut couldn't have been clearer. Hayut said:

> This is a person who has been convicted three times of offenses throughout his life, and he violated his duty to serve the public loyally and lawfully while serving in senior public positions…Having Dery in charge of two of the most important ministries in the government damages the image and reputation of the country's legal system and contradicts principles of ethical conduct and legality. [6]

As expected, the entire coalition raged against the court following the dismissal of Dery, using it as ammunition and justification for the need for a judicial overhaul. But for the opposition, and for most Israelis, the government's goal to abolish the reasonableness clause was another clear sign that a corrupt regime was about to change the entire structure of the judicial system out of personal interests. The 'reasonableness bill' became known as the 'Dery bill', as it was widely seen as law tailored personally to Arieh Dery. But it was also a way to remove the court's judicial oversight of the government. As Rhotman prepared the bill, another incident helped kickstart mass demonstrations across the country.

On 5 July, Tel Aviv Police Chief Ami Eshed announced his resignation, giving an unprecedented speech in which he claimed that he had paid a personal price for his decision to avert a civil war. Referring to National Security Minister Itamar Ben-Gvir who had demanded repeatedly that police crack down harder on demonstrators, Eshed said:

> I sinned by not being able to meet the expectations of the ministerial level, which included violating the rules, protocols, organizational structure and culture in decision-making and in operational judgment. We could have cleared (Tel Aviv's Ayalon Highway) in minutes at the cost of breaking heads and crushing bones. … We could have filled the emergency room in Ichilov (Hospital) at the end of every demonstration. I insisted time and time again during the protest that the Tel Aviv District under my command would prove that it can be done differently. It is possible and necessary to allow protest while also setting clear boundaries for it, in accordance with the law. Regrettably, for the first time in three decades of service I encountered the illusory reality in which achieving peace and order is not a required achievement, but exactly the opposite. [7]

The jaw dropping speech confirmed what demonstrators and opposition lawmakers had said for months about Ben-Gvir pressuring police to be violent. A few days later, Attorney General Gali Baharav-Miara and other senior officials in the Justice Ministry were summoned to a highly unusual cabinet meeting on law enforcement's handling of the mass demonstrations across Israel. The meeting, from which audio recording were later leaked to the Israeli media, will surely go down as one of the most outrageous in Israel's history. The most aggressive ministers in the cabinet, such as Ben-Gvir, Transportation Minister Miri Regev, Justice Minister Yariv Levin, and Public Diplomacy Minister Galit Distel Atbaryan, viciously attacked Baharav-Miara, accusing her of 'selective enforcement.' Several went as far as calling on Baharav-Miara to be fired. Likud minister, David Amsalem, was even more aggressive and condescending in his rhetoric, calling Baharav-Miara the most 'dangerous person in Israel in a speech in Knesset not long after. 'Get her out, and suddenly everybody who breaks the law will be punished, and we'll become a normal country,' he claimed.[8] The attorney general on her part argued, rightfully so, that it was not her job to pressure law enforcement to be more aggressive with demonstrators or to fill quotas for arrests or indictments of protestors. The mere fact the cabinet held a meeting about why demonstrations against the government weren't suppressed more, was unprecedented and outrageous. The calling for the attorney general's firing just added to the absurdity. Not surprisingly, the combination of the government's advancement of the 'reasonableness bill', Eshed's speech and ministers demanding the attorney general crack down on protestors only breathed new life into the demonstrations.

On 11 July, another 'Day of Disruption' rocked Israel, with hundreds of thousands taking to the streets again. Several highways were blocked by demonstrators, while thousands protested at Ben-Gurion airport. Over 70 people were arrested that day, and numerous incidents of police violence were documented. Despite a clearly more aggressive approach by the police against protestors following Eshed's resignation, Ben-Gvir demanded an explanation from the police's central district commander as to why right-wing and left-wing protesters were treated differently. He thereby defied a Supreme Court ruling from March which forbade him from interfering with police conduct on an operation level. But the most surprising, and biggest embarrassment for the government, came when the White House issued an extremely rare (if not unprecedented) statement about the demonstrations, calling on Israeli authorities to 'protect and respect the right of peaceful assembly.' The wording of the statement was chillingly similar to those issued by the Biden administration about the hijab protests in Iran, where authorities killed and jailed protestors. In the past it would have been unthinkable for the White House to issue such a statement about internal demonstrations in Israel. But the U.S.-Israel relationship had been severely damaged during the new Netanyahu government's first six months.

Netanyahu did everything he could to constantly stress that the relationship between the two allies was as strong as ever, despite numerous diplomatic fallouts. Biden, who is widely considered the most pro-Israel U.S. President ever, finally took his gloves off and removed any doubt about the seriousness of the crisis between Washington and Jerusalem when he said that Netanyahu's government had some of 'the most extreme' ministers he could remember from his decades in politics.[9] Notwithstanding the deteriorating relationship with Israel's most important ally, the Netanyahu government continued to advance the 'reasonableness bill.' Understanding that the bill was likely going to be passed in its most extreme form, with no consensus reached with the opposition, demonstrations grew bigger and more frequent. The week before the bill was set to be voted on, hundreds of demonstrators began marching in the blistering heatwave from Tel Aviv to Jerusalem. After five days, the march had grown to some 30,000 people walking to Jerusalem to hold a rally in front of Knesset, which drew an estimated 60,000 people. The same evening, a pro-reform rally was held in Tel Aviv by right-wing activists, also with roughly 60,000 people showing up.

Meanwhile, Netanyahu was hospitalized again, for the second time in one week, this time because of heart complications. He was rushed to hospital late Saturday night and had a pacemaker installed. With uncertainty about Netanyahu's health, Justice Minister Yariv Levin became acting prime minister. The drama could not be overstated. 48 hours before one of the most important votes in Knesset's history, the prime minister was hospitalized, while chaos erupted on the streets. But the most serious escalation was undoubtedly the announcement by over 10,000 Israeli soldiers in the IDF reserve who said they would stop showing up for duty if the law passed. The IDF chief expressed great concern over damage this would do to the IDF, pleading with the soldiers to reconsider. The refusal to serve was, however, met with disgust and loathing by ministers. Transportation Minister Miri Regev suggested that those refusing to serve should be jailed. This absurd claim despite half her coalition partners never serving a day in the army, being exempted as part of a status quo agreement for the ultra-orthodox.

On Monday 24 July, Knesset was scheduled to vote on the law a second and third time. Thousands of demonstrators gathered outside Knesset in the early morning hours, with hundreds blocking the roads leading to parliament. Police used water cannons to clear the roads and had to forcibly remove those who were lying on the ground. As the debate began inside Knesset, the chaos and clashes outside escalated. Netanyahu was released from hospital and drove straight to Knesset to take charge of the situation. All morning, President Herzog held marathon talks with the government and opposition in an attempt to reach a consensus on the bill. The chaos and uncertainty about the bill was evident inside the Knesset, where two senior Likud lawmakers admitted they truly didn't know if it was going to pass or not. Meanwhile the IDF chief, Herzl Halevi, was trying to get a meeting with Netanyahu before the vote, to give him a clear picture of the security situation in light of the mass refusal to serve. But Netanyahu, against all common sense, refused to meet Halevi, knowing full well what dire situation would be presented to him. As the vote began, a consensus still had not been reached. Last ditch attempts by Defense Minister Gallant were pointless. Netanyahu had made up his mind. He listened to the extremist camp of Levin and Ben-Gvir who refused to compromise whatsoever on the bill.

As the second vote passed, the entire opposition walked out of Knesset, boycotting the third and final vote. At 3:40 PM, the 'reasonableness bill' passed with 64 votes for and 0 against. The government's first judicial reform aimed at weakening the Supreme Court had passed, sparking an immediate outcry in the media, among opposition leaders and all sectors of Israeli society that had come out against it in the past six months. Former Mossad chief Tamir Pardo accused Netanyahu of knowingly destroying the country. Lapid and Gantz raged at Netanyahu for surrendering to extremists. As tensions spilled over outside Knesset, and with mass protests erupting in Tel Aviv and Haifa at the same time, Levin and others were seen smiling and taking a selfie inside Knesset, celebrating their 'win.' Levin hailed the passing of the law, saying the government had 'taken the first step in a historic process to correct the judicial system,' while Lapid said Netanyahu had become a 'puppet on the strings of extremists and messianists. This is a sad day, a day of our home's destruction, of needless hatred, and look at the coalition celebrating.'[10] As anger boiled over on the streets of Tel Aviv, and police using more force than ever against demonstrators, Netanyahu held yet another speech to the nation, calling on the opposition to begin negotiations over the remaining reforms. But the damage was done. The effects of the passing of the reform were felt immediately. Israel's Medical Association, representing 95% of all doctors, announced a 24-hour strike planed for the following day. The Credit rating agency Moody's Investors Service along with US investment bank, JP Morgan, issued clear warnings about the negative consequences to Israel's economy. And the crisis in the IDF only worsened with each day passing. 24 July 2023 would go down in history as the day Israel's democracy changed forever, putting it on a dangerous path toward authoritarianism. Netanyahu ignored warning signs about the dangers to Israel's economy, security, social cohesion, democracy, and relationship with allies and instead caved to extremist and far-right coalition partners to stay in power.

Notes

1   Emanuel Fabian and Alexander Fulbright, 'Gallant calls to pause judicial overhaul, citing "tangible danger" to state security', *Times of Israel*, 25 March 2023.

2   Ha'aretz, 'Israeli Opposition Leaders Slam Justice Minister's 'Court Protects Rapists' Comment', *Ha'aretz*, 28 April 2023.

3   TOI Staff, 'Likud MK: Barak would be hanged 'in other countries' for civil disobedience calls', *Times of Israel*, 11 June 2023.

4   TOI Staff, 'Minister: Barak's call for civil disobedience 'worse' than ex-president Katsav's rape', *Times of Israel*, 13 June 2023.

5   TOI Staff, 'Lashing "propagandists," justice minister refuses to back bill protecting reporters', *Times of Israel*, 29 June 2023.

6   Chen Maanit, 'Bombshell Ruling by Israel's Top Court Disqualifies Netanyahu Ally Dery From Serving as Minister', *Ha'aretz*, 18 January 2023.

7   Josh Breiner, 'Tel Aviv Police Chief Quits: I Paid a Price for Choosing to Prevent a Civil War', Ha'aretz, 5 July 2023.

8   Noa Shpigel, '"Get Her Out": Netanyahu Ally Says Attorney General Most Dangerous Person in Israel', *Ha'aretz*, 19 July 2023.

9   Fareed Zakaria, 'Biden on Netanyahu, Saudi Arabia and seeking reelection', *CNN*, 9 July 2023.

10 Jotam Confino, 'Knesset passes first judicial reform weakening High Court's power', *Jewish News*, 24 July 2023.

13

October 7

Today, Hamas sees a weak government that depends on supporters of terrorism and is unable to fight terrorism, strike at senior Hamas figures and restore peace and security to the citizens of Israel. There is no reason to wait for the next attack. This government must go home. We must immediately establish a strong national government headed by Netanyahu that will restore peace and security to the citizens of Israel.

This was just one of countless warnings by Netanyahu against the Bennett-Lapid government. Words which would come back and haunt him a little over a year later when Netanyahu had regained power and would replace Golda Meir as the prime minister responsible for the biggest catastrophe in Israel's history.

On October 7, millions of Israelis were woken by rocket sirens across southern and central Israel at around 6:30. It was a Saturday, so most religious people didn't have their phones or TV turned on, and therefore didn't know what was going on. Like most people, I was very confused, as rockets are usually only fired at Tel Aviv when Hamas or Islamic Jihad are at war with Israel. This came out of the clear blue sky. It took me a few minutes to grab my phone and check the news. In my morning haze I realized that something big was happening. The confusion and panic among Israeli journalists were not a good sign. Not long after, numerous unverified videos began circulating on social media, revealing apocalyptical scenes from the Gaza border communities. Dozens of armed Palestinians were seen breaching the border fence in cars, on motorbikes and on foot. Minute by minute the situation became more and more chaotic, with scenes of Hamas terrorists on pickup trucks in the city of Sderot, firing indiscriminately at civilians. Other videos from a music festival in an open field near Kibbutz Re'im, a few kilometers from Gaza, showed horrific scenes of young Israelis running for their lives as Hamas terrorists were hunting them down. Reports of terrorists landing in Israel with parachutes and appearing from the sea also began circulating.

It became clear in the morning hours that a massive, orchestrated terror attack had been launched by Hamas and Islamic Jihad, attacking dozens of Kibbutzim and moshavim on the Israeli side of the border. Army bases and outposts were attacked at the same time to dismantle the communication system and slow down the warnings sent to the central command. Terrorists had captured entire highways near the Gaza border and were shooting at any Israeli car that came near them. Then came the first reports about civilians dragged by Hamas back to Gaza. Social media was full of videos showing children, mothers, elderly and soldiers (some of whom were severely injured by gunshots) abducted to Gaza. Palestinian civilians were cheering and hitting the hostages as they were paraded on the back of trucks inside Gaza.

It took about six hours before the citizens of Israel heard from their prime minister. The message was, however, clear as day: 'We are at war.' This was no surprise. Millions of Israelis had run for shelter throughout the morning, while some were still fighting for their lives near the Gaza border. Thousands of soldiers, special forces and police were sent to the south to clear the area of terrorists who had taken control of entire kibbutzim. Some survivors of the massacre managed to hide in their homes in places like Kibbutz Kfar Azza and Kibbutz Be'eri, until Israeli soldiers managed to kill the terrorists who were destroying and killing everything on their way. Israelis hiding from terrorists were on live TV telling anchors about their situation through the phone. The magnitude of the horror became evident in the following days when the first journalists were allowed into Kfar Azza, Be'eri and the festival site where bodies were still shattered everywhere. Entire families had been burned alive in their homes; some had been executed, tortured and mutilated. Eyewitness accounts of gang rape began to surface. Everyone from toddlers to Holocaust survivors were among the many victims. 1,200 people were killed that day, most of whom were civilians. More than 250 people were kidnapped by terror groups, including citizens from around 40 countries.

What followed was a full-scale invasion of Gaza, as well as attacks on Israel by Hezbollah in Lebanon, the Houthi rebels in Yemen, and Iranian militias from Syria and Iraq. Israel was effectively fighting a multi-front war against all its enemies, with Iran pulling the strings. As the Israeli public shifted into emergency mode, with hundreds of thousands of reserve soldiers called up for duty, Benny Gantz's National Unity party joined Netanyahu to form an emergency government. A seemingly responsible move but also highly political. With Gantz and Gadi Eisenkot, two former IDF chiefs, joining the war cabinet, a strong signal was sent to a public fighting for its survival. The extremists in Netanyahu's government, most notably Smotrich and Ben-Gvir, would have little influence over war. This would also serve Netanyahu abroad, with Israel's allies seeing a responsible leadership instead of far-right extremists calling for the destruction of Gaza and resettling of Jews in the enclave.

Israel enjoyed widespread support among its allies in the beginning of the war, with leaders visiting Jerusalem and the sites of the atrocities. Western leaders made comparisons with the Holocaust, promising to stand by Israel in its justified war against a genocidal death cult in Gaza. But as the bombs started dropping in Gaza, and Hamas' health ministry raising the death toll every day, without clarifying the number of civilian casualties, Israel slowly began losing its support. Millions of pro-Palestinians marched every week in capitals across the world, pressuring their governments to cut ties with Israel. The term genocide was used very early on to describe Israel's war against Hamas, due to internal displacement of civilians as well as destruction of civilian infrastructure.

Once again, Hamas managed to outmaneuver Israel, destroying Israel in the PR war. It didn't take long for the world and the media to forget the atrocities of October 7 and instead focus on the civilian suffering in Gaza. Hamas successfully used civilians as human shields, while operating from hospitals, schools, mosques and UN facilities. Vast Hamas tunnels were found under Gaza's biggest hospital Al Shifa, as well as the UNRWA headquarter. UNRWA was also forced to suspend a dozen workers after Israel provided evidence of them taking part in the October 7 massacre. One worker was caught on video kidnapping an Israeli from Kibbutz Be'eri.

In late November a ceasefire deal was finally struck between Israel and Hamas that would see the release of 110 hostages (both Israelis and foreigners) and some 150 Palestinian prisoners. Hamas broke the ceasefire after a week when it failed to deliver the last batch of hostages and began firing rockets at Israel again. While the public was initially relieved that at least most of the women and children had been released from Gaza, frustration with Netanyahu and the government's handling of the war increased in the coming months. Not only did Netanyahu refuse to take personal responsibility for failing to prevent October 7, but his policy towards Hamas was finally exposed as a disaster. For years, Netanyahu had allowed suitcases with millions of dollars to enter Gaza from Qatar, giving Hamas the resources to strengthen its military capacity and build a roughly 500km long tunnel network. Netanyahu's theory was that Israel could buy peace and quiet by allowing Hamas to grow, and at the same time it would sabotage any prospects of a two-state solution. The stronger and more popular Hamas grew, the more it weakened the Palestinian Authority, which was the only organ able to make peace with Israel. As the war continued with no breakthrough in striking another hostage deal with Hamas, pressure began to grow on Israel internationally. The U.S. demanded more aid be delivered to Gaza, while France condemned Israel for the large number of civilians killed.

At home, pressure on Netanyahu grew day by day, with families of hostages taking to the streets in utter distress, desperation and anger over the government. Poll after poll revealed that most Israelis held Netanyahu responsible for the failure to prevent the massacre, while most people thought he should resign either immediately or after the war. His Likud party lost almost half its mandates in the polls. Gantz, on the other hand, almost tripled his mandates in every poll. Gantz also began to act indecently, clearly thinking about the day after the war and the likelihood of him becoming prime minister. He visited the White House and Downing Street in March, despite Netanyahu ordering him not to. In fact, Netanyahu went as far as instructing the Israeli embassies in Washington and London not to help Gantz with his visit, according to a source close to the government. At this point, Netanyahu had become intolerable for Israel's allies. Most of them thought he was lying to them, the source added, while Gantz was seen as a more moderate statesman to work with. One of the main criticisms was that Netanyahu had no plan for the day after the war in Gaza. In Israel, the issue of the hostages began to divide the nation as well. Smotrich and Ben-Gvir's camp openly opposed striking another deal with Hamas to free the hostages, arguing it would harm Israel's security if thousands of terrorists were freed. Smotrich went as far as saying that the freeing the hostages wasn't the most important issue; toppling Hamas was. Naturally, this was met with immense anger among the families of the hostages who felt like the government abandoned them on October 7 and now were letting their loved one's rot in Gaza. As usual, it became clear that Netanyahu's main goal was to stay in power by stalling for time and trying to keep the far-right members of his coalition happy.

Six months into the war, 134 hostages were still held in Gaza. Netanyahu's insistence that only military force would bring the hostages home failed. Mass demonstrations were held on a daily basis, with people camping outside Knesset.

14

Epilogue

Netanyahu is undoubtedly one of the most influential prime ministers in Israel history. He has served longer than any other leader, but more importantly, he changed the nation forever. He understood politics better than any of his rivals, using social media to his advantage, cutting cynical deals with extremists and outcasts to secure every vote possible. Winning six elections, spanning over three decades, there's hardly any other democratically elected leader in the world who can compete with Netanyahu when it comes to political success. His cynicism, shrewdness, shamelessness, communication skills, understanding of politics and survival instincts make him one of the most unique political leaders in modern age.

While his first term was characterized by relative responsibility, Netanyahu learned that the term 'divide and conquer' applied perfectly to Israel, a nation of tribes and parallel societies just waiting to clash. He eventually understood that getting absolute loyalty from the ultra-orthodox parties and the extreme right would provide him with crucial mandates, leaving very little chance for his rivals to create a government without them. It did, however, come with a big prize. Netanyahu gave the ultraorthodox parties billions of dollars earmarked for their communities, despite their refusal to modernize, join the army like everyone else, increase their participation in the workforce, and educate their children in other topics than the Torah. In some ways it doomed future generations of ultraorthodox men and women, who had little chance of creating a future for themselves on the job market with very little skills. It perpetuated the animosity felt by secular Israelis who continued to bear the financial burden, while sacrificing their sons and daughters to protect the country. With orthodox families often having at least six children, the community was on a fast track to eventually become a majority, leaving Israel with a bleak future.

To his supporters, Netanyahu brought stability to a nation at constant war with its enemies, helped Israel become a high-tech hub and made peace with Arab Gulf countries. But while he is celebrated as a king among his followers, Netanyahu is despised by his opponents, more so than other democratically elected leaders, maybe with the exception of Donald Trump. His role in the demonstrations against Rabin, where incitement was running wild as he was cheering on the crowd, tainted him among half of the Israeli population. He was immediately at war with the established media who never forgave him and who often did everything in their power to cover him negatively.

Nobody can deny that Netanyahu changed significantly from the prime minister he was in 1996 to the highly divisive figure he would become in 2023. Becoming the youngest ever prime minister in the 1990's, Netanyahu had a lot to prove, especially in the aftermath of the assassination of Rabin. Despite his loathing of Yasser Arafat, whom he referred to as a terrorist, Netanyahu not only shook hands with him, but continued to fulfil at least parts of Israel's obligations to the Palestinians under the Oslo Accords during his first term. While it infuriated his right-wing base, it earned him respect in Washington and the reputation of a statesman rather than a dangerous demagogue. But the respect abroad was not as important to him as pleasing his right-wing base. After all, they were the key to his power.

The backlash from cozying up to Arafat therefore became a crucial lesson for him in his later terms. Those who worked closely with Netanyahu throughout the years all describe him as highly intelligent and risk averse, despite launching several Gaza operations (a term used by Israel, while foreign media more often use the word 'war' to describe the operations). He was never looking for a war. In fact, most of the time he tried his best to avoid it, unlike other prime ministers, such as Menachem Begin and Ehud Olmert in 1982 and 2006 respectively.

Netanyahu's understanding of the Arab world proved right, at least to some extent. The Abraham Accords took most experts by surprise. Peace with Arab Gulf states could not be achieved before peace with Palestinians, most of them believed. Netanyahu proved them wrong. Realism and self-interest are just as prevalent among Arab and Muslims states than other countries around the world. As a politician, he worked harder than all his competitors, going the extra mile to stay in power. He knew how to use both the left, centre and right-wing parties to his advantage, which his governments from 2009 and onward illustrated. Common for them all were, however, a highly sophisticated maneuvering by Netanyahu to constantly walk the fine line between buying time and deflecting pressure from Washington vis-a-vis the peace process, and at the same time showing his base that he was the biggest right-wing nationalist on the political map. A leader in a 'different league.'

The Obama years were personally a disaster for Netanyahu, who became a loathed figure in the White House. But his insistence on flexing his muscles at the most powerful man in the world when it came to 'defending' Israel against it resulted in a rock-solid voter base, which became more and more obsessed with him. The beatings Netanyahu took in Washington and in the Israeli media for undermining Obama's efforts to reach a nuclear deal with Iran were used by him as proof that he safeguarded Israel no matter what. His Iran policy later turned out to be a complete failure. After convincing Trump to leave the nuclear deal, Iran ended up becoming a nuclear threshold state, with no viable and unilateral Israeli military option available. The settlement movement became increasingly aggressive and powerful. The number of settlers and illegal settlements skyrocketed under Netanyahu.

Meanwhile a systemic change took place in the security establishment, which allowed settler violence to slowly spiral, as confirmed by former IDF Deputy Chief, Yair Golan. Internally, minorities began feeling increasingly alienated under Netanyahu, culminating with the Jewish Nation-State Law, which once and for all stated that Israel was a Jewish state. During Israel's endless election cycles from 2019 to 2022, Netanyahu, despite his age, worked tirelessly on his campaigns. It would be in this period, however, that his decision to normalize the extreme far-right and catapult them into power would forever taint his legacy. It's true that parties like Religious Zionism, Jewish Power and *Noam* would've slowly grown bigger due to demographic changes (most of their voters are religious nationalists who tend to have more children than secular Israelis for example), and due to Israel's society becoming increasingly right-wing. But people like Itamar Ben-Gvir, Betzalel Smotrich, Avi Maoz, and Almog Cohen (to name a few) would not have yielded such great influence had it not been for Netanyahu. Their racist and homophobic remarks, aggressive push for annexation of the West Bank, loathing of the army, the media and the justice system caused tremendous damage to the country as well as the Palestinians. His governments turned a blind eye to extremist settlers committing pogroms and terror attacks against innocent Palestinians, allowing the West Bank to become the settlers' Wild West.

His 2022 government's racist policies and conduct toward the Palestinians was more an illustration of the increasing political isolation Netanyahu found himself rather than him acting according to his own core ideological belief. He is first and foremost a pragmatist, who has had many different ideologies over the years. In fact, it's commonly believed that Netanyahu loathed most of the extreme right-wingers in his government, who caused more headaches for him than any other coalition partners he ever had. Netanyahu knew he had to appease ministers like Ben-Gvir and Smotrich to stay in power, but it came with a great price. He found himself having to constantly distance himself from homophobic, racist and violent remarks by far-right ministers and lawmakers to somehow contain the tremendous damage they were causing internally in Israel as well as abroad.

The cold air between Netanyahu and Biden during the first nine months of his term stemmed from the judicial overhaul, terror attacks by settlers, aggressive conduct by Israeli police on Temple Mount, and of course inflammatory and violent remarks by ministers and lawmakers. The war between the media and the government had started long before the rise of the far-right in Israeli politics. Years earlier, Netanyahu paved the way for ministers and coalition lawmakers to attack the media in the most populist way possible, helping undermine trust in one of democracy's most important pillars. That is not to say that the Israeli media has undoubtedly leaned to the left since the establishment of the state. In many cases Israeli journalists were extremely opinionated, on par with American journalists. One could argue some were even obsessed with Netanyahu, doing everything they could to attack him. But to continuously brand the entire media landscape as 'propaganda' was nothing short of a classic populism. It's hard not to draw a direct link between Netanyahu's use of 'propaganda', 'Al-Jazeera' and 'fake news' to describe the media, and the many assaults committed by extreme right-wingers in recent years against journalists, often using that exact same slur as they viciously attacked them during broadcasts. The phenomenon is very similar to that of the settlers and hilltop youth, who feel that their political leaders have their back. The leaders' hateful rhetoric and actions against journalists and Palestinians translate into a carte blanche for assaults.

The same goes for the judicial system. He unleashed a gang of far-right populists against the system, doing everything to dismantle it piece by piece. Netanyahu's change of view on the judiciary is as profound as his policies toward the Palestinians. In his first terms, Netanyahu continued in Menachem Begin's path when it came to defending the Supreme Court and its independence. He shelved law proposals from radical members of his second and third governments that would have weakened the Supreme Court. He also made sure that Ayelet Shaked's 'judicial revolution' wasn't implemented. But things changed dramatically when the first corruption allegations surfaced. As it became clear that he was going to be indicted, Netanyahu mobilized his Likud party against the entire judicial system. Everyone from the attorney general to the state prosecutor and police were involved in nothing short of an illegal coup to topple him. The media and the left-wing were, of course, part of this. We will probably never find out if he believed this or if it was merely part of his strategy to defend himself. What we do know is that nearly a million people kept voting for him and Likud. His loyal followers either believed Netanyahu's accusations about the witch hunt and the poisonous and corrupt judiciary, or they simply didn't care enough. He was still 'King Bibi', the only true leader of Israel. There is still no proof that a deep state conspiracy, conducted by the media, left-wing, police and judiciary, tried to remove Netanyahu from power. But once again, a prime minister's accusations proved to carry significant weight. The 'poison machine', as it's often referred to by those opposing Netanyahu, repeated the same slogans about a 'coup' and a 'witch-hunt' against the prime minister. Most Likud lawmakers were eager to prove their loyalty, attacking the judiciary at every chance.

The campaign, led by Netanyahu and executed by Likud, caused tremendous damage to Israeli society, with a significant part of it believing that they live in a country where a tiny left-wing mafia decides everything. For that segment of society, the government's attempt to overhaul the judicial system was necessary to restore the balance of power. But a significant majority of Israelis were vehemently opposed to the government's 'judicial reforms', best illustrated by the weekly mass demonstrations and criticism from all important sectors of society. Likud solidified itself as the biggest party in Israel in the 2022 elections, but it didn't campaign on revolutionizing the judicial system. Nor did the other far right and ultra-orthodox parties. It is, however, no surprise that United Torah Judaism, Shas, Religious Zionism, *Noam* and Jewish Power loathe the Supreme Court and the power it yields. On the contrary, their goal is to weaken the court to implement their political agendas. Annexing the West Bank, immunizing soldiers and police, exempting ultra-orthodox youth from the army, allowing gender segregation in public places, discriminating against gays, nixing administrative detentions for Jews, imposing death penalty for Palestinian terrorists and deporting their families will only happen the day the Supreme Court loses its power.

All of the above run counter to the values of Likud, which was established as a right-wing and secular party with respect for law and order. Menachem Begin's, and by extension Likud's, respect for the Supreme Court's independence was ironclad. Likud is, however, not the same party today. In fact, one can argue that it has abandoned its core ideology and has become a far-right party. The days of Ariel Sharon, Dan Meridor, Yitzhak Shamir, Menachem and Benny Begin are gone. Since taking over the party in 2009, Netanyahu has managed to change the DNA of the party. Absolute loyalty to him would become the only currency needed to rise in the ranks of the party. Slowly but surely the party was filled with right-wing extremists whose ideology in no way resembled that of the old party. Netanyahu's problems became the party's problems. The more you attacked the media and judiciary, the more likely you would be to climb the ranks. And the few Likud members who dared speak out against the government's policies, such as Yoav Gallant, Yuli Edelstein and David Bitan, found themselves as punching bags for the younger and more aggressive Netanyahu loyalists. Likud under Netanyahu embraced populism, xenophobia, ultranationalism, and authoritarianism. Today, attacking the media, Arab Israelis, the judiciary, the Bank of Israel, the IDF, and of course the demonstrators who consist of both right and left-wing Israelis, is part of the Likud ministers and lawmakers' style. The more aggressive the better. Anyone and anything but Netanyahu are a legitimate target, as long as it serves his or Likud's interest, namely attracting voters.

It's hard to see how Likud would've evolved into what it is today had it not been for Netanyahu. Likud's 'natural' partners, ideologically speaking, aren't the fringe, racist and homophobic parties they formed a government with in 2022. The original Likud had much more in common with the values of *Yesh Atid*, National Unity Party, and *Yisrael Beitenu*, parties which all respect Israel's democratic institutions, the Supreme Court, the media, and of course LGBTQ and women's rights. Values which Religious Zionism, Jewish Power, *Noam*, United Torah Judaism and Shas all loathe, and which they are doing everything they can to either roll back, undermine or significantly weaken. But the arguably most destructive footprint Netanyahu is leaving behind him is the biggest security scandal in Israel's history; October 7. The deadliest attack against Jews since the Holocaust, in which 1,200 people were killed and 255 taken hostage in Gaza, shook Israel to its core, and was a direct result of Netanyahu's leadership.

As of August 2024, Israel was still fighting a war against Hamas and other terror groups in Gaza, as well as defending itself from attacks from Yemen, Lebanon, Syria, Iraq, Iran and the West Bank. Contrary to his many election promises, Netanyahu allowed Hamas to grow stronger than it had ever been before. Millions of dollars were sent in suitcases from Qatar to Hamas every month. Netanyahu's plan was to let Hamas flourish at the detriment of the Palestinian Authority. The stronger Hamas became, the easier it would be for him to say Israel had no partner to negotiate peace with, as most of Israel's allies accepted that Hamas could not be tolerated as the sole leader of a Palestinian state.

A master of status-quo, Netanyahu believed that his strategy to give Hamas breathing room would buy him time. But it wasn't just Netanyahu who failed miserably in keeping Israeli citizens safe. Weapons were smuggled across the border with Egypt, the world's largest network of terror tunnels were built across the entire Gaza Strip, and warning signs were ignored by defense and intelligence brass who arrogantly believed that Hamas would never have the capacity to carry out a major terror attack against Israel like the one that took place on October 7. But they all took personal responsibility for the failure to prevent the massacre. Netanyahu was the only one who didn't. There is little doubt, that Israel's enemies capitalized on the massive internal crisis caused by the judicial reforms which left the country weaker and more vulnerable than ever. Netanyahu therefore played a significant role in bringing Israel to its biggest societal and existential crisis ever.

Bibliography

Ayalon, Ami '*Friendly fire: How Israel became its own worst enemy and its hope for the future*' (Steerforth Press, Lebanon, New Hampshire, 2020).

Barak, Ehud, '*My Country, My Life, Fighting for Israel, Searching for Peace*, (Martin's Press, New York, 2018).

Kushner, Jared, '*Breaking History: A White House memoir*', (Broadside Books, Harper Collins, New York, 2022),

Landau, David, '*Arik: The life of Ariel Sharon*' (Vintage Books, a division of Random House, New York, 2014).

Netanyahu, Benjamin '*Bibi: My Story*' (Simon & Schuster, New York, 2022)

Peri, Yoram, '*Generals in the cabinet room: How the military shapes Israeli policy*' (United States Institute of Peace Press, Washington, D.C. 2006).

Pompeo, Mike, '*Never Give an Inch: Fighting for the America I Love*', (Broadside Books 2023, New York).

Ya'alon, Moshe, '*The longer, shorter path*', (Geffen Publishing House, Jerusalem, 2020).

Interviews

Alkidwa, Nasser: Palestinian ambassador to UN 1991-2005, Palestinian Foreign Affairs Minister 2005-06, Yasser Arafat's nephew.

Arafat, Naseer: Director of Nablus Cultural Heritage Enrichment Center

Beilin, Yossi: Deputy Minister of Foreign Affairs 1992-1995, Minister of Justice 1999-2001, Minister of Religious Affairs 2000-2001 (Labour party). and Atomic Energy 2009-2013.

Bushinsky, Aviv: Media advisor to Prime Minister Benjamin Netanyahu 1998-99, Chief of Staff for Finance Minister Benjamin Netanyahu 2003-04.

Golan, Yair: Deputy Economy Minister 2021-2022 (Meretz), Deputy IDF chief of staff 2014-2017, Commander of IDF Northern Command 2011-2014, Commander of the IDF Home Front Command 2008-2011.

Halevy, Efraim: National Security Council director 2002-2003, Mossad director 1998-2002, Israel's ambassador to EU 1996-1998.

Hayman, Tamir: Israeli Military Intelligence chief 2018-2022.

Hellinger, Moshe: Dr. Political Science at Bar-Ilan University.

Hendel, Yoaz: Director of Communications and Public Diplomacy for Prime Minister Netanyahu, 2011-12. Minister of Communication 2020-22. (Blue and White, Derech Eretz and New Hope).

Hijjawi, Sami: Mayor of Nablus 2022-

Ichay, Ran: Advisor to Foreign and Finance Minister Netanyahu 2002-2004, Israeli ambassador to Kazakhstan 2006-2008, Director General of the Prime Minister's Office 2010-2012, Director General of the Ministry of Jerusalem and Heritage 2016-2019.

Kariv, Dvir: Intelligence analyst in Shin Bet 1990-2012.

Malach, Gilead: Director of the Ultra-Orthodox in Israel Program at the Israel Democracy Institute

Meridor, Dan: Minister of Justice 1988-1992, Minister of Finance 1996-1997, Minister without portfolio 2001-2003, Deputy Prime Minister 2009-2013, Minister of Intelligence

Neiger, Motti: President of the Israel Communication Association (2006-2009), Associate Professor at the School of Communication at Bar-Ilan University.

Olmert, Ehud: Prime Minister 2006-2009, Mayor of Jerusalem 1993-2003

Oren, Michael: Israel's Ambassador to the U.S. 2009-13. Member of Knesset for Kulanu party 2015-2019.

Peri, Ya'akov: Shin Bet director 1989-1995, Minister of Science and Technology 2013-2015, Member of Knesset 2013-2018 (Yesh Atid party).

Rhotman, Simcha: Knesset member for Religious Zionism, Chair of Knesset Constitution, Law and Justice Committee 2023-

Shakshir, Husam: Deputy Mayor of Nablus 2022-

Shapira, Assaf: PhD in Political Science from the Hebrew University of Jerusalem.

Sharansky, Nathan: Minister of Industry & Trade 1996-99, Minister of Internal Affairs 1999-00, Deputy Prime Minister 2001-03, Minister of Housing & Construction 2001-03, Minister of Jerusalem Affairs 2003-05. Yisrael Ba'Aliyah 1996-2003, Likud 2006. Chairman of Jewish Agency 2009-18.

Tibi, Ahmad: Leader of Arab-Israeli Ta'al party, Deputy Knesset Speaker 2006-

Tucker, Anita: Gush Katif resident (1977-2005).

Weiman, Nadav: Staff sergeant in the elite IDF unit, Sayeret Nahal 2005-08. Senior Director in Israeli NGO 'Breaking The Silence' 2011-

Yatom, Danny: Mossad director 1996-1998, Chief of Staff for Prime Minister Ehud Barak 1999-2001, Member of Knesset 2003-08.

Glossary

Terms:

Aman: Israel's Military Intelligence
IDF: Israel's Defense Forces
Intifada: Palestinian uprising – 1987-1993 and 2000-2005
Knesset: Israel's Parliament
Mossad: Israeli intelligence agency
Shin Bet: Israeli Security Agency

Israeli parties:

Blue and White: Also known as Kahol Lavan in Hebrew, was created in 2019 as an alliance between Benny Gantz, Moshe Ya'alon, and Yair Lapid. Their ultimate goal was to present an alternative to Netanyahu's right-wing bloc. The alliance eventually collapsed when Lapid and Ya'alon withdrew from the party following Gantz's decision to form a government with Netanyahu.

Jewish Home: Known as HaBayit HaYehudi in Hebrew, was a right-wing religious Zionist political party in Israel. It was founded in 2008 and made up of a number of smaller but similar parties, all representing religious nationalists and settlers in Israel. The party advocated for the expansion of settlements in the West Bank and keeping Jewish heritage, traditions, and religious observance in all aspects of Israeli society.

Jewish Power: Known in Hebrew as Otzma Yehudit, is considered one of the most far-right political parties in Israel's history. The party was founded in 2012 with its political aim being to annex the West Bank and Gaza. It adheres to strict observance of Jewish religious law, but differs from the ultra-orthodox parties in its fundamentalist view on Zionism as well as pushing for a change in the Temple Mount status-quo, so that Jews can pray at the holy site. The party leader, Itamar Ben-Gvir, is among the most controversial politicians in Israel's history, with a long list of indictments behind him, as well as racist and homophobic views.

Kadima: Meaning "Forward" in Hebrew, Kadima was formed by Ariel Sharon in 2005 after he broke away from his Likud party. It was seen as a centrist party, positioning itself as a moderate alternative to the right and left-wing parties. Kadima focused on national security, socio-economic reforms and making peace with the Palestinians by conceding territory. It was formed after Sharon's disengagement plan which saw a full Israeli withdrawal from Gaza. The party gradually declined in influence and disbanded in 2014, with some of its members joining other political factions.

Kulanu: Meaning "All of Us" in Hebrew, was a centrist political party in Israel founded in 2014 by Moshe Kahlon, a former member of Likud. Like other centrist parties, Kulanu focused on issues like socio-economic reforms, housing affordability, cost of living, and social welfare. After a short period in one of Netanyahu's governments, Kulanu disbanded in 2019, with some of its members joining other political parties.

Labour: Known as HaAvoda in Hebrew, was for decades one of Israel's major political parties. Founded in 1968 as a merger between David Ben-Gurion's Mapai party, Rafi and Ahdut HaAvoda, the party played a historic role in forming Israel in the years to come. A socialist party with deep roots on traditional Zionism, Labour evolved over time to embrace more centrist positions on economic and security issues. It traditionally advocated for social welfare programs, workers' rights, and a negotiated settlement to the Israeli-Palestinian conflict based on a two-state solution. In the last two decades, Labour lost its popularity and has become one of the smallest parties in Israel.

Likud Party: Founded in 1973 by Menachem Begin and Ariel Sharon as a liberal, secular right-wing party. It became the first right-wing party to ever win an election in 1977, later referred to as an earthquake that forever changed Israeli politics. Despite being pro-settlements and with a hawkish position on the Israeli-Palestinian conflict, Likud became the first party to make peace with an Arab nation and to withdraw from Israeli occupied territory when it signed the Camp David Agreement with Egypt in 1979. Despite ups and downs in elections since then, Likud has become the most influential political party in Israel following decades of Labour dominance.

Netanyahu secured six election wins for Likud but he also changed the party's DNA, in particular its stance on issues like the Supreme Court and security.

National Religious Party (NRP): Also known as Mafdal (an acronym for Miflaga Datit Leumit, meaning National Religious Party in Hebrew), was a party with roots in the religious Zionist movement. Established in 1956, the party played a significant role in religious issues and settlements in the West Bank and Gaza Strip. Like other religious Zionist parties, NPR combined religious ideology with nationalist and Zionist principles, supporting Jewish settlements in the West Bank. In 2008, the NRP merged with the National Union party to form the Jewish Home party.

National Union: Another right-wing political alliance in the religious Zionist movement. Formed in 1999, the alliance brought together several smaller parties, including Moledet, Tkuma, and Hatikva, opposing territorial concessions and advocating for the annexation of parts of the West Bank and Gaza Strip. It also supported measures to strengthen Israel's security, such as increased military presence in the West Bank and Gaza Strip. The National Union was part of right-wing governments which included Likud and other religious nationalist factions. In 2008, the National Union merged with the National Religious Party to form the Jewish Home party.

Religious Zionism: Also known as the Religious Zionist Party. It was founded in 1998 under the name Tkuma, but the party later joined a number of right-wing alliances, such as National Union, Jewish Home and Yamina. It finally ran with Jewish Power and Noam, another far-right, religious and anti-LGBTQ party, as part of the Religious Zionist Party. Its leader, Betzalel Smotrich, is known for his racist and homophobic views as well as his tireless efforts to annex the West Bank.

Shas: An ultra-Orthodox political party that represents Sephardic and Mizrahi Jews. Founded in 1984 under Rabbi Ovadia Yosef, Shas is looking out for the interests of the religious Sephardic and Mizrahi communities, focusing on religious education, social welfare, and cultural preservation. It's based on Orthodox Jewish values and traditions, and it often supports conservative social policies. Shas has been among the most influential parties in Israel since its founding, sitting in both left and right-wing governments.

United Torah Judaism (UTJ): An ultra-Orthodox Jewish political alliance formed in 1992 and made up of two factions: Agudat Yisrael and Degel HaTorah. UTJ represents different streams of ultra-Orthodox Judaism and like Shas, it works for the interests of the Ashkenazi community, also focusing on religious education, and securing funding for religious institutions. It has also played a significant role in Israeli politics, especially in the Netanyahu years, helping him stay in power.

Yesh Atid: "There is a Future" in Hebrew, was established in 2012 by former TV journalist Yar Lapid. The party is considered centrist with a liberal agenda, focusing on issues such as socio-economic reforms, education, and national service. In recent years it has also focused on reducing religion in Israel, often attacking the ultra-orthodox parties for their refusal to serve in the IDF. After serving briefly in one of Netnayahu's governments in 2013, Lapid has become one of his fiercest rivals and critics, refusing to ever sit with him again.

Yisrael Beitenu: Meaning "Israel – Our Home" in Hebrew, was formed by Avigdor Lieberman in 1999 as a secular nationalist political party, representing the interests of Russian-speaking immigrants and secular Israelis. The party focuses on national security, immigration, and the rights of Russian-speaking Israelis as well as reducing religious influence in society. It's seen as one of the most hawkish parties in Israel when it comes to Palestinians. Lieberman is a strong supporter of targeted killings of terrorists as well as strengthening settlements. A former ally of Netanyahu, Lieberman has also refused to sit with him again.

Palestinian parties, organizations and terror groups

Fatah: Fatah is one of two major Palestinian political parties and the largest faction within the Palestine Liberation Organization (PLO). Fatah was founded in 1959 by Yasser Arafat and its platform is based on secularism and nationalism as well as pursuing a Palestinian state. It has become increasingly unpopular under Mahmoud Abbas' rule, due to widespread corruption and a refusal to hold elections since 2009.

Hamas: Founded by Sheikh Yassin in 1987 during the beginning of the first Intifada. Affiliated with the Muslim Brotherhood and with deep roots in Islam, the movement slowly gained popularity among Palestinians for its insistence on destroying the State of Israel through violence. Its fierce rivalry with Fatah culminated in 2007 when it took control over Gaza. It operates both in Gaza, West Bank and East Hamas is behind some of the worst terror attacks against Israelis, ranging from suicide bombs to mass slaughter of civilians on October 7. It is designated as a terror organization by a long list of countries and international bodies, including the U.S., Canada, Australia, UK, and the EU. Hamas is closely allied with Hezbollah and is receiving funding from Qatar

Islamic Jihad: Also known as the Palestinian Islamic Jihad (PIJ), is an Islamist terror organization founded by Abd Al Aziz Awda Fathi Shaqaqi in 1981. Like Hamas, it's also an offshoot of the Muslim Brotherhood. It's considered even more extreme than Hamas, but has grown in recent years, often collaborating with Hamas, most recently on October 7. It's responsible for a long list of terror attacks against Israelis, including suicide bombings. It opposes a two-state solution, and is using jihad to wage a holy war on Israel. It's closely allied with Hezbollah and Iran, and has offices in both Syria and Lebanon. Like Hamas, Islamic Jihad is designated as a terrorist organization by numerous countries and international bodies Islamic Jihad receives support from Iran and operates independently of the Palestinian Authority (PA), which controls parts of the West Bank. The group's activities have led to ongoing conflict with Israel and have been a significant obstacle to peace efforts in the region. Like Hamas, Islamic Jihad is designated as a terrorist organization by numerous countries and international bodies.

PLO: The Palestine Liberation Organization (PLO) is an umbrella organization that officially represents the Palestinian people. It was founded in 1964 by the Arab League, seeking to liberate Palestine by creating a Palestinian state. It used armed struggle to fight against Israel, but also committed terror attacks, most notably during the Olympics in 1972, when it killed 11 Israeli athletes. It shifted tactics over the years as it recognized Israel's right to exist in the Oslo Accords.

PA: The Palestinian Authority (PA) is the governing body established in 1994 as a result of the Oslo Accords between Israel and the Palestine Liberation Organization (PLO). PA is responsible for civil affairs as well as security in certain parts of the West Bank. It's the official governing body of the Palestinians, but has become increasingly unpopular over the years due to widespread corruption and anger among Palestinian over its cooperation with Israel.

Milton Keynes UK
Ingram Content Group UK Ltd.
UKHW040017120924
448207UK00002B/56